THE ESSENTIAL GUIDE TO PLANNING LAW

Decision-making and practice in the UK

by Adam Sheppard, Deborah Peel, Heather Ritchie
and Sophie Berry

First published in Great Britain in 2017 by

Policy Press   North America office:
University of Bristol   Policy Press
1-9 Old Park Hill   c/o The University of Chicago Press
Bristol   1427 East 60th Street
BS2 8BB   Chicago, IL 60637, USA
UK   t: +1 773 702 7700
t: +44 (0)117 954 5940   f: +1 773-702-9756
pp-info@bristol.ac.uk   sales@press.uchicago.edu
www.policypress.co.uk   www.press.uchicago.edu

© Policy Press 2017

British Library Cataloguing in Publication Data
A catalogue record for this book is available from the British Library

Library of Congress Cataloging-in-Publication Data
A catalog record for this book has been requested

ISBN 978-1-4473-2446-1 paperback
ISBN 978-1-4473-2445-4 hardcover
ISBN 978-1-4473-2448-5 ePub
ISBN 978-1-4473-2449-2 Mobi
ISBN 978-1-4473-2447-8 ePDF

Cover design by Lyn Davies
Front cover image: Getty
Printed and bound in Great Britain by CMP, Poole
Policy Press uses environmentally responsible print partners

Contents

List of figures, maps and tables

Figures

Maps

Photographs

Tables

List of boxes

Author biographies

Adam Sheppard is a lecturer in Development Management and Planning Practice for the Department of Geography and Environmental Management at UWE Bristol.

Deborah Peel is Emeritus Professor at the University of Dundee and Visiting Professor at the University of Wageningen.

Heather Ritchie is a Lecturer in Spatial Planning and Energy Policy in the School of the Built Environment, Ulster University.

Sophie Berry is a practising planning officer for the Regeneration, Investment and Housing department of Newport City Council.

List of acronyms

AMSC	Approval of Matters Specified as a Condition
AONB	Area of Outstanding Natural Beauty
BCN	Breach of Condition Notice
BGS	British Geological Society
BPN	Building Preservation Notice
CIL	Community Infrastructure Levy (England)
CPO	Compulsory Purchase Order
DAERA	Department of Agriculture, Environment and Rural Affairs (Northern Ireland)
DCLG	Department for Communities and Local Government (England)
DfC	Department for Communities (Northern Ireland)
DfI	Department for Infrastructure (Northern Ireland)
DOE	Department of the Environment (Northern Ireland)
DPEA	Directorate of Planning and Environmental Appeals (Scotland)
DRD	Department for Regional Development (Northern Ireland)
EEZ	Exclusive Economic Zone
EIA	Environmental Impact Assessment
ES	Environmental Statement
EU	European Union
JR	Judicial Review
LDC	Lawful Development Certificate
LBC	listed building consent
LDO	Local Development Order (England and Wales)
LPA	local planning authority
LRB	Local Review Body
MMO	Marine Management Organisation (England)
MPS	Marine Policy Statement
MTAN	Minerals Technical Advice Note
NAPE	National Association of Planning Enforcement
NDO	Neighbourhood Development Orders (England)
NPPG	National Planning Practice Guidance (England)
NPF	National Planning Framework (Scotland)
NPPF	National Planning Policy Framework (England)
PAC	Planning Appeals Commission (Northern Ireland)
PCN	Planning Contravention Notice
PiP	Permission in Principle (England)
PILS	Public Interest Litigation Support
PINS	Planning Inspectorate (England and Wales)
PPS	Planning Policy Statement (Northern Ireland – since replaced by the SPPS)
PPW	Planning Policy Wales (Wales)

RAWP	Regional Aggregate Working Parties (England)
RCJ	Rules of the Court of the Judicature (Northern Ireland)
RDS	Regional Development Strategy (Northern Ireland)
RSPB	Royal Society for the Protection of Birds
RTPI	Royal Town Planning Institute
SEA	Strategic Environmental Assessment
SI	Statutory Instrument
SPA	Special Protection Area
SPP	Scottish Planning Policy (Scotland)
SPPS	Strategic Planning Policy Statement (Northern Ireland)
SSSI	Site of Special Scientific Interest
TAN	Technical Advice Note (Wales)
TPO	Tree Preservation Order
UK	United Kingdom

Acknowledgements

The authors would like to express thanks to their family and friends for their support during the writing of this book, without which it would never have been completed.

They are also grateful to the anonymous reviewers of the book for their constructive and helpful feedback and suggestions.

Finally, special thanks for contributions, reviews and comments go to Nick Croft (University of the West of England, Bristol) and Izindi Visagie (Ivy Legal).

Foreword

For the time being, the United Kingdom remains united, but each nation state has different powers and potentially more so, as devolution increases. England, Northern Ireland, Scotland and Wales have slightly different institutions and instruments of planning, resulting in distinctive legal and policy arrangements. For scholars, this poses some questions. Where do they diverge? How does each nation state interpret the principles of town and country planning? Fundamentally, is there any threat to what is known as the British discretionary planning system?

This book attempts to address these issues. In a wide-ranging investigation, the four authors make this text distinctive, giving the reader a special insight by drawing on their own research and experience of each devolved administration. The differences are discussed, explained and integrated throughout the text, not separated into standalone chapters, and it allows for real comparison between the planning systems and approaches of each nation.

There are some difficult subjects brought to life through interesting case studies. From the Shetland Islands to Plymouth, from Derry/Londonderry to Suffolk, there is an enlivening inclusion of case law and how its interpretation has influenced planning law. In addition to core planning concepts and approaches to development management, there are chapters on enforcement, Judicial Review and the way in which plans and decisions are challenged through the Ombudsman. Waste and minerals are explained; and in order to be comprehensive, historic conservation as well as planning gain are also included. Another innovation is some explanation on the emergent law relating to marine spatial planning, which is now considered to be a vital part of planning law, where competing demands for use of the sea bed, coast and surface are being dealt with in a spatial manner.

Planning is a complex subject, not easily understood by many – including the public and politicians as well as students. Regulation and the examination of its impact on the environment are not always considered fascinating, but the dynamic and ever-changing aspects are brought to life in this readable book. It will act as an important reference text for those who want to understand the basics of planning law and need to compare the four nations. For use as a text book, and for students of planning, each chapter ends with a list of references for further reading.

It is refreshing to know that the four systems diverge only slightly in reality. The basis of British planning law remains intact, and whilst the terms (mainly the names of the plans and instruments and the scale at which planning is delivered) differ between nations, it is clear that they learn and take from each other as they review their approaches to planning.

The chapter on the history of planning law contextualises the subject and offers hope to town planners who are feeling dispirited about the erosion of regulation, and the attack by successive governments on town and country planning in general. *The Essential Guide to Planning Law* takes the reader back to the very beginnings of planning, allegedly in 2600 BC. Whilst this illustrates that planned and regulated cities are ancient, this can only serve to prove that humans rely on some kind of structure and rule of law to enable us to live side by side. So it is with the four nations of the UK: uniting around the common ambition to plan in the public interest; to control and regulate so that one person's ambition or privilege does not have a detrimental impact on another, nor upon society at large. This book explains very well why planning and regulation are in the best interests of the economy, the society and the environment of our four nations.

Janet Askew
October 2016

ONE

Planning law in context

Chapter contents

- Scope and aims of the book
- Managing the land resource
- Land-use planning
- Marine planning
- Institutional arrangements of planning
- Overview of the book

Introduction

This is not a law book about planning but a planning book that considers planning law and its application. We hope to provide you, through a 'straight' and factual presentation, with an essential knowledge and understanding of planning law and decision-making, and to do so in a readable and accessible way with reference to the main concepts, philosophies, systems, structures and arrangements within which planning law exists and decision-making takes place. This chapter frames the book and provides some of the context for its wider content.

Scope and aims of the book

The use and development of land is a critical concern for everyone in society. To this end, statutory land-use planning was introduced to ensure that land and property development served the greater public good, or public interest. History reveals that, without planning, land may be used inappropriately – as with ribbon development, or buildings in areas of landscape quality or areas prone to flooding – positive planning, however, can potentially serve the wider purpose of societal well-being.

At different times and in different places the physical effects of planning (or even its perceived absence) have been both controversial and emotive. In the popular press the planning system often tends to be cast as the villain of the piece, variously authorising the bulldozer to eradicate treasured buildings or flatten valued landscapes, failing to allocate sufficient land to provide local affordable housing for first-time buyers or permitting a controversial design. In allocating land for homes and places of work, in identifying where energy, information, communication and transport infrastructures should go, planning affects each of us on a daily basis. Yet its legal basis and statutory function as part of the wider governance framework of society are relatively poorly understood. Why is this? And why do so few people exercise their legal right to engage with the planning system in order to shape and influence the quality of the places where they live, work, raise their families, grow up and grow old? Why do some communities feel that they have to resort to protesting in order to make their voices heard?

Our aim in writing this book is to provide a simple introduction to the essentials of planning law for those working in the built environment, and also to support those interested more generally in planning and place-making. We hope that a wider understanding of how planning decisions are made in the United Kingdom (UK) may serve to enhance the quality of the built environment and reduce some of the conflicts that arise when development proposals come forward. We examine some of the challenges facing the use, development and management of the land resource in the public interest and we make the case for positive planning to become rather more central to public life.

Our main purpose is to explain what, why, when, where and how planning laws regulate development. We are thus principally concerned with the state activity known as development management (formerly development control). We explain why society has found such controls necessary; what planning law aims to achieve under different circumstances; how the system for implementing planning legislation has evolved over time; how planning law is intended to work in practice; and who is involved. Although planning is an important activity worldwide, we focus on the British planning system, and particularly on how the four national systems currently operate across the devolved UK.

We use the term 'devolved UK' to emphasise that different planning (and other) powers are held by the four administrations. Constitutionally, the partition of the island of Ireland into the Irish Free State (subsequently the Republic of Ireland) and Northern Ireland in 1921 paved the way for the creation of the United Kingdom of Great Britain and Northern Ireland in 1927, which formally united England, Scotland, Wales and Northern Ireland – listed in terms of the sizes of their populations. Despite certain important differences, a number of fundamental elements in each of the national planning systems remain the same; our focus is on core principles relating to planning law. In the historical parts of the text we refer loosely to Britain; where particular legislation applies, we refer to the relevant part of the UK (Map 1.1).

The book provides a general introduction to planning decision-making for the increasing number of people concerned with land and development, whether as students, local government councillors, practitioners or the general public. For example, you may wish to extend your house, you may be thinking about running a business from your home, or you may wish to change the signage for your shop: do you need planning permission or consent? Alternatively, you may have heard that a new shopping centre is planned near where you live, or be concerned about the erection of a wind turbine: how can you find out more detail about the planning application and contribute your views? You may be interested in the emerging field of marine planning. This book provides general and practical information about what is involved and what you can do. At the end of each chapter we point you to other resources and more detailed texts, as planning law is a highly sophisticated and specialised field.

Map 1.1: Map of the devolved UK

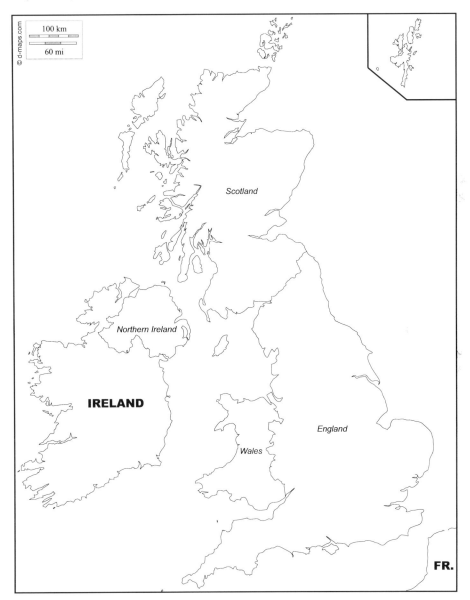

Source: www.d-maps.com/carte.php?num_car=5545&lang=en, copyright d-maps.com

The legal arrangements for planning and managing land have changed over time. Planning is variously referred to as land-use planning, town and country planning, town and regional planning or spatial planning and even neighbourhood or community planning. This terminology reflects both scalar dimensions (for example national, regional and local levels) and the complexity of land management itself. The latter involves dealing with the spatially interrelated nature of activities and different interpretations of land use and development at given points in time. The diversity of terminology should also alert you to the dynamic nature of law and the importance of keeping up to date with statutory changes, policy developments and the legal judgments interpreting planning legislation that make up the body of case law underpinning planning law in practice.

The continually evolving nature of the regulatory framework is important to recognise; change is constant and you should see this text as a starting point in terms not only of the content but also of the story of planning: things will continue to change. You will need to explore these changes, such as those arising from on-going evaluations of the effectiveness, efficiency and equity of particular planning systems, and also with respect to the wider constitutional changes occurring in the UK.

We encourage you to become familiar and confident with some of the thinking and language of planning law and to appreciate the legal context in which planning decisions take place. In the same way that planners and built environment professionals need to be comfortable with terminology relating to design, development finance or environmental protection, it is important for practitioners to be able to discuss developments and planning proposals in the light of their legal basis. We aim to explain and illustrate some of the principles underpinning the ethos and application of planning law within contemporary political and democratic contexts. Each of the authors has worked in the field of planning in the public sector and we have found it to be a dynamic and contested field of law, and one that tends to be politically charged.

Having a solid feel for the bases of planning law will enable you to engage in discussions about the rationale for and practical implications of the legal and procedural dimensions of planning in an informed way. It will also help to explain current debates in relation to marine planning. However, this book has not been written as a definitive interpretation of current planning law, and so, unless you have a reasonable working knowledge of planning law and property development you are strongly encouraged to seek professional planning or legal advice in relation to specific development proposals.

In order to get us started, this introductory chapter is designed to do four things:

1. to identify important issues in managing the land resource
2. to introduce the subject of land-use planning and the rules of the game
3. to provide an overview of the different scales and interests involved in planning
4. to outline the structure of the book.

Photo 1.1: Fracking has become a highly contentious planning issue, Co. Fermanagh, Northern Ireland

Source: Deborah Peel

Managing the land resource

Land, labour and capital are the basic factors of production for society. As an environmental asset, land is a precious resource for any community. It is the basic requirement for and source of food, warmth and shelter. As society has become increasingly urbanised and as we have become more sophisticated in terms of how we derive our support systems and services, our direct and daily relationship with the land has changed. Our perception of the land resource is also shaped by our sense of place.

Unlike environmental resources such as air and water, land is relatively fixed in supply and location. In absolute terms, it may be considered a finite resource; following the logic of sustainable development, land is a resource held in trust for future generations. These considerations raise complex philosophical, political and legal issues. Notwithstanding the importance of land, these questions are often ignored, misunderstood or misrepresented. How society values land and determines how to use or develop it has critical implications for individuals, neighbours, communities, societies and the wider ecosystems that support and sustain human life and well-being. In addition, the quality of physical development, in terms of siting, design and layout, for example, affects individuals' and communities' overall sense of place and quality of life. In many ways, these interrelated issues are not a new concern. As Chapter Three will explain, concerns about public health and safety drove early anthropocentric considerations for controls and by-laws that were intended to protect human health and create urban settlements that worked efficiently and effectively.

As our understanding of contemporary concerns, such as climate change, has matured and our appreciation of how society, the environment and economic development interrelate has evolved, our social construction of the land resource has become more sophisticated. Increasingly, society tries to find the best approach to discuss how to find ways of balancing the use and development of the land resource according to the principles of sustainability. Population growth and the shift of the majority of the world's people to urban living have focused attention on urban and regional planning, metropolitanisation and how to govern and make the best use of the land resource. These matters have highlighted the importance of public participation. Planning legislation provides important opportunities for consultation and for engaging interested parties in individual decisions.

Different political jurisdictions have variously designed their systems to plan for and control the use and development of land. These differences reflect the diversity of cultures and contexts in which legal principles and institutional arrangements have been established. Historically and practically, the UK provides an interesting example of how the legal arrangements for land-use planning have evolved over time. Two features in particular are of interest.

First, planning is informed and influenced by a wider body of environmental law. For example, through the UK's membership of the European Union (EU) for over 40 years the UK planning system has been shaped by a number of European Directives that provide legal controls over, for example, habitats, water and species. The expansion of environmental law may be explained in part by a growing sensitivity to ecological matters and a shift to an eco-centric approach to environmental management. One of the consequences of the UK's June 2016 EU referendum result and the decision for the UK to leave the EU – so-called 'Brexit' – is the potentially reduced influence of this European-wide legal framing context. Nonetheless, other international laws and protocols, such as the Ramsar Convention in relation to wetlands, provide important environmental controls. Moreover, national governments ultimately perform a critical role in devising and implementing their own environmental law regimes that may be more or less protective in their aim.

Second, and influenced by an expanding human rights agenda, such as in relation to access to environmental information and environmental justice through the Aarhus Convention, or the United Nations Convention on the Rights of the Child, increasing emphasis is placed on individuals' rights to participate fully and in an informed way in socio-environmental decision-making arrangements. From this perspective, the land-use planning system provides an important democratic forum in which individuals can participate in decisions that affect the places where they live, work and relax.

On the one hand, such trends suggest a potential mainstreaming of planning, perhaps indicating a degree of uniformity. On the other hand, an emphasis on citizens' rights invites putting locality and place at centre stage. These influences help to explain the evolving differences in the legal frameworks for planning across the four national administrations of the UK.

Many commentators would contend that planning involves the management of social, economic and environmental change. Everywhere around us, change is evident. Demographic changes, such as an aging population in many developed economies, and new family formations, create pressures on the type, availability and location of housing. Changing consumer preferences, such as for out-of-town retail facilities or online shopping, similarly place new demands on the development of transport infrastructure, whether for the private motor car or for the delivery van. Acknowledgment of the disadvantages of conventional carbon fuel sources has necessitated alternative approaches to energy generation. New housing on greenfield sites, new road or rail schemes or wind or solar farms on established landscapes are just some of the development dilemmas that the planning system is designed to mediate.

Planning law also gives land protection from development. Reasons for granting protection may include giving form, identity and structure to our urban settlements. The creation of Green Belts has been a long-standing feature of the British planning system, but such designations are subject to development pressures, as is illustrated by discussions in the media about the arguments for and against house building in the Green Belt. Such debates arise because there is a perceived housing shortage. Planning law provides the legal framework and democratic forum in which discussion of the evidence, and of the pros and cons of building in certain areas, can take place. What is your own view? People will often have different opinions about what and where to build and disagreements are very likely. Put simply, the purpose of planning law is to create a democratic, formal and consistent decision-making framework for determining how societies use, develop, protect and enhance the built and natural environments within a given jurisdiction. This democratic decision-making arena is informed by technical and professional information, processes and advice, and by legal opinion.

The scale, intensity and diversity of demands put on land by different groups and interests, the different values individuals and communities hold about how land should or should not be used, and for what purpose(s), represent some of the most fundamental challenges facing any society. Land is a limited 'commodity', and one that we rely on for all aspects of our lives. Contemporary debates about fuel and food security, or experiences of flooding and coastal erosion, for example, emphasise both how precious and how vulnerable the land resource is. Reflecting on the different and competing uses we make of land highlights the need for a set of legal arrangements for planning its use and development. If land-use change is proposed, how should society decide whether it is appropriate, and under what conditions?

Land can clearly be used in a variety of different ways: for food; for buildings, such as housing, schools and shops; for public infrastructure, such as transport routes, airports or dams; for leisure, such as football pitches, community cultural facilities or playgrounds; for the disposal or management of waste, such as landfill sites; or for exploitation of minerals, such as sand and gravel extraction. Alternatively, society can elect to leave land relatively 'undeveloped', designating it as a Local Nature Reserve or Area of Outstanding Natural Beauty (AONB), or conserving wilderness areas to protect biodiversity and support vulnerable species – for instance, through the creation of National Parks. In developing policies, plans and forms of legal protection, the UK has developed one of the most sophisticated forms of town and country planning legislation (Bell et al, 2013), and it is to introducing that system that we now turn.

Land-use planning

As the Royal Town Planning Institute (RTPI), the UK-based professional body for planners, explains, systems of planning are designed to guide the right development, to the right place, and at the right time. An important set of activities involves the preparation of dedicated planning documents and policies at various scales. This includes the preparation of and consultation on geographically specific development plans. Development plans allocate land and set out development proposals, providing a longer-term, forward-planning policy framework and decision-making context for determining the suitability of site-specific proposals.

We often see new building work going on around us, or changes in how buildings are used. Other land may be left empty or under-used, or left vulnerable to flooding and landslide. Buildings may be abandoned in a derelict state, become run down and, over time, characterise the degeneration of an area. Planners continually monitor change and the diverse array of individual development activities in a given council district, including the completion of new housing schemes, or changes in the retail profile of a given area, for example. Keeping an up do date evidence base of land availability, monitoring the overall balance of high street functions or interrogating population data are some of the vital and highly technical activities in understanding future requirements for retail, business or industrial space, or the need for homes, schools, hospitals and care facilities within a council area. Planners working in the public sector who perform this type of planning activity are called policy officers. They tend to describe their occupation as forward planning or development planning.

Planning legislation sets out the time frames, conventionally measured in four-year cycles, for preparing and updating development plans. As projected visions for a particular area, these plans are critical for individual property owners and businesses, such as house builders because they provide the plan-led context in which the market plans and manages its assets and makes investment decisions. We would suggest that it is the plan-led context and discretionary nature of planning in Britain that makes the tasks involved in obtaining planning permission (development management) so interesting, since each individual planning application is judged on its particular merits, taking into account the specific circumstances of that development proposal at that time.

The currency of the relevant policies of the development plan and the nature of the land uses and development surrounding a proposed development site are all relevant – or material – to the decision. As we will explore, working within a politically determined decision-making process, a local planning officer is required to gather all the relevant details, carry out a site visit, undertake consultation of interested parties and weigh up the individual considerations material to that specific case. The evidence is then subject to political approval by local councillors (also known as elected members). As we shall see, the tasks require very specific skills in information gathering, synthesis, analysis and professional judgement. Development management in the UK is certainly not a mechanistic exercise, although certain types of development are permitted and don't require formal planning permission. Planning laws, and the associated case law, define the relevant criteria for determining individual planning applications.

While planners working in development planning are concerned with providing future-oriented frameworks for development, often for plan periods that span decades, planners who specialise in development management operate to much shorter time frames. Planning legislation prescribes decision-making activities and time frames for determining individual planning applications in terms of weeks and months, because society depends on the availability of timely and appropriate development to provide jobs, homes and community facilities, for example. However, while society may demand faster journeys, more parking spaces, better mobile phone reception or more convenient shopping facilities, there are also (often unspoken) expectations that valued open spaces or treasured landscapes will remain undeveloped. Who decides? An appropriate balance must be struck, and in a timely, transparent, efficient and accountable way.

In the UK, land and property development is generally driven by private, market interests. In practice, the market expects the planning system to provide certainty, consistency, connectivity and coordination in relation to how different land uses and developments are spatially distributed, while individuals also look to planning to protect private property interests. Development management planners thus need to work efficiently and effectively in order to support the development industry and private developers to progress their individual business ambitions and development objectives in line with up-to-date development plans, and in the most appropriate locations. In this sense, planners are important enablers of development. But, at the same time as positively supporting the beneficial societal outcomes of development – such as quality built environments with a range of employment, leisure, educational and community facilities – development managers must also anticipate any potential adverse impacts or effects of development proposals. Identifying, anticipating and weighing up all the different considerations for each individual planning application involves investigating the conditions and context of the development site and collecting views from a wide range of different stakeholders. Decision taking involves the exercise of professional judgement and balancing all the relevant evidence in the wider societal or public interest. However, what the public interest means at any given time or place is contentious.

Certain demolition activities also constitute development. Similarly, planning legislation provides a legal framework for protecting and potentially enhancing our built heritage so as to conserve, preserve and enhance specific areas, buildings and other structures, and this is a specialised field in its own right. Such planning controls can restrict what individual property owners can do. In the case of a listed building, for example, prior consent may have to be obtained from the relevant local planning authority (LPA) for any external (or even internal) works. Failure to obtain consent is contrary to planning law and may constitute a criminal offence, so it is important to be aware of the requirements of the particular legal framework and the authorities and bodies involved. The legal remit of planning extends to the protection of trees and hedgerows and to control of the erection of bill-boards or the amount and style of advertisements. This regulatory framework is for the wider public interest and societal well-being.

The tensions, potential conflicts and legal arguments around the use and development of land arise primarily because of individual property rights. The notion that 'an Englishman's home is his castle' tends to carry an assumption that ownership of the castle means the Englishman can do whatever he chooses with his castle in terms of use or development. However, planning law regulates individual rights to develop and use land and property. In this book we will discuss and explain why and how society has developed planning law as a decision–making framework to help decide what types of development undertaken by private individuals or interests are or are not in the wider societal or public interest.

Figure 1.1: Key relationships involved in development management decision-making

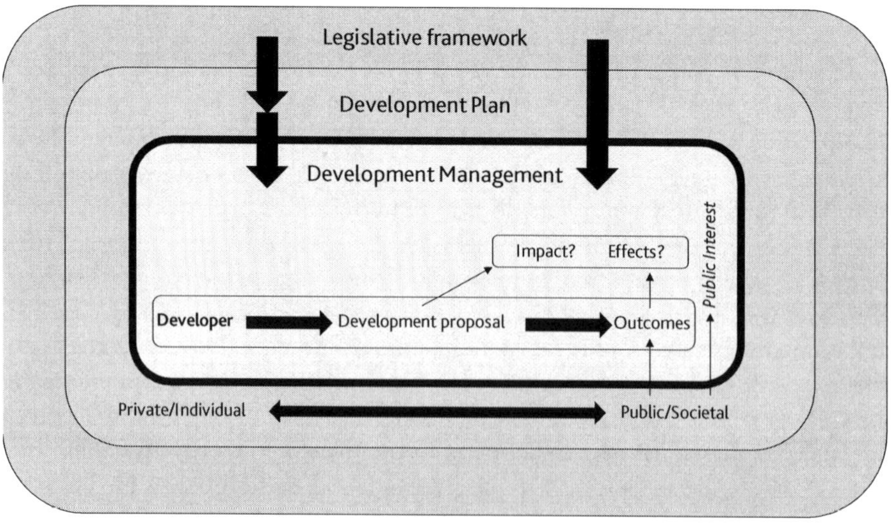

We will discuss the public interest in the light of wider planning considerations such as: the natural environment and the protection that planning law affords to the land resource and life systems it supports; the built environment and the historic, aesthetic and material values, for example, that we derive from our physical environments; and other less tangible but equally important cultural aspects that provide meaning, identity and a sense of place in our lives. Figure 1.1 illustrates the key relationships that, as we suggest, lie at the heart of development management decision-making.

Marine planning

As Chapter Three will elaborate, we have had various controls over land and a universal form of town and country planning for decades. Our seas and oceans are also a limited and scarce resource and are the subject of multiple and potentially conflicting uses. For example, the sea may be used for recreational purposes such as sailing, fishing, diving and jet-skiing; for shipping transportation; for commercial fishing; for national defence; and, increasingly, for energy exploitation such as wind, oil and gas. A fundamental question in relation to marine planning is: who owns the sea?

An established doctrine, 'Mare Liberum', translated as 'freedom of the sea', originated with Hugo Grotius, the so-called 'Father of International Law'. This rule has stood for open access to a 'common property' resource for over 400 years. The 'sea that belonged to no-one, free for all pioneers and explorers' has become a widely accepted norm in some quarters (Russ and Zeller, 2003, p 76). The notion of the seas being free and open has allowed their uncontrolled utilisation and exploitation. Indeed it can be argued that the very nature of the bundle of property rights pertaining to the marine environment and exploitation of the sea helps to explain what many see as the over-development and degradation of this resource. As we shall see, however, the perspective of 'Mare Liberum' has been challenged with the devising of new state controls, leading Russ and Zeller (2003) to identify what they have called a new doctrine of 'Mare Reservarum' (the reserved sea).

In understanding the exploitation of both the land and the sea a useful concept is the so-called 'tragedy of the commons' (Hardin, 1968). This refers to the over-use or over-development of a shared resource, such as common land. Where over-stocking of common land for grazing cattle, or over-fishing of the sea occurs, for example, the environment and users of that resource suffer. Two particular characteristics of common property resources help to explain this phenomenon. First, where on land a boundary fence may be erected, in a common environmental resource such as the sea control of access (exclusion) is difficult. Second, common property resources are subject to joint use and rivalry (subtractability) (Feeny et al, 1996). Depending on the circumstances, possible responses to the over-exploitation of resources may variously involve forms of self-regulation, the instigation of private property rights, state intervention and government control or a combination of these institutional arrangements.

Over-exploitation of the marine resource stems from how the particular bundle of marine property rights has evolved over time. In the context of the sea we can point to 'open access'; 'private property' (as enjoyed by the Crown Estate, for example); 'communal property', where defined rights held by certain groups or bodies may enable the exclusion of others; and 'state property', which empowers the state to regulate use of and control access to the marine resource (Feeny et al, 1996). In practice, the different rights may well overlap, and state–market–civil relations vary. Moreover, the Crown Estate enjoys particular rights, including the rights to explore and utilise the natural resources of the UK Continental Shelf (excluding oil, gas and coal) to a distance of 200 nautical miles – the Exclusive Economic Zone (EEZ) – and rights to the sea bed to a distance of 12 nautical miles. It also owns approximately 55% of the foreshore and around half of the beds of estuaries and tidal rivers in the UK. The rest of the ownership is vested in either public (local authority) or private landowners. We can begin to see how exercising controls over the various rights that exist in terrestrial and marine environments can become quite complex, as rights are differently bundled depending on the context.

As with the terrestrial environment, management of the marine resource is complex as a consequence of the nature of the different rights involved. Moreover, and following the arguments made by Feeny and colleagues (1996), the use and development of an environmental resource will likely be affected by the different motivations and characteristics of the individuals and bodies involved and how different resource users interact. Behaviours will also be influenced by the nature and culture of existing institutional arrangements, the ability to reform or create new rules of the game and how the regulatory authorities involved behave.

Institutional arrangements of planning

The legal arrangements for planning mean that there are a number of players and interests to be considered. Planning legislation sets out the statutory requirements, powers, time frames, rules and responsibilities for taking decisions, specifying the duties and roles of particular bodies and setting out how the general public can engage at various times. Our principal focus, the role of the development management planner in the decision-making process, is critical because in the UK planning tradition certain bodies are authorised in law to grant or refuse planning permission. In most council areas it is the LPA that makes those decisions, based on input from professional planners (officers) and locally elected politicians (councillors). (We will also make reference to certain specialist areas, such as mineral and waste planning, where separate authority exists.) Put simply, the role of the development management planner is to synthesise all the relevant information regarding an individual planning application to ensure that the effects and impacts of a particular development proposal do not adversely affect issues of wider public interest.

This section looks in a little more detail at the different players involved in planning, in order to set the context. A useful way of understanding the legal regime for planning is to think about the planning system as providing the 'rules of the game', so that landowners, investors, developers, businesses and local communities, for example, have a degree of certainty about what type of land uses and physical structures may be permitted in a particular area. We also outline what this means in practice by differentiating between the spatial scales and sectoral interests involved.

Different scales involved in planning

In this book we focus on the British planning tradition, and also tease out certain differences across the four constituent parts of the UK. Since 1999 we have seen the iterative – and often quite distinct – devolution of political powers across the UK: Scotland, Wales and Northern Ireland have variously taken the opportunity to reform and modernise their individual planning systems. There have always been subtle differences in the planning systems operating across the UK but under devolution these differences have become more accentuated. The result of the 2016 EU referendum and its implications on the nature of the UK's relationship with the EU will also alter the wider planning and development context. In terms of primary legislation, we address what the fluid constitutional context means in practice in more detail in Chapter Four, but the important point is that prevailing political priorities in the different parts of the UK have led to the emergence of different planning systems and legal arrangements. For the most part, the basic principles and terminology are similar, but there are subtle territorial differences that reflect different socio-cultural and development priorities.

This book considers those principles that transcend the separate jurisdictions of the UK, but we will also look specifically at England and the Westminster Parliament, the Scottish Parliament, the Welsh Assembly and the Northern Ireland Assembly. Each of these bodies has law-making powers with respect to land-use planning and each administration has devised subtle changes to reflect its particular circumstances. It is very important to be aware that the different LPAs that deal with planning decisions in England, Scotland, Wales and Northern Ireland operate under separate planning legislation. Should you be living or working in different parts of the UK, you need to make sure that you are observing the country-specific planning legislation. The Republic of Ireland, as a separate member state of the EU, has a different planning system. Therefore planning in Northern Ireland (the only part of the UK with a land border with another EU member state) introduces important local and strategic planning and development issues for cross-border working on the island of Ireland.

Throughout this book we make reference to different layers of government, paying particular attention to the legal powers and roles played by central and local government. This arrangement is very important in understanding the operation of planning law, since planning powers are variously allocated between central government and LPAs. From the perspective of planning as a state activity it is important to understand that planning also deals with both strategic and operational matters and that checks and balances variously operate across the different levels and in relation to other spheres of activity, such as economic development and infrastructure planning. Political oversight, right of appeal and judicial review, for example, offer mechanisms for ensuring the rigour and legitimacy of planning.

How spatial planning is organised across the four national administrations varies, with a growing focus on city-regional scales. For example, in 2006 Scotland adopted a hierarchical, scalar approach to deal with planning and development issues across Scotland and at the level of its 32 council areas. Separate arrangements exist for its two National Parks. This approach is intended to enable proportionate powers to be exercised over development schemes of national and strategic importance; city-regional development issues, which tend to cut across local government council boundaries; and local planning concerns. Within this broad context, planning laws address both major and minor developments, namely:

- a territorial-wide plan – the National Planning Framework, now in its third iteration and covering the full extent of the territory;
- four strategic development plans (covering the principal city-regions of Aberdeen, Dundee, Edinburgh and Glasgow);
- 32 local development plans.

The Independent Review of the Scottish Planning System (Beveridge et al, 2016) questioned the effectiveness of the strategic development planning level in practice. What such thinking means for the increasing development pressures on metropolitan areas remains to be seen. However, it is a core principle of planning decision-making in the UK that decisions are best taken at the local level.

Throughout this book we are primarily concerned with the development of individual sites or buildings at the local level. The site-specific nature of development underlies our focus on the development management aspects of planning – whether this involves how a building or piece of land is used, for example, or what form a particular development takes. We will elaborate the practical aspects of securing planning permission or consent in relation to the important role that development plans play in that process.

Different interests involved in planning

Given that land is ultimately a shared resource, the role of planning is to mediate between the different property rights and interests. Various actors, from landowners to local or international corporate developers, elected politicians and appointed officers, such as planners, other government bodies, such as those involved with transport or environmental health, and local communities and interest groups, such as the Royal Society for the Protection of Birds (RSPB), each have a role to play in different development scenarios. For ease of explanation we will be concerned with three broad sectors: the public, private and third sectors.

First, there is a tendency to portray planning as solely a public sector activity. The public sector (or state) dimension is quite complex, comprising a hierarchy of levels of government and different statutory bodies. As we will discuss later, central government exercises certain statutory controls over local government – for example, there are rules in place so as to avoid an individual local authority effectively granting planning permission to itself. There are also occasions where central government considers a development to be of national importance and thus uses call-in powers to determine the application at the national level. For the most part, however, we will focus on the functioning of LPAs and the ways in which individual planning officers decide on applications for planning permission. We will consider what this arrangement means in terms of the legal requirements to consult other bodies of the state, such as a statutory body concerned with environmental protection, and relationships with locally elected politicians, variously called local councillors or elected members. This relationship between officers and elected members is particularly interesting and codes of conduct have been developed over time to support the functioning of planning law.

Second, proposing, regulating and managing development has to be a collaborative activity and requires the relevant public and private parties to be actively involved. The private sector is critical to the development process because, it is argued, ideas, innovation and investment stem primarily from the market. While development proposals may be made and funded by the state, in this book we focus on how the planning system responds to applications by individual householders, volume house builders and corporate enterprises. A core challenge facing those predicting the future land-use requirements of a particular society is that needs and desires change. Although a particular local area may need more affordable housing, a particular investor may wish to build a number of executive homes. The profit motive underlies the majority of development decisions; land is a scarce resource and developers will wish to extract the most profit from any proposal. The job of the planning officer (as the state's representative) is to ensure that the private interests of the developer do not adversely affect the wider interests of society. This balancing act lies at the crux of development management and may be considered the basis of the professional planner's administrative role.

Third, civil society or the voluntary (or third) sector also has a critical role to play. In addition to the general public, we characterise this diverse sector as comprising a range of different private individuals and organisations (such as the National Trust or Friends of the Earth) with different financial and political support. All such bodies, whether they be charities, think-tanks, advocacy groups or campaigning organisations, contribute to wider public debates about planning, as well as provide responses in relation to specific development proposals. As we discuss in Chapter Eleven, planning law provides very particular arrangements for who can and cannot challenge planning decisions. Thus, while a developer (the first party) can appeal a planning decision, a third party cannot. The issue of third-party rights of appeal remains a point of controversy.

Over the course of the book we consider the implications of how planning legislation regulates development and change from three broad perspectives:

- the *state*, that is, what government and authorised parties are empowered and required to do under the law;
- the *market*, that is, how individual developers, including commercial interests, landowners, businesses and householders, are affected by planning legislation and in what ways they can challenge and appeal against decisions;
- *civil society*, that is, the general public/non-state actors, and the legal rights people enjoy under planning legislation to be consulted on planning applications, whether as neighbours, communities, special interest groups or private citizens.

Overview of the book

In the remainder of this book we outline the basic principles underpinning planning law and guide you to sources of information that will be helpful in navigating the legal arrangements. Figure 1.2, 'The essentials of planning law at a glance', provides a simplified overview of the principal elements we will cover. Whether you are an active citizen, a local politician or a professional working in the built environment, we hope that this book will be a useful introductory text.

Chapter Two outlines the changing nature of planning law and introduces some key terms. In particular, it considers the term regulation and how planning may be variously socially constructed.

Chapter Three places planning law in a historical context, explaining how the legal arrangements have evolved and matured over time.

Chapter Four presents the planning contexts across the devolved UK, outlining the policy and development planning arrangements.

Following this setting of the context, Chapters Five to Seven concentrate on decision-making activities and, specifically, on how we regulate and control development. Chapter Five introduces core concepts and terminology, defining the meaning of 'development'. Chapter Six deals with development management, explaining how different development proposals are processed and what constitutes 'permitted development'. Chapter Seven deals with the role played by planning conditions and with aspects of planning gain.

Chapters Eight and Nine look at other forms of planning control that manage different forms of change in the built and natural environment. These controls often operate in parallel with the core planning permission system. Chapter Eight considers the special planning arrangements that exist for waste, minerals and marine planning. Chapter Nine covers specific arrangements for the control of matters such as advertisement, conservation and listed building consents (LBCs) and Tree Preservation Orders (TPOs).

Chapter Ten covers enforcement. This is where permission or consent for development has not been obtained and where it is necessary, after the event, to regularise – or to take action against – development. Enforcement plays a very important role in terms of validating planning as an activity, since it confirms that action by the state (for example the LPA or, in some cases, the police) will be taken against those who do not comply with the laws of planning.

Chapter Eleven first looks at how developers can appeal against a decision. It then looks at the arrangements to challenge how a decision has been reached (Judicial Review [JR]). This area of planning law addresses procedural aspects. We also comment on complaints procedures and the role of the Ombudsman.

The final chapter concludes with some observations about how what we have learned about planning law fits into the bigger picture of managing the land and marine resources. In particular, we reflect on the importance of joint working, public participation and how well the planning system performs as a core part of the democratic system. Given the changing socioeconomic context, and important constitutional and environmental drivers in train, we also speculate on some likely implications for planning legislation, specifically in relation to emerging areas, such as well-being, community planning and a focus on aligning public services to deliver strategic outcomes.

Figure 1.2: The essentials of planning law at a glance

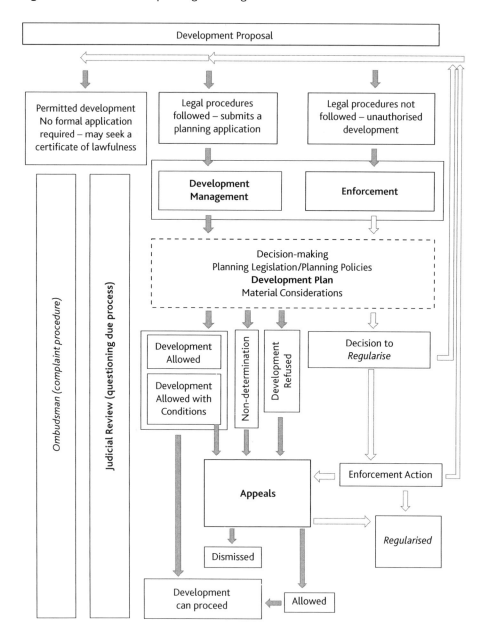

Recommended reading

Throughout this book we will point you to further reading and sources. Some general texts we would suggest are:

Cullingworth, B., Nadin, V., Hart, T., Davoudi, S., Pendlebury, J., Vigar, G., Webb, D. and Townshed, T. (2015) *Town and country planning in the UK*, 15th edn, Abingdon-on-Thames: Routledge.

Greed, C. and Johnson, D. (2014) *Planning in the UK: An introduction*, Basingstoke: Palgrave Macmillan.

For consideration of the process of development in a design- and finance-aware discussion:

Adams, D. and Tiesdell, S. (2013) *Shaping places: Urban planning, design and development*, Abingdon-on-Thames: Routledge.

For more detailed discussion of environmental law:

Bell, S., McGillivray, D. and Pederson, O.W. (2013) *Environmental law*, 8th edn, Oxford: Oxford University Press.

TWO

The nature of planning law

Chapter contents

- Ideologies of modern planning law
- Legal and planning systems across the devolved UK
- Sources of planning law
- Legislation
- Case law
- The social construction of planning law
- A political-economy approach to planning law
- Regulatory aspects of planning
- Types of regulation
- Reform and modernisation of planning under devolution
- Towards better regulation
- Chapter summary

Introduction

This chapter introduces some key terminology and aims to help you to understand and contextualise some of the basics of planning law. We identify certain key drivers that over time have influenced the reformulation of planning law in the UK. The chapter will both help you to understand the day-to-day legal arrangements shaping development management decision-making and the importance of legislation and case law, and provide you with a robust grounding in the wider context of planning law and some of the nuances of regulation and what regulatory regimes seek to achieve. You will then be able to engage in on-going debates about the relevance of environmental regulatory arrangements to meet present-day challenges and will appreciate the prevailing pressures and economic drivers for the reform of planning law and the related modernisation of the planning system.

Chapter One offered an overview of the dynamics of the land-use planning system and explained why we have planning laws. In this chapter we go into more detail about the social context in which planning law is conceived, designed, made and implemented. The chapter identifies some of the main ideological and theoretical stances that help to explain planning as a particular type of state regulation and the reasons why planning laws are continually evolving. We also outline some important terminology related to planning law. (Some people criticise planning for using 'planning jargon', but we would argue that in practice there are certain key legal terms and concepts that are set out in the planning legislation and through case law. These terms form part of the accepted language of planning.) Also in this chapter we introduce the idea of social construction as a way to explain planning law as a social practice, subject to contestation and reformulation. We begin, however, by outlining McAuslan's (1980) three ideologies of modern planning law, which continue to provide a solid basis for understanding the evolution of land-use planning and some of the fundamental tensions involved.

Ideologies of modern planning law

Systems of law exist to enable structure, order and control over behaviours and to protect or advance certain rights. As we discuss in more detail in Chapter Three, the form and management of built and natural environments have been influenced over centuries through the introduction and practice of various types of legislation and the interpretation and application of law. As theories of planning have evolved, so the legal arrangements for planning have matured, and vice versa.

In his seminal work, *The Ideologies of Planning Law*, McAuslan (1980) identified three ideologies that, taken together, inform the nature of modern planning law. He argued that, over time, different rationales have been advanced to justify the existence of planning law. These legal rationales have gained prominence – or indeed dominance – at different points in time, reflecting changing circumstances. Initially the aim was the protection of private property; then the introduction of state controls in the post-war period asserted a concern with the public interest;

Figure 2.1: McAuslan's (1980) ideologies of planning law

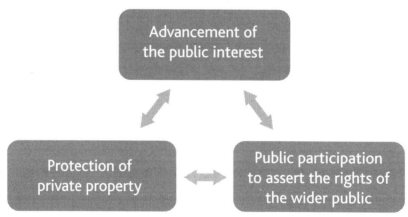

Source: Adapted from McAuslan (1980).

and from the late 1960s in the UK there was an emphasis on public participation as a way to better assert the rights of the wider public.

We examine the historical development of planning law in the UK in more detail in the next chapter, but McAuslan's thinking alerts us to three broad justifications for the modern planning law regime. Figure 2.1 presents these ideologies as equally weighted, but one can easily imagine how one ideology might be advanced as more or less important, or be subject to capture by a particular interest that is keen to give greater weight to one aspect of planning law. Planning systems thus vary across time and space, and in the light of dominant interest groups.

Legal and planning systems across the devolved UK

Legal systems vary around the world; Newman and Thornley (1996), for example, identify various 'families'. Across Europe most legal systems are based upon civil law, but in England and Wales there is a common law tradition. Civil law is modelled on the basis of the core principles being referable, effectively meaning that legal principles are written and stated in text. Civil law is provided by jurists, whose work provides the primary source of law, and the system is often referred to as a codified system because of the manner in which law exists. In contrast, in common law systems the law is built up by judges and their individual judgments. It is the decisions of the Courts, alongside the relevant planning legislation, that cumulatively provide the legal framework for planning decision-making. Scotland (Scots Law) has a hybrid system combining civil and common law features that is relatively more distinct. There is an important similarity in planning decision-making arrangements across the present devolved UK that merits discussion, and that is the nature of the British planning tradition, which is based on a discretionary planning system.

Regulatory planning systems

Within a regulatory system of planning the regulations in place prescribe precisely what is controlled by a planning system, what is permitted in given circumstances and what conditions, requirements and limitations exist. Regulatory systems are sometimes called zoned systems because the manner in which this form of system is translated into practice is often through zoned plans that prescribe what a given area is designated for, and what can and cannot happen within the designated space (or zone). This approach may be seen as limiting flexibility in favour of creating greater certainty.

Discretionary planning systems

Within a discretionary system, as in the UK, the decision-making process is very different in many respects. The scope of control is defined in the first instance through planning legislation (a regulatory element within the system), with subsequent legal interpretation provided by judges in the Courts (case law). The Courts therefore play a hugely important role in planning in the UK. Through their arguments and decisions judges provide the detail and clarity to interpret the meaning and spirit of legislation. Thus, through the building up of a body of case law the decisions of the Courts have helped the operation and application of the planning system to be understood and practised (Wood et al, 2011).

A word of caution

Notwithstanding these broad distinctions, it would be far too simplistic to state that a planning system is either a regulatory model or a discretionary one. For example, the United States operates on a common law legal system but has a regulatory planning system in operation, bringing together a zoned planning system with the power of the Courts to establish clarification, interpretation and the basis for decisions (Wood et al, 2011). Considerable care should thus be taken before making any categorical assumptions about the nature of particular systems of law or models of planning system. As we discuss again in Chapter Three, we can place planning systems on a spectrum from regulatory to discretionary. Thus, forms of discretion will exist within regulatory systems, even if this is only the ability to replace a plan (or element of a plan) early so as to allow a different future to be realised. Similarly, a discretionary system will have some regulatory elements. In the UK, a regulatory arrangement exists through the various planning legislation, and there is no question that the system of permitted development rights (discussed in Chapter Six) represents a regulated element within a discretionary model.

Sources of planning law

Two sources of planning law underpin the planning systems operating in England, Wales, Scotland and Northern Ireland: legislation and case law, the former comprised of primary and secondary legislation. Before we look at these two sources we first introduce the individual legislatures (law-making bodies) operating in the four administrations.

Legislatures of the devolved UK

Devolution in the UK enables Scotland, Wales and Northern Ireland to govern their own territory, subject to the reserved matters held by Westminster. Planning matters for England are covered by the Westminster Parliament, which also has responsibility for certain UK-wide matters. The extent of the legislative powers to the devolved governments varies, with Scotland having relatively more extensive legal independence as compared to Wales and Northern Ireland. Since the late 1990s a range of powers have been progressively transferred to national parliaments and assemblies following referenda in Scotland and Wales (1997) and Northern

Ireland (1998). The resulting legislatures are, respectively, the Scottish Parliament, National Assembly for Wales and Northern Ireland Assembly.

The degree of legislative autonomy and the extent of the matters devolved to each country varies. Broadly, the areas for which the Scottish Government, Welsh Government and Northern Ireland Executive are responsible include health, education, culture, the environment, transport and local government, whereas the UK-wide government remains responsible for foreign affairs, defence, social security, macro-economic management and trade, and for all other state matters in England. In terms of legislation, town and country planning is an environmental matter and is thus devolved.

Although separate governments were established under devolution following the referenda, devolution has taken place over different time frames. Under the Scotland Act 1998, the Scottish Parliament was given powers to make legislation in devolved areas, including town and country planning. Under the Government of Wales Act 1998, however, the Welsh Government was not granted competence to pass Acts, and so to make primary legislation in the area of town and country planning. This occurred a little later in 2011, following the commencement of Part 4 of the Government of Wales Act 2006 (Cave et al, 2013). Prior to this, the Welsh Government used policy to shape the planning system to fit the Welsh context. Significantly, the Planning (Wales) Act 2015 is the first major piece of primary legislation to be passed by the Welsh Assembly.

In Northern Ireland, the Planning (Northern Ireland) Order 1991, and the earlier 1972 Order, set out the role of the (former) Department of the Environment (DOE) with regard to planning functions for formulating and coordinating policy, but did not confer law-making powers (Cave et al, 2013). Because of the political situation in Northern Ireland arising from the period known as 'The Troubles' planning arrangements have evolved at a very different pace from elsewhere in the UK. Wider public sector reform and local government reorganisation, however, have meant that planning has been a core part of a major legislative agenda and programme for change associated with the Review of Public Administration in Northern Ireland under devolution.

Legislation

Legislation is law made through Acts by the responsible legislature. For planning matters in the UK the power to legislate is in most respects a devolved matter. In order to fully understand the nature of devolution, and the impact and role of legislation within the individual national planning systems, it is necessary to explain the significance of the two main types of legislation, namely, primary and secondary legislation.

Primary legislation

Primary legislation sets out the basic legal framework for an area, such as town and country planning. As explained above, each of the devolved nations now has the necessary powers to make its own primary legislation on environmental and planning matters. Primary legislation in the UK is comprised of Acts, made following the passage of a Bill through the respective legislature. In some instances an Act comes into force immediately, or after a transitional period that is generally set out in the Act. In other instances, however, an Order must be made to commence a particular part of an Act. Therefore, when viewing legislative documents, one must take care not to assume that all parts of an Act are actively in force. Where an Act covers more than one administration, such as the Town and Country Planning Act 1990, which covers both England and Wales, some of its parts may be in force in one nation but not in another. The primary legislation associated with town and country planning covers all aspects of the planning system, including, for example, prescribing the requirement to prepare local plans, defining the meaning of development, setting out how different types of planning application should be determined, defining enforcement powers and establishing the arrangements for appeals.

A further significant point about primary legislation is that often, instead of stating the full details associated with a given matter, an Act will instead provide power for further detail to be specified in subordinate or secondary legislation, usually in the form of Regulations or an Order. In effect, primary powers can at times be quite broad, thereby allowing secondary legislation to be amended or updated at different times, or shaped to the context of a particular devolved nation. This arrangement is held to provide efficiency and a degree of flexibility.

The creation of primary legislation can be a very lengthy process. The Housing and Planning Act 2016 in England took 150 days to complete the processes of the House of Commons and House of Lords. The complete end-to-end process can therefore take a considerable period of time. To take the drafting of the Planning (Wales) Act 2015 as an example, an independent advisory group first published its recommendations, *Towards a Welsh Planning Act* (Welsh Government, 2012a). These recommendations were followed by months of public consultation, formal assessment and scrutiny by the Assembly before the legislation could be passed. In practice, it took almost three years for the Planning (Wales) Act 2015 to receive Royal Assent. This Act is in addition to the Town and Country Planning Act 1990 (which preceded devolution in the UK and applies to England and Wales). This cumulative process is a key point to bear in mind; new legislation does not always replace or stand separately from the existing regulatory framework: it can adapt it. The 2015 Act amends some of the sections of the 1990 Act as they apply to Wales, rather than replacing the Act in its entirety.

Secondary legislation

Secondary legislation is subordinate to the main Act in force and specifies the details of a particular law. The ability to make secondary legislation provides governments with flexibility to change the law through Statutory Instruments (SIs) without having to go through the lengthy process of getting an Act through Parliament. While the primary legislation sets out the broad framework, secondary legislation, for example, may include: the details of what is required to ensure that a planning application is valid; the practical details of appeal procedures; or detailed requirements of consultation in relation to the submission of a planning application.

From this perspective, SIs are important in providing the necessary legal detail under which a particular (planning) Act works (operates) in practice. SIs are important because they flesh out (make provision for) the operation of particular Acts. Thus, for example, while Part 2 of the Planning and Compulsory Purchase Act 2004 ('the Act') established a system of local development planning in England, it was the subsequent Town and Country Planning (Local Planning) (England) Regulations 2012 that set out the detail for the operation of that system. As the Explanatory Note accompanying those Regulations explains, certain parts:

> prescribe the form and content of local plans and supplementary planning documents (to be prepared by local planning authorities) and prescribes which documents are to be local plans. The Regulations also prescribe the process for preparation of the local plans and supplementary planning documents. (SI 2012 No. 767, p 23)

We can see from the style and tone of the language that the Regulations are prescriptive – or mandatory – in terms of who does what, when and how. Taken together, then, the primary and secondary legislation in force across the UK provide the framework and detail for how each planning system should operate.

Case law

Under the UK's discretionary system, case law is the second source of planning law. As with other aspects of public administration, planning decisions may be challenged through the Courts. Judges' decisions are, then, important in providing clarity and understanding of the planning system, its terminology and decisions taken. The Courts exist to ensure procedural correctness and for the interpretation and application of legislation.

In strict administrative terms the nature of the law varies only marginally between the systems of England and Wales and those of Scotland and Northern Ireland. Land law is one area, in particular, where differences exist, such as in the interpretation of freeholds and leaseholds. For our purposes, however, there are sufficient similarities for us to discuss broad principles of decision-making.

Moreover, the nature of the issues being considered means that case law has relevance across the devolved UK. In practical terms, the volume of the English and Welsh body of case law also means that these decisions often dominate planning law discussions concerning case law. Although English and Welsh case law will not be binding outside of England and Wales, it remains valuable as precedent, offering insights into how earlier learned individuals have understood and interpreted legal issues. This approach leads to consideration of planning law as a particular social practice.

The social construction of planning law

Debates in society, whether in the media, in universities and research centres, in Parliament or grassroots politics, in clubs and societies, in streets or sitting-rooms, in popular culture and the arts, individually and cumulatively influence thinking about the role and rule of law. As a social practice, law is actively shaped by societal thinking. Even though the common law tradition provides a solid and relatively stable body of case law and a shared understanding of certain core concepts, the aims and purposes of planning are socially constructed.

Social construction is a way of understanding and jointly creating (constructing) meaning. As a way of understanding our shared social reality of planning law, this approach to engaging with the world requires us to appreciate that institutional arrangements and the norms and social practices underpinning these arrangements can be rejected, maintained or reformulated by those involved; different configurations of planning law could be advanced to address alternative objectives. In other words, planning law and the associated legal systems and paraphernalia do not exist in a vacuum, separate from human beings and immutable for all time, but are products of social interactions. Systems of planning law are situated in time and place, and by the societies they serve.

The nature of planning law and how laws work in practice is then subject to dominant ideas, influences and values – as McAuslan's (1980) ideologies demonstrate. Societies develop legal frameworks in line with shared beliefs, traditions and values. These may very likely be promoted through political channels. In this way legal arrangements may become accepted, normalised and routinised – or they may be viewed as technically out-dated, un-useful or obsolete. By way of example, we can point to how planning controls over certain types of early factory usage became redundant. As technological improvements are made, the adverse impacts of certain land uses may be overcome and legal provisions may then be relaxed.

Arguments for and against the design of planning law and practice are very differently represented, depending on broader political and ideological values with respect to how much control the state should exercise over the free market, and to what extent private interests should be controlled in meeting wider societal interests. The history of planning legislation clearly shows on-going efforts variously to consolidate, amend, revoke or repeal various legislative provisions so as to better fit contemporary requirements. Thus, as contexts have changed, so have ideas about the role of the state, how planning should be organised and what the remit of planning law should be. A political-economy perspective is one way to structure a time-line for thinking about how planning law has changed.

A political-economy approach to planning law

A political-economy perspective pays attention to the interplay between politics, economics and law. Inter-disciplinary in its focus, a political-economy lens provides us with a way of understanding state–market–civil relations and, importantly for our purposes, the role of regulation in society. An appreciation of how politics, economics and law interrelate in a particular society is vital if we are to understand what planning law is intended and designed to do at any given time and why institutional arrangements then assume particular forms.

At one level, a political-economy perspective explains why different institutional arrangements and operational dynamics exist under capitalist, socialist or communist economic systems. Specifically, studying planning law through a political-economy lens means that we are required to ask probing questions about the nature of the wider intellectual and political debates that are concerned with the land resource and how land is used and developed. Debates over planning law inevitably involve the power and influence of property rights. Context is everything.

Values, beliefs and political imperatives generate greater or less legitimacy for specific legal planning provisions. In the post-Second World War period a conventional presentation of competing political traditions is as left wing (Labour) and right wing (Conservative). While these distinctions are certainly much more nuanced in practice, particularly when one takes into account the nationalist parties of Wales and Scotland and the various political parties in Northern Ireland, the left–right distinction makes a general point concerning the role of regulation in society. Giddens (2013, p 70), for example, characterised the political beliefs of 'right' and 'left' as: 'The neoliberals want to shrink the state; the social democrats, historically, have been keen to expand it.' Fundamentally, the nature, form and purpose of planning law will be determined by which political viewpoints and ideologies hold sway.

We will not go into detail here on the implications of these political debates for planning (see some suggested texts at the end of this chapter), nor identify all the different types and effects of regulation. Suffice it to say that our perspective is that land-use planning forms an integral and necessary part of the state's regulatory and governance apparatus to control the actions of the free market in the public interest. This is only one view, however, and not everyone necessarily agrees with this line of reasoning.

Arguments against statutory planning present evidence that planning regulations are costly to business, cause time delays, involve unnecessary paperwork and reduce the amount of land available for development. From a neoliberal perspective, such state bureaucratic arrangements are sometimes provocatively criticised as 'red tape'. This helps to explain why planning law is subject to pressures for change, particularly with respect to simplification of procedures and regulations.

It is generally accepted that the setting up of the welfare state, of which the Town and Country Planning Act 1947 was a part, benefited from a post-war consensus between the political parties. A shared agenda based on social-democratic principles enabled a process of reconstruction, even if there were party-political differences at the margins. During the late 1960s a degree of civil unrest challenged established state–market–civil relations, prompting efforts to enhance public participation in planning – ideological shifts identified by McAuslan (1980). As Giddens (1998) explains, the social-democratic period of political consensus began to be severely undermined after the mid-1970s, to be replaced by neoliberal thinking.

As a consequence of these broad ideological shifts, during the 1980s and early 1990s, in particular, there were systematic efforts to reduce planning controls (see, for example, Thornley, 1993). Under the administrations of prime ministers Thatcher and Major, in particular, emphasis was placed on creating a planning law framework, such as Enterprise Zones and Simplified Planning Zones, that made land-use and development decision-making easier. Legislation was also used to create alternative legal planning bodies, including Urban Development Corporations. These initiatives were consistent with neoliberal thinking that emphasised the need to modernise state–market–civil relations, including the privatisation of certain state-owned bodies, such as British Telecom, or the sale of council-owned housing.

The election of a Labour government under Tony Blair as prime minister in 1997 has been described as offering a 'third way' (Giddens, 1998). This idea suggests an attempt to merge the broad approaches of Left and Right with respect to designing and managing state–market–civil relations. The agenda of reform and modernisation that complemented political devolution at that time – and that has shaped planning law since the turn of the millennium – may then be seen as being influenced by some of the preceding social democratic ideals, as well as (new) neoliberal ideas about what constitutes an appropriate modern state apparatus. Subsequent administrations have influenced the nature of contemporary forms of planning, such as through the localism agenda under the Conservative–Liberal Democrat Coalition. As we shall see in the final chapter, ideas about the perceived ideal legal arrangements for planning appear to be becoming normalised under established neoliberal influences to reduce state controls.

If you are engaged in planning – whether as a developer, a private sector planner or a local government planning officer, or certainly as a local councillor – you will be unable to avoid the truism that 'planning is political', and there are interesting debates to be had in relation to the appropriate reach of the state. The continuing interest in creating an appropriate planning regime to provide certainty and consistency in decision-making about the use and development of land suggests that the fundamental benefits of planning law are accepted, even if improvements could be made to the workings of the system. As the on-going development of case law illustrates, however, it is issues of interpretation and application of planning law, and the types of controls exercised, that make this such an interesting and dynamic area in which to work.

Regulatory aspects of planning

Putting regulation into effect can be quite a complicated social practice, involving a number of different aspects. Bell et al (2013, p 228) in their comprehensive book, *Introduction to Environmental Law*, state:

> In practice, environmental law is made up of more than mere rules that forbid pollution and other forms of environmental harm. The process of environmental regulation begins before laws are made, when policies are established that can be translated into laws. Once in place, environmental laws have to be given practical effect through the establishment of environmental standards, and systems of administrative decision-making and enforcement. Thus, the system of environmental regulation involves many different aspects, including the setting, application, and on-going review of environmental standards.

If we accept that planning law performs a useful societal function, we then need to understand the different forms and roles that regulation plays. Understanding why we regulate and how we regulate can help us to reflect on the merits and effectiveness of regulation. In short, in making the case for planning law, we need to ask questions like: Is this working? Could we do better? Have we prevented harm occurring? Have there been any unintended consequences? Have we achieved the desired outcomes? Is planning fit for purpose? Is the system proportionate? These are the sorts of questions that inform contemporary modernisation and reform agendas about the nature and extent of regulation and control.

Anticipatory, continuing and adaptive controls

We have already made reference to regulations, in the sense of rules (see also Chapter Three, which considers the related role of building regulations). The word 'regulation' is sometimes used in other ways, as in planning 'regulates' (zones) the amount of land that is allocated or available for a particular use; that is, planning regulates the supply of land. Planning policies also regulate (control) where development is located – such as not in a Site of Special Scientific Interest (SSSI). LPAs and related environmental protection agencies, such as the Scottish Environmental Protection Agency, may be referred to as regulatory bodies. Given that planning law complements a much bigger field of environmental law, it is important to appreciate that regulatory approaches take different forms. In this section we make some general points to help explain how laws and regulations work and why reform and modernisation of (planning) legislation have attracted such attention.

It is helpful to position planning law as integral to a wider body of law concerned with environmental protection, and it is worth heeding the distinction highlighted by Bell et al (2013) in terms of two general types of regulatory mechanism: anticipatory controls and continuing controls. Planning is an anticipatory form of control in that use or development of land is prohibited unless planning permission is granted. In effect, the relevant LPA determines whether planning permission should be granted. This type of anticipatory control means that potential environmental (or indeed social) harm can be avoided. Permission has to be granted before action can take place.

Continuing (or operational) controls, on the other hand, relate to on-going controls or conditions over land and property use and development. For example, the LPA may request that certain activities, such as the operation of a quarry, take place during certain hours. As we shall see in Chapter Seven, the use of planning conditions can enable development to proceed without harm being caused. In our example a condition might be used to control the traffic, noise and air pollution caused by the movement of lorries.

A related regulatory category, adaptive management controls, is effectively a combination of anticipatory and continuing controls (Bell et al, 2013). Adaptive management regulatory measures concern developments where a temporary permission is granted so as to assess the impacts of development over a restricted period. Such a 'trial run' would enable any effects from development to be given more detailed consideration. What these distinctions help to illustrate is the different uses and purposes of regulatory controls and some of the different time frames involved. Where major developments are concerned, potential developers may find that they have to comply with a range of different pieces of legislation. It is important to understand where planning law fits in this jig-saw.

Types of regulation

In practice, the planning system involves different types of regulation. Figure 1.1 (p 10) represented the role of decision-making and development management as managing development outcomes to maximise the public interest and minimise or eliminate the adverse effects of the impacts of development. Planning law may thus be understood as goal-conflict regulation, since, in regulating development, its role is to manage potential conflict between an individual (private) interest and the public interest. As we shall see in more detail in Chapter Six, in practice, planners seek to collate the necessary evidence, present the information in a clear, concise and transparent way and use the available participatory mechanisms to debate (and hopefully resolve) the trade-offs. Such resolution is not always easy to achieve. For example, the goals of planning law may involve aspects of environmental regulation (such as protection of a plant or animal species or landscape, or controls over pollutants or emissions) and/or social regulation (for example, public safety or public health).

Decision-making in planning involves balancing these different regulatory aims, and administrative (or process) regulations exist in order to set out the decision-taking processes (rules of the game). The stipulation of regulatory controls is in order to manage the achievement of defined policy goals and to provide certainty (to the market, civil society and other state actors), for example in terms of how particular decisions will be taken. Importantly, some of the matters that appear to fall under the planning regime may well be regulated by other forms of environmental law. There is occasionally a risk of overlap (or underlap) in different consenting regimes, such as civic licensing, road construction and building standards. Clarity and communication are critical so as to avoid improper use of regulatory controls or acting beyond one's powers (ultra vires). Figure 2.2 summarises the four principal types of regulatory activity we are concerned with in this book. Goal-conflict regulation indicates that planning is concerned with the mediation of outcomes, generally involving communication in order to negotiate trade-offs, while process regulation is concerned with the functioning of the planning system and ensuring that due process is followed (see Chapter Ten, for example, in relation to JR).

Figure 2.2: Regulatory activities of planning

For some time an important policy improvement agenda emanating from the level of the EU has concerned the development of better regulation. Set against the political imperative of enhancing Europe's competitive advantage, this political ambition to improve the efficiency and effectiveness of state regulations seeks to reduce the perceived burden of regulation. Ideas about improving regulatory performance have filtered down into the EU member states and led to a range of projects and programmes to reduce 'red tape'. Whether the ideas for better (or smarter) regulation have been driven by EU thinking or are rather more home-grown and UK-based, we suggest that the general focus, particularly since the turn of the millennium, has been on streamlining the respective statutory planning systems and stimulating growth and development following a period of economic recession. Against this background, the modernisation and reform agenda associated with the post-devolution period merits separate attention.

Reform and modernisation of planning under devolution

The drive to reconfigure the role and purpose of the state that was introduced under the Conservative governments of the 1980s and 1990s continued under the subsequent Labour governments. While the political rhetoric varied and there were different policy ambitions, the reliance on neoliberal ideas endured. The outcome of the political debate was further changes to planning law – changes that were palpable across the UK, given the devolution of political powers to Scotland, Wales and Northern Ireland, and that were elaborated in the individual programmes for government (see, for example, the February 2009 special issue of *Planning, Practice & Research*).

Underlying the twin concepts of reform and modernisation under the Blair administrations were changes to the style and culture of state governance. For example, in 2006 the Prime Minister's Strategy Unit encapsulated the ambition as follows:

> The Government has a clear vision: everyone should have access to public services that are *efficient, effective, excellent, equitable, empowering and constantly improving*. Achieving these goals would make significant progress towards the Government's wider objectives of greater social justice and a higher quality of life for all. (Cabinet Office, 2006, p 4 – our emphasis)

A number of important drivers were identified, including: social, economic and technological changes; public expectations; and changing attitudes. Ideas for changing how the planning system operated involved a major rethink about the effectiveness of the respective planning laws. Changes to the legal arrangements were not considered to be sufficient on their own and a programme of legislative change tended to be accompanied by a parallel emphasis on culture change in how the system was operationalised. This programme of change witnessed an emphasis on top-down performance management; an increased focus on public engagement and capacity building; and encouraging partnership working between the state and the private sector.

Subsequent institutional arrangements, particularly under devolution, have encouraged the use of clear spatial hierarchies, performance frameworks, such as a balanced scorecard approach introduced by the Heads of Planning Scotland (2012), and duties to cooperate. Taken together, these measures have sought to improve the operationalisation and implementation of the planning system.

Towards better regulation?

We conclude this chapter with the response from the RTPI in Scotland (2012) to a consultation exercise on a Better Regulation Bill in Scotland (since enacted as the Regulatory Reform (Scotland) Act 2014). This response set out 10 tests for better regulation. As debates about the appropriateness of planning regulations continue, we suggest that these tests provide a useful starting point for thinking about regulation, both on an individual basis and as part of a complex system. Regulation, according to the RTPI in Scotland's consultation response, needs to be:

1. proportionate
2. effective
3. fully resourced and affordable
4. integrated with any positive and proactive approaches supporting its objectives (for example, development plans)
5. efficient
6. evidence based and clear
7. consistent
8. joined up with other regulatory regimes to ensure that there are no contradictions or overlaps
9. enforceable
10. verifiable.

In short, to be effective, any regulatory system must enjoy the trust and respect of the society it is intended to serve. Planning law is no different and, as contexts change, so too must the planning regime.

Chapter summary

This chapter has looked at the nature of planning law in the devolved UK. It has introduced key terminology and law-making bodies and processes. Society's legal frameworks and regulatory arrangements are socially constructed; thus, at any given time legal frameworks for planning are shaped by prevailing political values and priorities. In practical terms, planning law is interpreted and developed through case law and worked out by planners operating the system. In practice, the primacy of a particular ideology means that how state, market and civil relations are configured will vary, depending on whether market-based or state-based responses to economic development and growth, or environmental protection demands, or social priorities, take precedence. Changes in government priorities and the dominance of certain political values have altered the nature and prominence of planning as a distinct sphere of state regulatory activity, and an emphasis on better and proportionate regulation will likely result in further reforms of the system.

Recommended reading

For more information on the workings of Parliament and law-making, see: www.parliament.uk

For a general introduction to the post-war evolution of planning theory:

Taylor, N. (1998) *Urban planning theory since 1945*, London: Sage.

For a consideration of the nature of planning within different political contexts and through specific periods of reform of change, see:

Clifford, B.P. and Tewdwr-Jones, M. (1998) *The collaborating planner: Planning in the neoliberal age*, Bristol: Policy Press.
Planning Practice & Research (2009) published 24(1) a special issue providing a collection of papers critically reflecting on a decade of New Labour planning reforms.
Tewdwr-Jones M. (2008) 'The Complexity of planning reform: a search for the spirit and purpose of planning', *Town Planning Review*, vol 79, no 6, pp 673–88.
Thornley, A. (1993) *Urban planning under Thatcherism: The challenge of the market*, Abingdon-on-Thames: Routledge.

THREE

The development of planning law

Chapter contents

- Early forms of planning
- Early controls in the ancient world
- The emergence of controls in Britain
- Developments in the 19th century
- Developments in the early 20th century
- 1947 and universal control
- Chapter summary

Introduction

In this chapter we identify some of the roots of the modern planning system in the UK, taking in the ancient world, the medieval period, the influence of royal proclamations, the role of Parliament and the rise in importance of local government. In tracing the scope of planning controls from an initial concern with health and safety to a system incorporating aesthetics and wider social goods, we look beyond the first legislation with 'planning' in its title. By considering earlier forms of control over the built environment, one can better understand the different rationales for planning controls, appreciate key concepts and ideas and recognise the main arguments for and against contemporary state intervention. The idea of the 'state' intervening in the private rights of individuals is not necessarily accepted, and some people argue that the state should not 'interfere' with market forces or private rights. By considering how the UK planning system evolved over time, it is easier to understand the case for planning and appreciate the justification for its existence.

Early forms of planning

There is a tendency to start the history of planning in the UK in the middle of the 19th century, with the development of public health legislation. In terms of the modern planning system, such a starting point is quite correct. As noted by Peter Hall:

twentieth-century city planning, as an intellectual and professional movement, essentially represents a reaction to the nineteenth-century city. (Hall, 1996, p 7)

However, the story of 'planning' and of planning law can be identified much earlier, particularly if we look to the origins and evolution of state intervention in and control of the built environment, rather than just to the emergence of the modern planning system. It is important to note here that the idea of a planning system is somewhat amorphous; we are talking here about interventions in the built environment by the 'state', such as it may be. From this perspective, intervention may be undertaken through a variety of legal and administrative systems. Historically, intervention could have been through decrees issued by monarchs or other powerful leaders. Today it will typically be through government legislation and public administration. Moreover, in the UK the built environment is managed not only through the statutory land-use planning system but through a raft of related controls, including building regulations, environmental health legislation, licensing, highways legislation, land law and contracts.

As a species, humans have tended to organise and 'plan' the way they live. Choices about where and how to organise collective living have been informed by issues of protection and defence, access to food and water, shelter from the weather, exchange of goods and services and so forth. We can point to a legacy of rules concerning how the built environment should be managed to support the notion of 'planned' settlements.

In around 2600 BC, for example, the Bronze Age fortified cities of the Harappan civilisation (present day Pakistan, northwest India, and some regions in northeast Afghanistan), including Lothal, Dholavira, Rakhigarhi, Kalibangan and Mohenjodaro, represented some of the world's first important urban centres. Such settlements were 'planned', controlled and managed with leadership and administration, and provide examples of planning-related activities within early civilisations (Singh, 2008). A relatively more structured approach to planning for particular purposes to support human endeavour can also be traced back a long way:

> there would seem to be general agreement that the oldest example of town planning as yet discovered is that of Kahun, in Egypt – a town constructed for the purpose of housing the workmen engaged in building the pyramid of Illahun, and dating from about 2500 B.C. (Aldridge, 1915, p 12)

In relation to our story of 'planning regulation' and the origins of modern statutory planning in the UK we must therefore cast our net wide and consider a variety of controls over structures, place and space. In so doing, we can better explain how and why we have the particular system of planning controls in operation today.

Early controls in the ancient world

It cannot be said with absolute confidence where the first regulation to manage the built environment emerged. However, one of the earliest codes of law relating to buildings is that of the 6th Babylonian King of Mesopotamia, Hammurabi, in approximately 1754 BC. Hammurabi was a 'man of law' and created a code of 282 laws covering a wide range of matters to underpin his rule. Some of these laws, in a very simple and limited way, allowed for the built environment to be controlled. Of particular interest are laws 228 to 233:

> 228. If a builder build a house for some one and complete it, he shall give him a fee of two shekels in money for each sar of surface.
> 229. If a builder build a house for some one, and does not construct it properly, and the house which he built fall in and kill its owner, then that builder shall be put to death.
> 230. If it kill the son of the owner the son of that builder shall be put to death.
> 231. If it kill a slave of the owner, then he shall pay slave for slave to the owner of the house.
> 232. If it ruin goods, he shall make compensation for all that has been ruined, and inasmuch as he did not construct properly this house which he built and it fell, he shall re-erect the house from his own means.
> 233. If a builder build a house for some one, even though he has not yet completed it; if then the walls seem toppling, the builder must make the walls solid from his own means.
> (Yale University, 2008)

Clearly, this regulatory framework is a relatively limited legislative construct, essentially specifying payment and construction standards (on pain of death!); but it points to two important aspects in the active management of the built environment and wider issues of public safety: the state protecting private interests and providing the means to seek compensation.

The search for safety controls and quality standards is a core driver for this type of law. In early legislation such as the Code of Hammurabi, we also see recognition of the concept of justice. This highlights the importance of justice as a core principle of planning systems: the state is acting in the interest of some party. Initially the focus was on private interests and the rights of individuals but, as we shall see, planning's emphasis ultimately shifts towards the public interest and ideas of social justice.

Box 3.1: Private rights and state intervention

The idea of our rights to, and relationships with, land is important to our understanding of the interaction between land and people, land and planning, and people and the state. Landownership involves a legal relationship between humankind and the land. Cultural attitudes concerning landownership vary significantly around the world, ranging from a position where land is not something that can be 'owned', through to the more common capitalist land- and property-market model wherein land is owned by someone or some party (including potentially the state), with potential for the existence for others of certain 'rights' to this land . From the perspective of planning, in some respects this bundle of rights transcends landownership; in many contexts, including the UK, landownership is primarily relevant from the perspective of implementation and delivery – planning decisions are 'carried by' or 'run with' the land, not the landowner.

The existence of certain 'rights' over land is important to our discussion, since ownership and legal interest in land confer certain rights; these rights are impacted upon where state intervention occurs. This book is specifically focused on development management and as such is particularly concerned with development rights and how the state intervenes (some might say 'interferes' from a particular political perspective) with the rights of people and their association with land, whether by ownership, tenancy, interest, occupation or use. We are thus interested in the wider relationship of humankind to land and the different relationships between private interests and other rights in or over land, including (but not limited to) ownership. What role does the state play in protecting, controlling and potentially restricting these rights?

We can see further early examples of systems of control over the built environment and private rights in the ancient civilisations of the Greeks and Romans. Rules and regulations relating to urban planning began to emerge in ancient Greece, during the 8th to 6th centuries BC. Central to their development was the idea of the state intervening in private interests to provide a legal framework of rights. Importantly, it can be argued that this approach was informed by wider and more holistic motivations for social justice. In particular, the idea of 'wholesomeness' of the environment emerged as a core tenet and was key to the introduction of regulations in ancient Greece. Attaining wholesomeness was not something to be left to the free market, but was to be managed through state intervention (Aldridge, 1915). This idea of state intervention out of necessity is important and is a dynamic that presents itself repeatedly, including in the emergence of 'pure' planning legislation in the UK in the middle of the 19th century.

The idea of wholesomeness found in the early regulations of ancient Greece is also significant in considering the nature of state intervention. Much of the early regulation that forms our narrative is private–law based, that is to say, a legal system based around requirements, controls and dispute resolution linked to land interests and rights. The consideration of wholesomeness is something bigger; it moves us into public law and state intervention in the public interest, together with ideas of social justice.

Ancient Greece had a very different geography, reach and organisation as compared to modern Greece. Moreover, the controls that emerged in ancient Greece certainly did not extend universally. Nevertheless, they represent a further demonstration of human attempts to manage the built environment. The realities of urban places in ancient Greece were disordered and squalid, but, where controls were applied, builders and occupiers were subject to by-laws safeguarding light, air, water, structural aspects and fire safety in new construction (Aldridge, 1915). Although they were relatively limited and simplistic, parallels can already be drawn with modern amenity standards and building controls over the built form.

Later, during the Roman Empire, in 450 BC, we find an example of laws relating to land rights. The 'Twelve Tables' were a formalised set of laws. Table VII considered land, and at a very basic level addressed some aspects of property rights. A number of further controls were introduced by various Roman emperors. For example, Emperor Cicero (106–43 BC) introduced a law stating that no man might destroy, un-roof or dismantle an urban building unless he was ready to replace it by a building at least as good, or had received special permission from his local town council. Later examples are the regulations introduced in Rome under Emperor Nero (54–68 AD) which dealt with light, air and space around buildings; construction using permanent materials; and height restrictions, with a building to be no higher than twice the width of the street it fronted. This thinking extended controls over the surrounding built environment.

Box 3.2: Ancient and modern: the dawn of planning law?

Insights into the scope of modern planning law can be drawn from the built environment controls introduced by the Mesopotamians, Romans and ancient Greeks. During the period of the Roman Empire, however, and despite their expansive and ordered reach, controls were relatively limited in their application and much of the built environment was uncontrolled. The importance of the ancient world is not that universal control began but, rather, a legislative framework for setting quality standards and controlling individual structures and the built environment started to develop.

The ancient period is important for understanding contemporary planning law because of the drivers that underpinned the emergence of different rationales for and forms of control. The early focus was on legislating for private rights and interests, but some sense of social justice and public law is present, including ideas around health, well-being and the nature and integrity (wholesomeness) of the built environment. Such ideas are key aspects underpinning the nature and justification for planning systems today, although new terms or concepts, such as sustainability, and eco-systemic or holistic thinking, tend to frame contemporary planning law discourse.

Britain in the Middle Ages

The Norman Conquest in 1066 was important because of the impact the subsequent period had upon the development of the legal construct of the nation (including landownership). Under the Norman influence there was eventual divergence from the established Anglo-Saxon (Germanic) model of regulation and statute based civil law and the development of a common law legal system with judicial precedent. This legal tradition underpins the systems of law found across the UK, albeit Scotland has a hybrid system of civil and common law. From a planning perspective this common law system means an approach that embraces judicial precedent equally with statutes.

In terms of our time-line and tracing the evolution of planning law in relation to urbanisation, the Middle Ages in Britain are important. Falling between the ancient and the modern worlds, the medieval period is also sometimes referred to as the 'Dark Ages'. The significance of this latter term is to differentiate the 'great' civilisations of the ancient world and Modern civilisations (which are held to represent the 'light') from the intervening period (the 'darkness'). As evocatively described by Aldridge (1915, p 33):

> The barbarians and semi-barbarians who swept like a flood over Western Europe were not dwellers in cities and in the ceaseless wars waged by them the art of city building had no chance of development.

Understood in this way, there was something of a hiatus in the emerging art and science of planning.

The term 'Dark Ages' may be considered erroneous in some respects, for although a 'vacuum' was created by the collapse of the Roman Empire, into the void ultimately emerged the system of law that underpins our planning systems today. As Aldridge (1915, p 33) continues:

> slowly and surely two new forces came into being. First, the spread of Christianity with, as an ultimate consequence, the establishment of a class of peaceful man, dwelling in religious housing and possessing both the leisure and desire to study; and second, the establishment of small kingdoms governed by rulers capable of developing the arts of civilisation and possessing sufficient strength and military capacity to secure periods of peace for their subjects.

There is evidence that early in the 13th century certain building controls emerged in London. It is not surprising that London attracted specific attention. As in the ancient world, the controls were, understandably, focused upon areas of population concentration and driven by the need for intervention. Hence, as in Athens and Rome before, London became subject to the introduction of certain forms of control over the built environment. Significantly, in 1212 London's first Mayor (linking directly to the current Lord Mayor of London – as distinct from the office of Mayor of London established in 2000), Henry Fitz Ailwin, initiated building controls. These regulations directly concerned the prevention of fire or rebuilding after fire had occurred.

In 1275 a key development was the setting up of the Assize of Nuisance. A part of the Assize Courts system in place at that time, the Assize of Nuisance represented a set of regulations concerning property rights and the management of nuisance in relation to property and its use. The remit of the Assize of Nuisance covered walls, gutters, privies, windows and pavements and the procedures to be followed to settle disputes (Booth, 2003). It was relatively limited in scope and application, but is of note for being an early example of an ordered system of control for the management of the built environment in Britain, albeit firmly based on private rights and interests.

Subsequently, a number of royal proclamations expanded the scope and nature of controls in quite a dramatic way. Significantly, these controls extended beyond an established core concern with nuisance, property rights and construction in the interests of safety and the prevention of fire. Controls that emerged over the next 300 years variously considered population growth, density, appearance and resource management. While we can question the motivation for and efficacy of some of these controls, the part played by the monarchy during this period is of particular note.

For example, Queen Elizabeth I introduced some interesting changes, starting with a proclamation, and then an Act of Parliament in 1593 that stated that no buildings could be erected on new foundations, only on the foundations of existing buildings. In today's terms, this control may be seen as place-specific, since it specifically focused on addressing emerging concerns relating to the increasingly rapid growth of London and Westminster, and stretching to an area of three miles beyond the city gates. The same Act also prevented the subdivision of houses to accommodate new households, highlighting the key emphases of this new control, namely, population growth, density and housing conditions (Booth, 2003).

In 1605 King James I made a proclamation that included a requirement for new buildings to be constructed of stone or brick. On the one hand, this continued the tradition of controls driven by a concern with fire prevention and health and safety. On the other hand, a different driver for control is of potentially greater interest for our story. At that time Britain was experiencing significant deforestation, primarily as a consequence of ship-building, housing and other timber construction, together with a general reliance on wood for fuel. As such, a shortage of timber for construction was a significant risk, and the 1605 proclamation was driven in part by the necessity to preserve timber supplies. This focus can thus be considered as an early form of environmental resource management. Moreover, the 1605 proclamation expanded controls beyond the individual building, since it addressed issues of the street frontage, specifically, stating that buildings must be 'uniform' in order and form. A subsequent proclamation in 1618 covered further construction standards (Booth, 2003). Thus, we can see how a succession of royal proclamations progressively extended the scope of controls over the built environment from issues of harm, health and safety to aesthetics, quality of life and resource management, and expanded state intervention from a concern with single buildings to the streetscape as a whole.

A final point relating to what may be considered a period of monarchical influence is the 1630 proclamation of Charles I, which focused on further aspects of construction. Of specific interest here was the strengthening of the role of the Commission for Buildings, which had a remit to enforce controls (Booth, 2003), thus illustrating the importance of making provision for bodies or organisations with the necessary authority and power to exercise and enforce controls. This requires us to think about how different institutional designs and practical expertise in relation to the preparation and implementation of planning controls have come about.

After the English Civil War of 1642–51 Parliament was central in bringing about change. Here, we can highlight the Rebuilding Act of 1667, which followed the Great Fire of London of 1666. This legislation represents an important step in the emergence of modern administration, since it introduced surveyors to settle disputes. In his discussion of the origins and nature of British planning controls

Figure 3.1: The development of controls

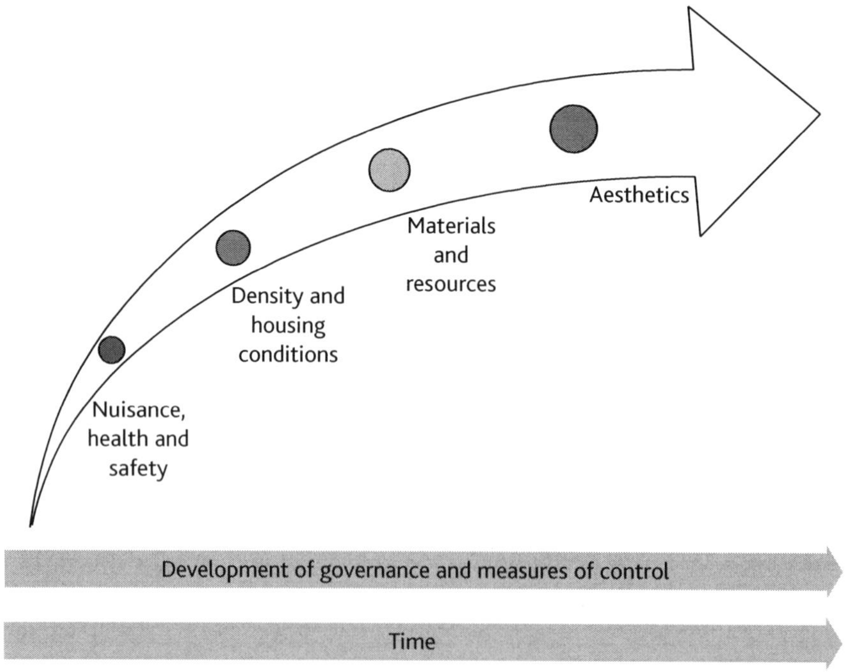

Aesthetics

Materials
and
resources

Density and
housing
conditions

Nuisance,
health and
safety

Development of governance and measures of control

Time

Booth (2003), notes the importance of this step in the development of the modern system of local government and the role of 'professionals' in the regulation and management of the built environment.

These early forms of control are important because they represent the emergence of state intervention to control the built environment and a move from limited concerns about nuisance and private property rights to a situation where the state is intervening through legislation in the interests of resource management, population growth, density, housing conditions and aesthetics.

It is evident that the scope and remit of intervention increased over time as the implications of non-intervention became clear. Such considerations remain very current, even if they are now expressed in slightly different ways. While the motivations for some of the early legislation may be debateable, they represent stages in the development of planning law from a relatively limited form of private law to a rather more publicly oriented legal construct. This period also saw initial attempts to establish the necessary administrative structures and expertise to enforce the new controls.

Developments in the 19th century

It is during the 19th century that we can identify the beginnings of a relatively more comprehensive 'planning system'. The story thus far is underpinned by necessity: the evolution of state intervention was partly driven by the perceived necessity of responding to or addressing events and circumstances that existing private arrangements either could not or would not respond to adequately (Gilg, 2005). During the 19th century the impacts and effects of the Industrial Revolution, particularly in relation to housing and living conditions, were a powerful driver for change and led to a scale of necessity for state intervention not witnessed before.

During the Industrial Revolution the pace and extent of land and buildings use and development transformed the urban landscape, particularly in the burgeoning urban centres. Critically, the rapid urban expansion – often driven by revenue creation, took place in a context of very limited regulatory controls. Poor housing conditions and the associated poor health and low life expectancy led to growing fears of social unrest There was also a parallel concern in some quarters that an unhealthy workforce was not the most productive one; in other words, it was recognised that poor environmental conditions had an economic cost (Cullingworth et al, 2015). Thus a new social construction of urban environmental and social problems and a case for more state intervention began to be articulated.

A particularly strong argument for change stemmed from improvements in medical knowledge. For example, in 1855 John Snow provided evidence that cholera was water borne. It was argued that the spread of disease could be controlled by better sanitary arrangements. New forms of control and planned environments were being advocated by philanthropists, conservation campaigners, professional bodies representing architects, surveyors and engineers, enlightened industrialists such as Titus Salt (Saltaire, 1853), Cadbury (Bournville, 1878) and the Lever brothers (Port Sunlight, 1887), and reformers such as Ebenezer Howard, Raymond Unwin, Barry Parker and the Garden City movement (Cullingworth et al, 2015). Taken together with developments in the powers and capacity of local government, the accumulating body of evidence and heightened societal awareness:

> eventually resulted in an appreciation of the necessity for interfering with market forces and private property rights in the interests of social justice. (Cullingworth et al, 2015, p 17)

This period is particularly significant because a general acknowledgement of the failures of unregulated private interests and markets underpinned arguments for and acceptance of legitimate state intervention to control private interests. However, we must be careful not to overstate the general acceptance of government controls over private property! For some people, private interests should simply not be 'interfered with' by the state; the very idea of the state holding planning powers is fundamentally unacceptable. As they see it, the question is not how much power the state should have in relation to the control of land and development but whether the state should have such power at all. Others view state controls of otherwise uncoordinated, market-led development serving private interests as essential to securing the wider public good.

What emerged during the 19th century was a broadly 'regulatory' system of control based upon by-laws. As noted in the previous chapter, planning systems across the world occupy a spectrum, variously exhibiting 'regulatory' elements, or following a 'discretionary' approach, as in the UK. A regulatory system is one where a development plan is produced that provides a framework for managing change that must be adhered to and that is binding. The making of the plan effectively represents the planning decision and the planning application is an administrative test against this plan. Change from the plan provisions would typically require revisions to the plan a scenario which could also lead to the involvement of the Courts. In a discretionary system, although a development plan exists, this plan is the primary factor in decision–making, not the sole basis for it. Discretion exists to make a decision through a planning application that does not accord with the development plan where other material considerations indicate this should be the case. The decision is therefore the determination of the planning application. Today's discretionary-modelled planning system is very different from the practice adopted in the middle of the 19th century, and was a by-law-modelled construct and more oriented towards a regulatory system.

From the mid-1800s legislative change occurred as Britain attempted to respond to urban growth and social, technological and economic change. Municipal reforms were introduced by the Local Government Act 1858. However, it was the Public Health Act 1875 that allowed local authorities to create by-laws to address health issues in existing urban areas, rather than any planning legislation.

For new developments and redevelopment of slum areas, building regulations prescribed street-widths and the layout and design of new housing, including heights and structure.

Developments in the early 20th century

A strong case can be made that certain early by-laws advanced the importance of better living conditions in new urban areas. Indeed, what may be viewed as the first dedicated planning acts (1909, 1919 and 1932) all built upon this early form of development control, variously expanding and extending the scope and application of by-laws. We now consider efforts to create more comprehensive, statutory planning mechanisms.

Box 3.3: Limitations of planning by-laws

The by-law model was criticised not only for its focus on new areas of development but for being overly restrictive and inflexible. As an example, in 1906 Unwin and Parker required a separate Act of Parliament simply to introduce a cul-de-sac into their Hampstead Garden Suburb plan because the extant by-law did not make provision for it. Although the various by-laws were seen to be helpful in controlling the effects of poor development, they were also identified as a flawed mechanism. In 1909 Unwin commented:

> by means of our much abused bye-laws [sic], the worst excesses of overcrowding have been restrained ... and yet the remarkable fact remains that there are growing up around our big towns vast districts, under these very bye-laws, which for dreariness and sheer ugliness it is difficult to match anywhere, and compared with which many of the old unhealthy slums are from the point of view of picturesqueness and beauty, infinitely more attractive. (Unwin, 1909, p 3)

The legislation passed in 1909 may be considered the first 'planning act', in the sense that its title included the words 'town planning'. The Housing, Town Planning, etc. Act 1909 had wide-ranging objectives that reflected the drivers for change existing at the time. It set out the scope of planning controls and the different roles of the state in executing the legislation. John Burns, President of the Local Government Board, introduced the aspirational objectives of the 1909 Act as being to enable:

> the home healthy, the house beautiful, the town pleasant, the city dignified and the suburb salubrious.

The 1909 Act put the home at centre stage and referenced planning in the context of everything from the physical environment through to health and the very morals of society. It can thus be seen as embracing a certain emphasis on public interest and social justice that it was felt could be realised through legislation. Despite certain limitations, the Act clearly elevated the position of planning in the field of public law, as well as addressing private interests. We can thus say that the 1909 Act was a step change from the early thinking of the Assize of Nuisance. Nevertheless, despite the Act's grand aspirations, and as with earlier controls, its focus can be considered as primarily confined to housing and new development proposals. Its potential to control and impact positively on existing developed areas was therefore limited.

The subsequent 1919 Act extended the scope of planning and is of note because it required councils with populations of 20,000 or more to produce 'schemes'. Significantly, this legislation provided state subsidies for housing, which enabled the growth of the council housing sector. The 1932 Act further expanded the 1919 provisions by introducing planning powers to cover existing developed land, an important step towards universal control. Finally, a further piece of legislation during this period that merits attention is the Restriction of Ribbon Development Act 1935. As its title implies, this Act was concerned with addressing unregulated urban expansion and the consequences of unrestricted building along transportation routes, so-called ribbon development. Those interested in advancing planning as a form of state intervention were responding to emerging issues and the negative effects of urban expansion as a result of un- or under-regulated development (Cullingworth et al, 2015), and the 1935 Act highlights a defining feature of the legislation of this period in that it was symptomatic of a reactive approach to planning. Furthermore, while these various pieces of legislation represented important conceptual advances, little controlled development came forward in practice, partly because of the inadequacies of the administrative process, but also due to the implications of 'betterment' in relation to the introduction of schemes under the 1919 legislation.

Box 3.4: A note on betterment

'Betterment' is effectively the increase in land value as a result of general population growth and, specifically, the granting of planning permission. State intervention in the 'land market' through the exercise of planning controls can impact on the value of land, either increasing or decreasing it, depending on the perceived development potential of a parcel of land. The preparation of development schemes had the effect of the state influencing private rights, landownership and land values. The form of planning system that emerged in the early 20th century resulted in betterment potential being lost as a result of lands not being identified for development by the planning arrangements. As a consequence, the state was liable to pay compensation to the landowner for the loss of the potential betterment. How to resolve this conundrum and deal with the betterment–compensation question was a key challenge for the embryonic planning system in the post-Second World War period (Moore and Purdue, 2014; Cullingworth et al, 2015).

Although the 19th and early 20th centuries witnessed the intellectual case and statutory basis for planning, the legal arrangements put in place did not translate well into practice. The by-law approach was restrictive and relatively narrow in application. Subsequently, the emerging controls were undermined by the associated financial implications of planning for land development. In short, the design and scope of planning law offered inadequate controls over existing developed areas and the countryside. Crucially, wider socioeconomic and political changes highlighted the need for a more sophisticated form of planning system.

The intellectual case for the planned use of the land resource and the regulation of urban and rural development was formed against the background of the First World War. Prior to, during and in the years immediately following the war, important social, economic, technological and political changes were taking place to various degrees and with significant consequences. These changes were highly differentiated, both socially and spatially, but included: a growth in demand for adequate housing; improved building standards; the desire to achieve homeownership; the expansion of means and modes of transport, enabling 'commuting'; the introduction of holidays, opening up the potential for leisure development; a breakup of established landownership patterns; and a decline in the agricultural sector. Moreover, constitutional changes were afoot. As already noted, the partition of the island of Ireland ultimately resulted in the creation in 1927 of the United Kingdom of Great Britain and Northern Ireland. Against the backdrop of these socioeconomic changes, the worldwide economic depression of the 1930s highlighted even further the weaknesses and limited nature of the early planning legislation and paved the way for a major advance in the story of planning law.

Box 3.5: The Plotland movement

Before we leave this discussion of early 20th-century formal, top-down planning law experiments, we wish to mention a parallel, bottom-up or informal approach to development. This stemmed from a growing desire on the part of those able to do so to 'escape' the city for some form of personal (rural) arcadia. An often overlooked but symbolically significant response to the changing situation in landownership and management was the plotland movement. Described perhaps a little unfairly by Gilg (2005, p 7) as 'grubby', the plotland movement was a manifestation of the circumstances of the time. Tapping into the 'quest for arcadia' (Hardy and Ward, 1984), the term 'plotland' comes from the nature of the development activity. Typically, low-quality land sold off by farmers and estates was purchased by speculators and then resold on a plot-by-plot basis.

The result was a significant number of unauthorised settlements along the south and south-east coast of England and along the Thames estuary. These unauthorised developments varied significantly in layout, form, scale, quality, provision of infrastructure and degree of permanence. They also came in all shapes and sizes. Homes ranged from former train-carriages and huts to bungalows. Opinion of their appropriateness and quality varied. For some, they were an abhorrent and illegitimate form of development located in beautiful landscapes, lacking adequate infrastructure, often poorly sited and liable to flooding. To others, they represented escape, hope, freedom, optimism and happiness (Hardy and Ward, 1984). The advent of the Second World War and the subsequent post-war legislation saw the removal of many 'plotland' settlements, but some remain, such as Dungeness and Jaywick. These examples of unauthorised development merit visiting, if only to reflect critically on how forms of local, bottom-up development impact on the strategic management of the land resource.

1947 and universal control

Prior to the Second World War an intellectual and political case for a more sophisticated and comprehensive control of land use and development was beginning to be made. It was argued that any new system needed to provide both flexibility and certainty, but also to respond to the changing demands of modern society. Moreover, the socioeconomic, demographic and physical conditions arising from the Second World War increased the need for transformative thinking. Times were changing; socialist thinking was also gathering momentum (Gilg, 2005). As a consequence of this blend of influences, the planning controls that emerged in the immediate post-war period as part of the wider welfare state apparatus can be considered as revolutionary.

During the Second World War, and in anticipation of post-war reconstruction, extensive research was undertaken to explore how to deal with and manage these changes and how the government could and should respond. Possibly the most significant of the anticipatory Second World War research projects are:

1. the Barlow Report 1940, which focused on economic, social and strategic issues and population distribution across the UK's regional geography;
2. the Scott Report 1942, which considered the implications of the rural context in a climate of economic decline and new development pressures, and recognised the potential of National Parks;
3. the Uthwatt Report 1942, which sought to resolve the issues associated with compensation and betterment in land values.

Informed by these seminal reports and other initiatives related to addressing the effects of war damage and the setting up of an extensive social welfare infrastructure (including the National Health Service), proposals were made to introduce far more radical state controls on planning and development. However, private enterprise continued to resist the growth of the state (Gilg, 2005). The 1940s can nevertheless be considered a decade of innovation with respect to planning law and new planning acts were conceived to provide a statutory basis for development control. These included interim controls in Northern Ireland

(1944) (enhanced in the early 1960s by further legislation); and a new statutory basis for planning and development management in England and Wales (1947) and in Scotland (1948).

The new planning legislation in the UK brought about a significant change: the nationalisation of land rights. Land and property remained in private ownership but the right to undertake 'development' (as defined by the legislation) now resided with the state. In other words, any statutorily defined development required permission, or consent, of some kind from the state. This requirement applied to all land. This fundamental change in the right to develop land and property was a momentous step in the evolution of British planning thought and practice and highlights the public law/public interest emphases of the emergent planning systems. Thus began universal control.

So as to maximise the potential success of the new system, no compensation could be claimed for the refusal of a planning application, and wide powers were given to LPAs to control advertisements and to protect heritage assets (Moore and Purdue, 2014). The betterment issue was addressed by providing a £300 million fund to compensate landowners for loss of potential value resulting from planning action; this was a one-off opportunity to claim, directly associated with the nationalisation of land rights (Cullingworth et al, 2015).

One of the most significant shifts associated with the 1947 model of planning law was the move from the principally regulatory by-law form of control to a more comprehensive and discretionary model, based upon a development plan that provided the land-allocation and policy-led context for guiding the siting, nature and form of development. Although prior to this arrangement degrees of discretion had existed in the way development was controlled, this new style of planning legislation represented a fundamental shift in British planning practice, and henceforth the UK planning law tradition would be based primarily on a discretionary rather than a regulatory, system. Since then, the majority of planning decisions are made based upon a series of policies and land-allocation proposals as set out in the relevant development plan and in the light of other material considerations. Instead of a binding plan relating to specified and delineated areas and a regulatory system with which developers needed to comply, the new approach extended the scope and potential for development because it increased the available land area and invited negotiation over development proposals. As such, the development plan became the most significant factor in the determination of a planning application.

The significance of exercising discretion with respect to individual development sites means that attention can be paid to issues on a site-by-site basis and in relation to evolving circumstances and other pertinent matters relating to a particular locality. The importance of exercising discretion as part of an administrative process is that it gives the decision-maker scope to take into account other material considerations relevant to the proposed use or development of land and buildings.

In concluding this section, we note other significant developments that took place at this time, including the New Towns Act 1946. Forms of legal protection were extended to Green Belts, National Parks, Areas of Outstanding Natural Beauty and agricultural land. As such, it is perhaps not surprising that the immediate post-war period has been seen as one of genuine revolution and enormous change in terms of planning law (Gilg, 2005). Society was also changing and the modern planning system was born in a period of large-scale state intervention that was generally not only accepted but also desired. The planning system of 1947 was part of the zeitgeist and general political consensus.

Clearly, the new approach took time to put in place. Practical experience and changing circumstances led to changes, some of them quite far reaching. Initially, the physical and socioeconomic consequences of the Second World War shaped what can be viewed as a first phase of planning controls, which were characterised by an emphasis on reconstruction and state-led (re)development. Wider social and technological changes, a break-down in the post-war political consensus, and concerns with scale and for public participation to better guide (rather than prescribe) development characterised a second broad phase in planning thought and practice. Notably, the Town and Country Planning Act 1968 (England and Wales)/1969 (Scotland) sought to provide a relatively more proportionate and 'tiered' approach to the decision-making context, with strategic 'structure plans' and more detailed 'local plans' providing the policy context (Cullingworth et al, 2015). Subsequently, an alternative political ideology resulted in the nature and extent of universal state planning controls being reduced and curtailed in certain specified areas. These area-based approaches were provided in defined places where regeneration and economic development priorities were an imperative. On a more general basis, however, the Planning and Compensation Act 1991 re-emphasised a 'plan-led' approach to managing the use and development of land, providing the context for reform and modernisation of the various planning systems under devolution. The 1991 Act was an important milestone, and despite changing political ideologies, the essential spirit of the 1947 planning tradition continues to underpin the legal constructs in place today.

Chapter summary

This chapter has provided some historical context to the development of planning controls. Initially, controls were introduced in a piecemeal and reactive fashion, primarily driven by a concern with private interests, standards and compensation. Specifically, we have shown how the scope of control and state intervention has evolved, from an initial focus on nuisance and private property rights to a system concerned with environmental management, management of population growth and density, improvement of housing conditions and aesthetics. The chapter has also highlighted how controls have shifted from a concern with the individual building to the streetscape and wider environment. Central to this chapter was introduction of the thinking behind the Town and Country Planning Act 1947, and which 70 years later remains the touchstone of our legal planning system.

Recommended reading

Aldridge, H. (1915) *The case for town planning*, London: The National Housing and Town Planning Council.

Booth, P. (2003) *Planning by consent: The origins and nature of British development control*, Abingdon-on-Thames: Routledge.

Gilg, A. (2005) *Planning in Britain: Understanding and evaluating the post-war system*, London: Sage.

Pendlebury, J. (2015) 'The evolution of town and country planning', Chapter 3 in Cullingworth et al, *Town and country planning in the UK*, 15th edn, Abingdon-on-Thames: Routledge, pp 17–35.

FOUR

Planning, plans and policy in the devolved UK

Chapter contents

- The current legislative contexts
- Plan-led systems
- National, regional and strategic plans and policy
- Local development plans
- City-regions, metropolitan areas and 'above-local' scale planning
- Neighbourhood plans in England
- Marine plans
- Chapter summary

Introduction

This chapter explores in greater detail the legislative context in place at the time of writing (July 2016) and outlines how planning is organised across the devolved UK. We consider the various systems and structures of government and plans in place for designing and implementing planning regulations, again noting that planning is a dynamic field and liable to change. In addition to the legislation, we highlight the importance of understanding the various institutional arrangements to support development planning and the roles played by national policy and territorial planning and by local policy in guiding, shaping and managing change. We also consider the emerging framework for marine planning, which is related to and draws on terrestrial experience.

As in the previous chapter, across the UK a plan-led system is in place, meaning that plans and policy 'lead' (or direct) decision-making within a discretionary decision-taking context. The purpose of a plan is ultimately to enable something to happen in a particular way, or in such a manner as to derive a particular benefit. As such, plans variously protect, conserve, manage, enable, deliver and support land and property development. The specific arrangements for development planning differ in practice in England, Wales, Scotland and Northern Ireland, reflecting the different local government arrangements in operation and different approaches to planning and the distribution of power and decision-making. We now consider the planning law frameworks of the four administrations. The discussion is organised in relation to primary and secondary legislation, regional-wide (territorial) planning policy and guidance, and operational aspects. Given our focus on development management, we pay particular attention to contextualising the geography of local government

The current legislative contexts

England and Wales

It is appropriate to consider England and Wales together because, from the legislative perspective, they have been very closely aligned until recently, when some divergence has become evident.

Primary legislation

The primary legislative frameworks for the planning systems in England and Wales are broadly the same (Cave et al, 2013). The main planning acts in force are: the Town and Country Planning Act 1990; the Planning and Compulsory Purchase Act 2004; the Planning Act 2008; the Localism Act 2011 and the Planning and Housing Act 2016 (both of which apply only in England); and the Planning (Wales) Act 2016.

In England, the Localism Act 2011 provides neighbourhood planning powers and a duty for cooperation between authorities. The move towards localism in England is intended to give communities more autonomy and responsibility to address the needs and wants in their specific area, the scope of which would not necessarily be identified by central government or councils governing the wider district in which a community is located. Wales does not have an equivalent Act to this, but on-going discussions concerning local government include the role and potential of the neighbourhood scale of planning; reform is likely, and, with this, it is likely that greater autonomy and responsibility will come.

Where parts of the Planning and Compulsory Purchase Act 2004 and Planning Act 2008 are not in force in Wales, the Welsh Government has the option to commence these if its want the provisions to apply to Wales. For example, in June 2015, Part 4 of the Planning and Compulsory Purchase Act was commenced in Wales to apply Sections 171E to H of the Town and Country Planning Act 1990 as it applies to Wales to enable Welsh LPAs to serve temporary stop notices in respect of unauthorised development. This legislation has been in force in England since 2005.

Secondary legislation

The main pieces of secondary legislation related to planning are those governing permitted development rights and the operation of the development management system. There are differences here between the English and Welsh systems as different Orders, or different versions of them, are in force. Secondary legislation associated with other aspects of the planning system, for example regulations in respect of advertisements, rules for planning appeal procedures and fees for planning applications, also exist.

For England, particularly significant secondary legislation includes (not an exhaustive list):

- the Town and Country Planning (General Permitted Development) Order 2015
- the Town and Country Planning (Development Management Procedure) (England) Order 2015
- Neighbourhood Planning (General) Regulations 2012 (as amended)
- the Town and Country Planning (Use Classes) Order 1987 (as amended).

For Wales, the particularly significant secondary planning legislation includes (not an exhaustive list):

- the Town and Country Planning (General Permitted Development) Order 1995 (as amended)
- the Town and Country Planning (Development Management Procedure) (Wales) Order 2012;
- the Town and Country Planning (Use Classes) Order 1987 (as amended).

The array of secondary legislation in force in England and Wales, and differences between them, can sometimes make deciphering planning legislation difficult – not just for the lay person, but also for planning professionals. Moreover, various updates have been made to secondary legislation over the years. In the absence of a consolidated version of these changes it is easy to become confused and frustrated as to what is actually the prevailing legislation at a particular time. The lesson here is that one cannot always assume that the content of a legislative document found through an internet search is the most recent legal position, or even any longer in force, if ever enacted. Consolidated versions of Orders that have been in force for many years, and updated regularly, would make life much easier for everyone who wants to avoid falling foul of the legislation. The Town and Country Planning (General Permitted Development) Order 1995 is a prime example of this. For example in Wales this Order remains in force despite several updates, in recent years these include changes in relation to renewable energy generation The Town and Country Planning (General Permitted Development) (Amendment) (Wales) (No.2) Order 2012, householder permitted development rights The Town and Country Planning (General Permitted Development) (Amendment) (Wales) Order 2013 and non-domestic permitted development rights The Town and Country Planning (General Permitted Development) (Amendment) (Wales) Order 2014 all under different amendment orders, whilst permitted development rights in England are also similarly convoluted with recent amendments included in the Town and Country Planning (General Permitted Development) (England) Order 2016.

Operation of the planning system

In England the structure of local government is as varied as it is complex. In some areas there are three tiers of local government: county councils; district/borough/city councils, and parish/town councils (DCLG, 2015a). Map 4.1 shows the local government boundaries for England. County councils have strategic responsibilities in relation to town planning, and determine applications for transport, minerals and waste, as well as development on their own land, for example schools. This responsibility also translates to enforcement powers in respect of these matters.

Reflecting the principle that planning is best dealt with at the local scale, most planning takes place at district level. Local councils are thus responsible for preparing local plans, determining planning applications and enforcement. Parish or town councils also have a role to play at the very local scale. In London, despite the boroughs being unitary authorities, in most respects the Greater London Authority performs a strategic-wide role and sits above this level, holding significant powers in areas such as transport and planning. Areas that include such designations as a National Park have a National Park Authority to oversee many functions and responsibilities. Some structural variations exist elsewhere, in response to devolution of powers and partnerships at the sub-regional scale. Given the increasing emphasis on the metropolitan scale, Manchester is a good example of the scaling-up of planning, since the Greater Manchester Combined Authority comprises 10 local authorities brought together to form a statutory combined authority.

The May 2016 Queen's Speech, setting out the proposed legislative programme for government for Westminster, included a new Neighbourhood Planning and Infrastructure Bill, specifically targeting economic recovery, housing provision and infrastructure, as well as addressing aspects of resourcing neighbourhood planning to further empower local people. This Bill heralds further changes to the planning system, including, potentially, a reduction in the use of pre-commencement planning conditions.

Before the Localism Act 2011, the role of parish and town councils in the planning system in England was to comment on planning applications. In addition to this function, they now have power to make Neighbourhood Development Plans to form part of the development plan alongside the local plan for the area, and also to make Neighbourhood Development Orders (NDOs), which can grant permission for certain developments without the need to apply for planning permission. These aspects of planning law are discussed further in Chapter Six.

In Wales, matters may be regarded as far simpler; only a unitary authority structure exists, with community councils operating at the community scale. The responsibility for planning functions in Wales is through its 25 planning authorities, comprising 22 local authorities and three National Park Authorities. From a statutory land-use planning perspective, these authorities develop local plans and policy, determine planning applications and are responsible for enforcement of planning control.

Map 4.1: Local Government in England

Source: www.d-maps.com/carte.php?num_car=5545&lang=en, copyright d-maps.com

The local government structure in Wales has been under review, and it is possible that the number of authorities will be reduced through merging existing authorities driven by a desire for increased efficiency of resources and improving public service. Finally, community councils are also found throughout Wales but do not have plan-making powers. Map 4.2 shows the present boundaries of the 22 local authorities in Wales.

Map 4.2: Local Government in Wales

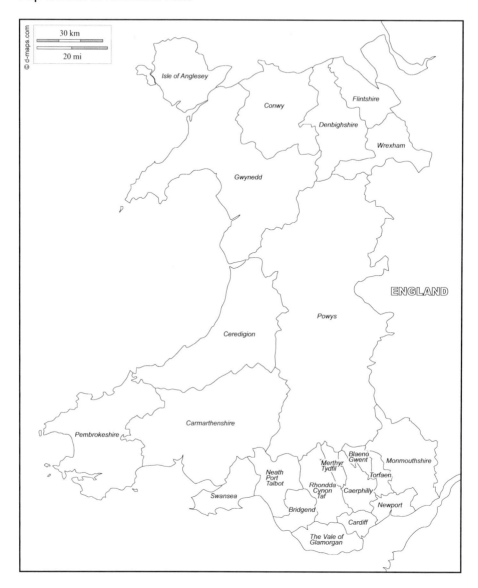

Source: www.d-maps.com/carte.php?num_car=15929&lang=en, copyright d-maps.com

Scotland

Primary legislation

The legislative framework for the planning system in Scotland is set out under the Town and Country Planning (Scotland) Act 1997, which was substantially amended by the Planning etc. (Scotland) Act 2006.

Secondary legislation

There exist a range of secondary legislative orders and regulations within the Scottish planning system, including:

- the Town and Country Planning (General Permitted Development) (Scotland) Order 1992 (as amended)
- the Town and Country Planning (Use Classes) (Scotland) Order 1997
- the Town and Country Planning (Development Management Procedure) (Scotland) Regulations 2008.

Operation of the planning system

As noted in Chapter One, Scotland has a hierarchical planning system. The local planning system, including the making of local plans, development management and enforcement, is operated through 32 local authorities (Map 4.3). There are two National Parks in Scotland, although their specific planning arrangements are different from other local authorities. Scotland also has four Strategic Development Planning Authorities (SDPAs). Introduced under the Planning etc. (Scotland) Act 2006, SDPAs (similar to the example of Manchester in England) are intended to provide a strategic and cross-jurisdictional perspective. In practice, groups of LPAs work together to produce Strategic Development Plans for sustainable economic growth in Scotland's four largest city-regions. They presently comprise: Aberdeen City and Shire; Glasgow and the Clyde Valley (Clydeplan); Edinburgh and South East Scotland (SES Plan); and Dundee, Perth, Angus and North Fife (TayPlan).

A root-and-branch review of the Scottish planning system in 2016 identified the strategic layer as requiring potential improvement, so the precise form and remit of the strategic scale of plan making may change. In contrast, and linked to wider reforms taking place in Scotland with respect to integrated public service delivery (community planning), the Independent Review of the Scottish Planning System (Beveridge et al, 2016) also recommended that there was scope for the emerging locality plans to be given statutory status by forming part of the local development plan. This line of thinking is predicated on active community engagement. Moreover, the findings of the Independent Review suggest that acquiring statutory status would only occur where it can be demonstrated that locality plans play a 'positive role' in delivering development requirements. In the light of neighbourhood planning experience in England, this thinking indicates a clear motivation to link communities more directly with development planning and reiterates a concern with scale. Legislative change is imminent. In its 2016 Programme for Government, the Scottish Government announced a Planning Bill early in the Parliamentary session with the stated aim of producing a high-performing planning system intended to enable housing and infrastructure delivery and promote quality of place, quality of life and the public interest.

Map 4.3: Local Government in Scotland

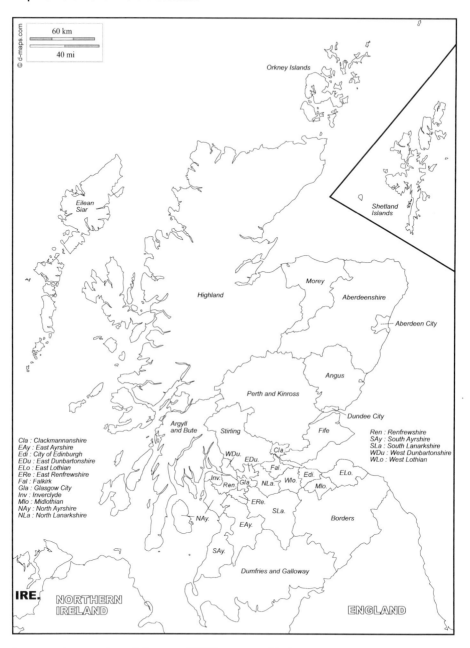

Source: www.d-maps.com/carte.php?num_car=15879&lang=en, copyright d-maps.com

Northern Ireland

Primary legislation

In Northern Ireland planning law has developed differently and has followed a different time–line. Until recently, the Planning (Northern Ireland) Order 1991 was the main legislation for controlling development. In contrast to the emphasis on local government decision-taking powers elsewhere in the UK, and with the exception of legislative powers, all planning powers rested with the (former) Department of the Environment (DOE), a central government department. Following a sustained period of legislative change, a fundamental restructuring and rescaling of government arrangements the Planning Act (Northern Ireland) 2011 now provides the primary legislation.

Secondary legislation

A raft of new subordinate legislation has been made under the 2011 Act to provide the detail for the new primary legislation. Some of the main pieces include:

- the Planning (General Permitted Development) Order (Northern Ireland) 2015
- the Planning (General Development Procedure) Order (Northern Ireland) 2015
- the Planning (Use Classes Order) Northern Ireland 2015
- the Planning (Local Development Plan) Regulations (Northern Ireland) 2015.

Operation of the planning system

The 2011 legislation has involved radical change. Prior to that, the majority of development planning and control was carried out at central government level. Activities were the responsibility of the Planning Service, an executive agency of the DOE. Political devolution and the setting up of the Northern Ireland Assembly in 1998 allowed a number of steps to be put in place to enable further decentralisation of planning powers. Nevertheless, Northern Ireland's particular history and the nature of the power-sharing government mean that the culture, experience and arrangements for planning at strategic and local levels, and in terms of managing urban and rural development, differ from those elsewhere in the UK.

In contrast to the rather more concentrated central government arrangements elsewhere in the UK, planning has tended to be somewhat dispersed in Northern Ireland, with regional development, rural development and regeneration falling to different government departments. This arrangement involves different party-political department control. Until 2015 the DOE was the department responsible for planning controls and local government. The DOE was subject to the overall direction and control of the Secretary of State for Northern Ireland (that is, Westminster) and the relevant Minister from the Northern Ireland Legislative Assembly, to whom oversight of the department was delegated. To all intents and purposes, until April 2015 planning decisions were taken under the authority of the Minister for the DOE.

Crucially the entire planning system has now been reformed and restructured from a unitary system, where all planning powers rested with the DOE and the Planning Service, to a new two-tier model of delivery. As part of wider reforms of public administration in Northern Ireland and the redrawing of local government boundaries from 1 April 2015, responsibility for planning was devolved to 11 new councils (the first tier), with the Northern Ireland Assembly retaining strategic and ultimate control for planning (the second tier). The transfer of planning powers to councils coincided with significant reforms and improvements to the planning process that were introduced through the Planning Act (Northern Ireland) 2011 and associated subordinate legislation. As elsewhere across the devolved UK, there is an expectation that locally elected members, professional planners and local communities will work together in planning their areas.

The transfer of the majority of planning functions (local development planning, development management and enforcement) to new district councils involve not just the redistribution of functions but working, through the creation of a new planning system for Northern Ireland at the local level. While the legal framework in Northern Ireland mirrors that operating in the rest of the UK, it is clear that the system is in a transitional period, involving structural reorganisation, the design of new roles and elaboration of new responsibilities, and the building of new expertise and relationships between officers, elected members and communities. Such a catalogue of activities is a reminder that creating planning laws is but a part of a much bigger picture.

Moreover, in May 2016, the number of central government departments in Northern Ireland was reduced. The Department of Agriculture, Environment and Rural Affairs (DAERA) now has responsibility for environmental protection and regulation, including marine planning, while urban regeneration, built heritage and local government (including community planning) fall under the Department for Communities (DfC).

More importantly, for our discussion, however, the majority of strategic planning activities were transferred to a new Department for Infrastructure (DfI), which has also assumed functions from the former Department for Regional Development (DRD). Planning functions are split between two divisions: (i) the Strategic Planning Division, which is responsible for processing planning applications deemed to be of regional significance or those which may be 'called in' from the local councils; and (ii) the Planning Policy Division, which develops planning legislation and policy in line with ministerial direction, as well as providing advice and guidance to councils on design, policy and practice. The DfI is responsible for:

- determination of regionally significant and 'called-in' planning applications
- the Regional Development Strategy (RDS)
- regional planning policy
- planning legislation

- performance management
- oversight of and guidance for councils.

The 11 councils are responsible for local development planning, development management and planning enforcement. Moreover, under the Local Government Act 2014 each of the councils has a duty to create a long-term vision for its area for the social, environmental and economic well-being of its community. This vision is set out in a 'community plan', which must be taken into consideration by the council when preparing its local development plan.

In practice, the reconfiguration of central government departments in Northern Ireland has seen the amalgamation of different functions, with a view to facilitating joined-up and coordinated working. Nonetheless, there will clearly be a need for effective communication across departmental portfolios with respect to planning because the related areas of environmental protection (DAERA) and community planning (DfC) are in separate departments (Cave, 2016).

Map 4.4: Local Government in Northern Ireland

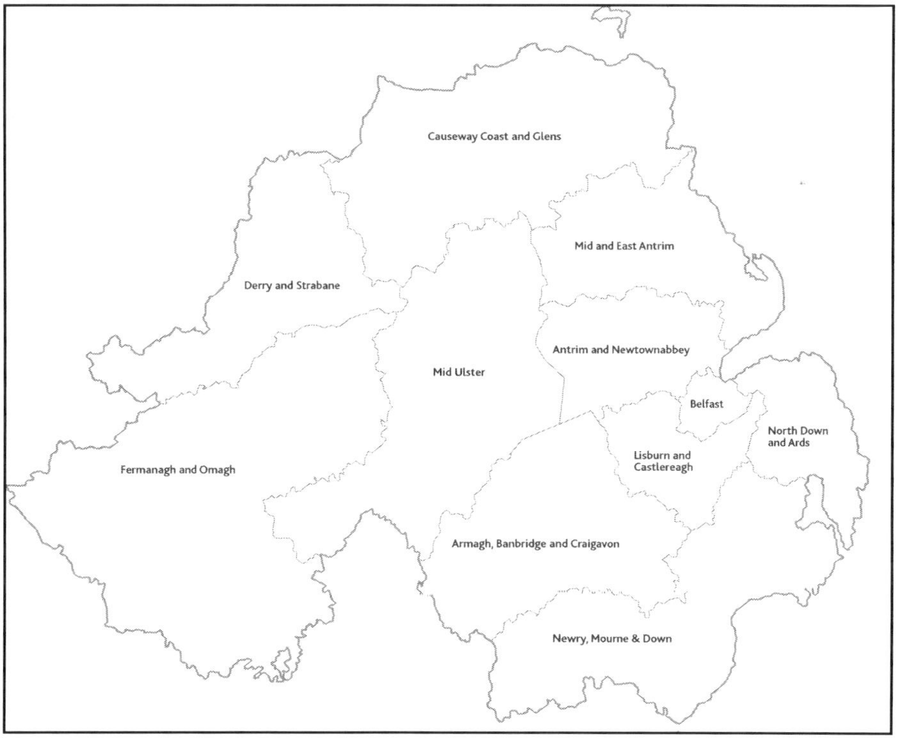

Source: Contains public sector information licensed under the terms of the Open Goverment Licence v3.0.

Plan-led systems

Having outlined the legislative frameworks for planning across the devolved UK, we now outline the development plan arrangements that are intended to provide the investment and development land-allocation and policy context for consistent decision-making. A related term that is useful in understanding the plan-led approach is forward planning, which reflects the aspirational nature of development plans, since they aim to guide future development, discourage undesirable development and set a strategic direction for the plan period of typically 15–20 years.

Being plan-led means that decisions for planning permission, where it is required, must conform to the development plan that sets out planning policies in relation to the development and use of land and buildings within the plan area. Although the precise terminology varies, we are principally concerned with the detailed plans made at the level of the LPA and to which, for our purposes, we give the generic title 'local development plans'. In practice, however, development plans and policy are made at a range of tiers. Where relevant, these different tiers must also be taken into account. For example, in England, Neighbourhood Development Plans are of equal status to the local plan. In Scotland, it may be relevant to take a strategic development plan and the *National Planning Framework* (NPF) (Scottish Government, 2014a) into account. As such, working in a multi-tiered and hierarchical planning context may involve taking strategic or national plans, regional plans and local or neighbourhood plans into account when taking a decision. It is important to be careful, as the term development plan invokes this loose family, as the following extract from a plain-English guide to planning illustrates:

> The planning system is plan-led and any planning application must be determined in line with the development plan (Local and neighbourhood plans and, where relevant, the London Plan) unless other material considerations indicate otherwise. (DCLG, 2015a, p 15)

A consistent feature across the devolved UK is that national legislation requires local authorities to produce local plans for their respective areas to regulate and shape development over a period of time. These local development plans are informed by policies produced at national level, which identify priorities that must be addressed and taken into account in local plan making, and contain locally specific policies that, taken together, are a material consideration in the determination of planning applications.

As a result of the requirement to produce their own plans, LPAs are, in the main, structured so as to have a dedicated group of policy planners, who are tasked with developing local planning policy and monitoring progress in respect of those policies and associated target indicators, in addition to the planning officers who deal with the day-to-day case load of planning applications. The production of national plans and policy guidance provides opportunities for governments to ensure greater consistency between LPAs and to ensure that planning policy works to achieve a range of national strategic matters. Certain central–local tensions exist. The 2016 Independent Review of the Scottish Planning System (Beveridge et al, 2016), for example, queried the extent to which planning policies articulated as national policy need to be reiterated in local development plans.

National, regional and strategic plans and policy

The purpose of the national (and or regional) planning tier is essentially to assert strategic spatial priorities and provide an overarching framework to guide the process of local development plan making. This central–local balancing act enables strategic (territorial) direction to be given for infrastructure needs, for example, while allowing discretion for local plan-making to better meet local community needs, conditions and circumstances. However, national policies and strategic plans do not simply provide a policy steer for those working in forward planning, since they are a statutory component of the development plan; they are material considerations in determining planning applications. Moreover, national or regional policy documents are often supported by detailed secondary advice and guidance, which are regularly referred to by planning officers making decisions in respect of planning applications or investors making development decisions. Such documents can be in the form of government circulars or more informal guidance. For reasons of space, we make only limited reference to these information sources, but they can be very useful in understanding the application of law in practice.

National-level planning policies across the devolved UK all place a strong emphasis on securing sustainable development. Consequently, planning policies are prepared with the objective of achieving the values and principles of sustainability. As a result, economic development, social cohesion and environmental enhancement and protection feature strongly in local development plans. As noted in the previous chapter, the scope of planning controls has expanded over time. Unsurprisingly, then, the nature of the planning policies in development plans covers a wide range of topics.

An examination of the national planning policy documentation across the devolved UK reveals commonality in several broad areas. In turn, these policy areas are reflected in local plans as LPAs strive to meet the policy standards set at national level. Major policy areas have tended to be sector specific in practice and include housing supply; enhancement of the natural environment and protection of habitats; and climate change mitigation and adaptation, which ranges from renewable energy to flood risk. Other important strategic policy aims include design quality, protection of historic buildings, infrastructure for transport and telecommunications, business and employment, leisure development, enforcement and advertisement control, retail, regeneration and health. The manner in which strategic policy objectives are translated into development plans at the local tier tends to vary. Moreover, in recent times, there has been a move to streamline national policy by producing single national policy statements. Below, we tease out some interesting nuances in UK practice with respect to national policy, national guidance and national (or territorial) plans.

England

National planning policy in England is the responsibility of the Department for Communities and Local Government (DCLG). In contrast to elsewhere in the devolved UK, England has no England-wide spatial plan. In March 2012, however, DCLG produced the *National Planning Policy Framework* (NPPF) (DCLG, 2012), which aims to reduce the complexity of the planning system by replacing the previous, sector-specific planning policy statements and guidance. The NPPF sets out the government's policies for planning and how these are expected to be applied. The policies must be taken into account in the preparation of local development and neighbourhood plans and, as noted in the document itself, the policies laid out in the NPPF are a material consideration in the determination of planning applications. Although the NPPF is a very important document within the English planning context, it does not act in isolation. It must be read in tandem with other documents, including policy relating to waste, travellers, schools, sustainable drainage systems, parking and starter homes.

The National Planning Practice Guidance (NPPG) that sits alongside the NPPF is an interesting development because of its extensive nature, comprehensive reach and 'live' format. In contrast to previous forms of written guidance and government circulars, which tended not to be updated and thus became out of date, this approach makes use of technological development. Since it exists electronically, it can be revised as required. You are strongly encouraged to take a look at the NPPG, for which the internet link is provided below, under 'Further reading'.

Wales

In terms of national-level policy, the Welsh Government prepares *Planning Policy Wales* (PPW) (Welsh Government, 2016), which is currently in its eighth edition. As elsewhere, this national planning policy must be taken into account by LPAs when preparing local development plans and determining planning applications.

PPW is supplemented by 21 Technical Advice Notes (TANs) that provide more detailed subject-specific guidance on different policy areas. Unlike PPW (which has had several iterations), many of the Welsh TANs have been in force since prior to 1998. This situation reflects the relatively limited law-making powers enjoyed by Wales until quite recently, and the reliance on policy to shape planning. Although much of the substance contained in the TANs remains relevant, some of the information is now dated. The introduction of the Planning (Wales) Act 2015 has created the impetus to revise the guidance where necessary. For example, TAN 22 (Sustainable Buildings) has been cancelled, since responsibility has transferred to Building Regulations and the construction stage of development is no longer dealt with as early as the planning application stage. The inclusion of TAN 20 (Planning and the Welsh Language) is an example of how planning and planning guidance need to reflect the uniqueness of regional and local conditions. Indeed, the importance of the Welsh language has been further reinforced through clarification in the Planning (Wales) Act 2015 that the impact on the use of the Welsh language can be a material consideration when determining a planning application.

The Planning (Wales) Act 2015 is the first piece of primary legislation passed by the Welsh Assembly Government. It builds on and amends existing and primary legislation, rather than offering wholesale reform. It aims to strengthen the plan-led approach, enable effective enforcements and appeals and support the development of a modernised planning system, notably including improving the development management system. The Act provides for the preparation of a National Development Framework to update and replace the *Wales Spatial Plan* (Welsh Government, 2004). This new Framework will (as in Scotland) identify developments of national importance and effectively reinforces a commitment to territorial (Wales-wide) development planning.

Scotland

Scotland has a long history with respect to preparing strategic planning policy guidance. The publication of the coastal national planning guidelines in 1974 addressed the onshore, landward developments associated with the production of North Sea oil and gas. The strategic coastal guidelines involved grouping onshore oil- and gas-related development into specific zones. Sixteen preferred development zones and 26 preferred conservation zones were designated in order to provide a strategic framework at a pan-Scotland scale (Rowan-Robinson et al, 1987). The measure was subsequently revised in form and extended to a range of strategic planning issues, including agricultural land, out-of-town retailing and skiing. Later, more recent concerns with aquaculture (fish-farming) and marine planning have further expanded the scope of development management, and also led to the publication of Scotland's first *National Marine Plan* (Scottish Government, 2015).

The trend towards a single national policy statement, rather than a suite of sector-specific policies, has also been adopted in Scotland. Published in 2014, the *Scottish Planning Policy* (SPP) sets out the Scottish Government's priorities for the operation of the Scottish planning system. As with the NPPF (in England) and PPW (in Wales), the SPP (Scottish Government, 2014b) aims to promote consistency in the planning application process across Scotland by guiding the preparation of development plans, encourages quality of design in development and is a material consideration in the determination of planning applications and appeals.

The 2014 SPP sits alongside the 2014 NPF. The NPF is currently in its third revision and provides a statutory framework for the country's long-term spatial development, including identifying 14 national developments, such as major road infrastructure and hydroelectric schemes. The SPP sets out the policies that will help to achieve the NPF and the Scottish Government's overarching purpose of:

> creating a more successful country, with opportunities for all of Scotland to flourish, through increasing sustainable economic growth. (Scottish Government, 2014b, p 4)

Importantly, then, the SPP has a core role to play in Scotland's outcomes-based approach to public policy and, as highlighted above, to (particular) ideas of sustainability. The SPP also provides an important insight into the status of such policy, since it carries 'significant weight' in the decision-making process and in plan preparation. Moreover, the specific assertion of *place-making* as a principal and overarching policy again highlights how the scope of planning continues to evolve:

> Where 'must' is used it reflects a legislative requirement to take action. Where 'should' is used it reflects Scottish Ministers' expectations of an efficient and effective planning system. The Principal Policies on Sustainability and Placemaking are overarching and should be applied to all development. (Scottish Government, 2014b, p 3)

Planning Advice Notes (PANs) play a similar role to TANs in Wales, and for similar reasons a number of them have been revoked or new guidance has been or is being produced in the light of reform and on-going modernisation of the planning system. Two policy guidance statements that perhaps merit attention in relation to development management are *Designing Streets* (Scottish Government, 2010), which covers new or existing streets and *Creating Places* (Scottish Government, 2013), which focuses on the importance of architecture and design.

Northern Ireland

Following the UK-wide approach to streamlining national policy guidance, and in anticipation of the restoration of planning powers to local councils and the introduction of a reformed two-tier planning system, the (former) DOE produced a *Strategic Planning Policy Statement* (SPPS) for Northern Ireland in September 2015. This single policy document consolidated and replaced 20 Planning Policy Statements and is intended to enable orderly and consistent development across Northern Ireland. The SPPS (DOE, 2015) must be taken into account in the preparation of local development plans and is material to all decisions on individual planning applications and appeals. Stipulating the aim of furthering sustainable development, the 2015 SPPS sets the strategic direction for the 11 councils to bring forward detailed operational policies within their local development plans. At the time of writing, none of the new district councils has yet completed this process.

We have already noted that the Northern Ireland planning system is in a period of transition in terms of new organisational structures and 'rules of the game'. This is not to say, however, that Northern Ireland does not have a useful body of technical or supplementary planning guidance, including Development Control Advice Notes. We can safely assume that these will be updated as relevant. Moreover, it is worth highlighting that place-making and stewardship have already been identified as key to raising place standards across Northern Ireland. Specifically, we would point to the *Living Places: An Urban Stewardship and Design Guide* (DOE, 2014), which highlights the mutually reinforcing nature of design and stewardship in creating and keeping quality places viable, clean and safe, and also highlights the importance of related controls over air quality and parking, for example.

At the strategic level, there have been two iterations of the RDS in Northern Ireland: *Shaping Our Future* (DRD, 2001) and *Building a Better Future* (DRD, 2012). The RDS is the spatial (territorial) strategy for Northern Ireland and, as elsewhere, its purpose is to deliver the spatial aspects of the Programme for Government. It complements the *Sustainable Development Strategy* (Northern Ireland Assembly, 2010) and informs the spatial aspects of the strategies of all government departments. The RDS is a long-term plan that recognises the important role Belfast plays in generating regional prosperity and that Derry/Londonderry is the focus for economic growth in the North-West region. Intended to ensure that all places benefit from economic growth, the RDS reflects the government's commitment to balanced sub-regional growth and recognises the importance of key settlements as centres for growth and investment.

Infrastructure planning

At the time of writing, England and Wales continue to have a joint approach to major infrastructure planning and have developed an accompanying series of National Policy Statements that seek to provide relevant guidance (Table 4.1). Although these are planning-related documents to date, they have been produced by the government department with responsibility for the given area – for example, energy policy was developed by the (former) Department for Energy and Climate Change. The July 2016 Westminster Cabinet reshuffle witnessed a change in the government policy direction, which may lead to different policy emphases to stimulate the UK economy and, potentially, a different strategic planning path for industrial policy.

Table 4.1: National policy statements (as at June 2016)

Energy	Transport	Water, waste and waste water
Overarching energy Renewable energy Fossil fuels Oil and gas supply and storage Electricity networks Nuclear power	Ports Airports National networks	Water supply Hazardous waste Waste water treatment

Source: Compiled by author from https://infrastructure.planninginspectorate.gov.uk/legislation-and-advice/national-policy-statements/

In Scotland, a recent report (Rydens, 2015) reviewed existing and emerging practices in infrastructure delivery that are enabled through the planning system. The report pointed to a tension between the short-term, market need for infrastructure and the longer-term infrastructure and investment needed to sustain community well-being. It confirmed that the principal weakness in planning for infrastructure is the uncertain financial and support arrangements. Significantly, it described planning as a 'choreographer' of other agency delivery mechanisms, rather than as discharging a deliberate and direct role. The Independent Review (Beveridge et al, 2016) subsequently highlighted the critical role to be played by the planning system in providing certainty, consistency and efficiency to secure the necessary investment in both physical infrastructure and human capital. Such discussions draw attention to the important relationship between strategic and local development planning and management.

Local development plans

Status in the plan-led system

National and local development plans are intrinsically linked. Local-tier plans are guided by national-tier plans and policy to enable a strategic approach in parallel with a local response. Local development plans are considered to be at the heart of the British planning system. Their role is to set out a vision and framework for future development of an area over a sufficiently long period of time (such as 15 years), addressing the immediate needs and opportunities in an area, while providing sufficient flexibility for change. Specifically, local development plans should set out what is intended to happen in the area over the designated plan period, where and when this will occur and how it will be delivered.

Local development plans should include proposals maps of allocations of land for specific purposes, identify areas of opportunity and constraint, such as flooding or protected habitats, and use strategic policies to achieve the objectives defined at the national tier. Local development plans are vital in determining local development management planning decisions in relation to site-specific applications for planning permission. As we will discuss in more detail, the specific planning policies relevant ('material') to the determination of a particular planning proposal are stated in both the officer's report ('report of handling' in Scotland) and the 'decision notice'.

In its planning policy guidance for local development plans in England, DCLG stresses the need for collaboration between local authorities and across boundaries to enable local plans to address strategic matters for long-term planning. In England, local government is expected to demonstrate effective collaboration throughout the plan-making process and this style of planning is intended to be continuous for the life of the plan. In order for LPAs to do this, a number of surveys and viability assessments must be carried out within particular strategic areas. These include Strategic Housing Market Area Assessments to judge future housing need, land availability studies for housing and employment, assessment of infrastructure need and capacity, examination of the demand for and location of minerals within an area, flood risk assessments, collection of evidence regarding historic assets, landscape character appraisals, tourism strategy evaluations, transport and access assessments, retail studies, employment studies and, at the time of writing, sustainability appraisals with respect to the EU Directive on Strategic Environmental Assessment (SEA).

The importance of local-tier development plans cannot be over-stated. They are intended to provide place-specific detail and are a primary consideration in the determination of planning applications. Within the context of the plan-led system, the generic British planning tradition essentially works on the principle that planning applications will be determined on the basis of the land-allocation and (adopted) policy context of the plan – unless there is good reason (and 'other material considerations') why an alternative decision should be taken. Local development plans therefore underpin how a given area should evolve and be managed over the duration of the plan period.

Plan preparation and adoption process

The process of regularly preparing, drafting and adopting a local development plan involves several stages. The details of this process vary across the devolved UK but generally comprise: evidence gathering and consultation by the local authority to identify the main issues (including information on possible candidate sites for development) so as to enable an informed drafting of plan policies; publication of a draft plan for further consultation; analysis of comment made during public consultation and subsequent plan refinement; and submission of the draft plan for public examination. The character of wider public and stakeholder engagement tends to vary across the stages from early involvement to consultation, feedback and negotiation, information updates and justification.

Before the policies of a local development plan can be 'adopted' the draft proposed plan must go through an examination stage carried out by an independent body from the national scale of government, that is, the Planning Inspectorate (PINS) in England and Wales, a reporter appointed by Scottish Ministers in Scotland and the

Planning Appeals Commission (PAC) in Northern Ireland. This examination stage ensures that all the relevant evidence, consultations, representations, community engagement and policies have been taken into account by a local authority and 'due process' has been followed in drawing up the development plan (for example, it complies with statements of conformity which set out how plans must comply with national legislative requirements).

The examination of a proposed local development plan involves testing for 'soundness' and legal compliance, including assessment of whether there is evidence of adequate cooperation (including between adjacent LPAs) and consideration of how the planning authority has responded to any representations from the general public, consultees and other interests. The examiner's report may recommend further modifications and, finally, adoption. Figure 4.1 summarises a generalised local development plan adoption process in the UK.

Figure 4.1: The local development plan adoption process

Given the plan-led emphasis of development management decision-making in the UK, the currency and accuracy of local development plans is all important. A criticism of the planning system is that not all local authorities have up-to-date adopted plans. Questions then arise as to the extent to which the policies of that plan are material to development management decision taking and what 'weight' such policies carry. In Northern Ireland, for example, planning decisions will be made with regard to the suite of development plans prepared by the (former) DOE while the 11 councils go through the process of having their own local development plans adopted. We will look in more detail as to what is material in any given case, but remember that national-tier policies may also be relevant when considering a local development issue.

City-regions, metropolitan areas and 'above-local' scale planning

Thus far, we have drawn attention to national and local policies in relation to the decision-making context. These aspects of the planning system highlight questions about the most appropriate scale at which to plan and with what authority. Moreover, although we have focused on political devolution with respect to Scotland, Wales and Northern Ireland, powers are also being devolved to certain English cities under devolution deals. Here we make some brief remarks about the strategic or metropolitan tier of planning, since, on the one hand, power is being devolved (that is, pushed down), while on the other hand plan-making is potentially being up-scaled. Such a 'scissor movement' may reduce controls over small-scale development.

As we have seen, the uncontrolled expansion of urban areas, such as London during the Industrial Revolution, was an important influence in asserting the case for planning. Moreover, the reality of people's lives means that they travel and operate beyond the boundary of the local authority where they live – for their work, leisure, education and so on. Such behavioural patterns also reflect the nature of housing and labour markets. As noted above, infrastructure provision requires a strategic approach to improve connectivity. Contemporary arguments for strategic or city-regional plans are thus based on the logic that joint working and collaborative plan making between areas can potentially produce mutual benefits, economies of scale and more efficient planning. It is also anticipated that this type of working will improve knowledge sharing, support innovation and, ultimately, enhance economic performance.

Mention has already been made of the four Strategic Development Plans in Scotland, enabled through the 2006 legislation. In similar vein, the Planning (Wales) Act 2015 provides for local authorities to form Strategic Planning Areas with adopted development plans and that will have regard to both national and local plans. The Welsh Government (2012b) recommended two city-regions: South East Wales and Swansea Bay. It also pointed to the need to improve cross-border communication in North-East Wales.

In Northern Ireland the economic development importance of the cities of Belfast and Derry/Londonderry has also been highlighted with respect to an interest in promoting regional balance through the RDS. Moreover, there has been sustained work on the island of Ireland to promote cooperation between the spatial strategies of the Republic of Ireland and Northern Ireland, notably in terms of a Belfast–Dublin strategic corridor, for instance.

In England the city-region concept is less developed in terms of a coherent national strategy and, over a number of decades, regional planning has variously risen and fallen in popularity. The new Greater Manchester Combined Authority is an interesting innovation in terms of a supra-council that has planning powers to help coordinate the region's regeneration, economy, housing and transport priorities. More widely, there is support for partnership and joint working initiatives that focus on the 'above local' or 'sub-regional' scale. Specifically, there is a legal 'duty to co-operate' on LPAs in preparing their local plans, and a requirement to work together on strategic planning matters such as housing delivery. At this point it is hard to predict how strategic planning will respond to the UK not being a core member of the EU and what the result of the UK EU referendum, and Westminster government's commitment to put 'Brexit' into effect potentially will mean in practice for relatively more peripheral and poorer regions.

Neighbourhood plans in England

In contrast to taking a strategic perspective, in this final section we consider planning at the lowest tier and the expanding range of actors involved in plan preparation. The Localism Act 2011 introduced new rights and (limited) powers to allow local communities to shape development in their areas by producing their own neighbourhood plan. The so-called 'Qualifying Bodies' are responsible for drafting the plan. These bodies may be based on parish or town councils where these exist or, by agreement, through another body; or may involve community groups in the form of Neighbourhood Forums in non-parished areas. Such forums must be formally recognised by the local authority to enable them to function as a neighbourhood planning body.

Neighbourhood plans are intended to establish general planning policies for the development and use of land in a neighbourhood area and form part of the statutory development plan. Working with the relevant local authority, Qualifying Bodies can also pursue a Neighbourhood Development Order to provide for 'permitted development rights' within a defined geographical area (see also Local Development Orders in Chapter Six). A Community Right to Build allows communities to gain planning permission for specific proposals without going through the planning process in the traditional manner. This approach can be used to provide, for example, family homes, affordable rented housing, sheltered accommodation and community facilities.

Neighbourhood plans form part of the development plan and are thus shaped by that policy context. They must therefore be in 'general conformity' with the host local plan; must have regard to and comply with relevant national and strategic policies; and must be compatible with Human Rights requirements and (to date) related European obligations. Where there is no up-to-date local plan in place, a neighbourhood plan can still be prepared, but it must be in general conformity with all the policies set out in the NPPF. If a local plan is subsequently adopted using more recent evidence, for example housing statistics, the local plan policies could override the neighbourhood plan. There is clearly an important issue of coordination and timing with respect to the preparation and adoption of multiple plans.

Neighbourhood plans are required to go through an independent examination. This process is different to that for local plans and may be seen as far less rigorous. As a consequence, aggrieved parties, such as developers, have sought to quash neighbourhood plans through the High Court. After the examination there is a referendum involving local residents. If the neighbourhood plan meets certain criteria and is supported by 50% or more of the electoral turn out the plan can be adopted. The neighbourhood plan then attains the status of being 'made'.

Box 4.1: Neighbourhood planning in action

The requirement to be in conformity with the local plan and to adhere to such matters as housing allocations have been felt by some to undermine the fundamental spirit of 'localism'. Nevertheless, neighbourhood plans are increasing in England and some are now well established. The neighbourhood plan 'made' for the Exeter St James neighbourhood area covers a 15-year period and sets out a number of priority projects as the focus for community action. The main objectives are to: define a local hub; restrict 'Houses in Multiple Occupation'; encourage development to meet community needs and support and maintain community facilities in the area; manage the impact of traffic and encourage sustainable transport; and improve the natural and built environment. A total of 25 policies in the neighbourhood plan seek to support these objectives.

Community-level plans are a relatively new addition to the development plan landscape, and the effectiveness of neighbourhood plans in England is subject to research and evaluation. With no obligation to have a neighbourhood plan in place and, given the amount of community time and money required to prepare them, neighbourhood plans will likely be retained and supported only if they are seen to create added value for communities. Moreover, evidence collected as part of the Independent Review of the Scottish Planning System (Beveridge et al, 2016) also highlighted a concern that relatively more affluent communities are better equipped to engage in such voluntary processes. As such, this approach may reinforce inequalities. There may also be a tendency for local communities to promote protectionist agendas. Nonetheless, it is evident that momentum is building in Scotland to advance the potential for communities to bring forward their own local place plans. In Northern Ireland, the statutory link between community planning and land-use planning opens up the potential for plan preparation at the neighbourhood level. As we shall see when we look in more detail at development management, the status of the policy environment is all important for decision-making in a plan-led context.

Marine plans

Our oceans are fundamental to the health of the planet. The sea is critical to the functioning of the water cycle and determines the Earth's climate. Humans rely on the sea for food, but we know that certain stocks have been over-fished and that the sea has become a major sink for various waste. The accumulation of plastics, for example, is a particularly insidious form of pollution. Public awareness of the broad area of marine planning (variously referred to as marine spatial planning, or maritime planning) is increasing as the range of use and development pressures placed on the sea have expanded and awareness of marine problems has heightened. The case for the necessity for state intervention in managing marine development and use in the public interest is gathering momentum (Peel and

Lloyd, 2004). As the legislative and plan context for the marine resource evolves, we can see some of the intricacies relating to coordination across the devolved UK, and how reserved and devolved powers operate.

Recognition of the fragility and vulnerability of the marine resource in the light of the reality of the increasing and competing economic uses and development potential of the sea has resulted in a number of international efforts to better plan and manage the marine environment. Indeed the introduction of formal marine planning legislation may be seen as demarcating a new vision, requiring a different mind-set for how we think about and use the seas. Initially, concerns for marine health drove the need for controls aimed at protecting the sea. An early example are the controls over Australia's Great Barrier Reef (Day, 2008). As arguments around the causes and implications of climate change have gained traction and as we understand more about the marine ecosystem the case for legislation and planning policies has become more sophisticated.

The extension of statutory planning controls over aquaculture in Scotland, for example, may be seen as important in demonstrating links between terrestrial and marine planning. Specifically, the Planning etc. (Scotland) Act 2006 introduced a new category of 'development' into the principal (1997) legislation to include existing marine fish-farms. The additional controls out to 12 nautical miles were deemed necessary in order to better regulate the expanding sector of aquaculture and to improve strategic coordination. LPAs are already responsible for land-use planning down to Mean Low Water Springs. The aquaculture controls highlight, however, that offshore development has onshore development implications.

The Marine and Coastal Access Act 2009 is held to represent a milestone in environmental regulation in the UK and to be one of the most important and long-awaited pieces of UK conservation legislation in nearly 30 years (Meas, 2009). It establishes a comprehensive regulatory and planning system for the UK's marine environment, integrating a number of previously fragmented sectoral approaches and covering, inter alia, minerals extraction, fisheries, energy provision and generation, and recreation. The Marine and Coastal Access Act 2009 has thus been welcomed for several reasons. First, it received cross-party support, giving it political legitimacy and suggesting a broad consensus for managing the marine resource in a relatively more informed way that meets the needs of a range of stakeholders and the wider community, and advancing sustainability principles.

Second, the nature of the legal arrangements seems to offer a one-stop-shop approach (Plant, 2003) in terms of providing a more streamlined approach to the various consent, control and licensing regimes. Such an approach can, arguably, provide a relatively more coordinated and integrated framework for controlling impacts and make it easier to bring development forward. In practice, the elaboration of the legal and policy arrangements for marine planning across the devolved UK has taken place with the four nations working separately and in parallel, although with significant efforts to assemble and share a supporting evidence base for the marine environment.

Third, the Marine and Coastal Access Act 2009 provides the legislative basis for implementing the ecosystem approach (Jones, 2009). An ecosystem refers to the range of interactions and interrelations in a given area. The nature of the ecosystem goods and services afforded by the marine varies. In terms of services, the marine environment offers: 'provisioning services' (for example, food, seaweed fertiliser, pharmaceuticals and tourism revenue); 'supporting services' (for example, capturing energy from the sun, nutrient recycling and sediment formation); 'regulating services' (for example, climate regulation and breaking down waste); and 'cultural services' (for example, non-material benefits such as the well-being effects of seascapes, or maritime heritage) (Scottish Government, 2015).

The Marine and Coastal Access Act 2009 provides for the exercise of controls over territorial waters and offshore waters out to the EEZ. In practice, the Marine and Coastal Access Act 2009 has a particular geographical remit in relation to the constituent parts of the UK. This position reflects the nature of the reserved and devolved matters under the present devolution settlement. Part 3, chapter 1, section 44 of the Act states that a 'marine policy statement' (MPS) is a document in which:

> the policy authorities that prepare and adopt it state general policies of theirs (however expressed) for contributing to the achievement of sustainable development in the UK marine area.

The joint adoption of a UK-wide MPS (DEFRA, 2011) by the four UK administrations represents a significant step forward in establishing a high-level policy context for the development of marine plans across the UK with the intention of securing 'clean, healthy, safe, productive and biologically diverse oceans and seas' (Scottish Government, 2015, paragraph 3). The articulation of high-level objectives promoting sustainable development is intended to support the integration of marine planning across the UK (Ritchie and Ellis, 2009). The High Level Marine Objectives set out in the MPS (DEFRA, 2011) are elaborated through a series of regional or sub-regional arrangements in the form of development plans that are created by the Marine Management Organisation (MMO) for English waters, the Marine and Fisheries Division (part of DAERA) in Northern Irish waters, Marine Scotland for Scottish waters and the Welsh Ministers, who act as the marine planning authorities in Wales for Welsh waters.

In Scotland, offshore waters are covered by the Marine and Coastal Access Act 2009, whereby the UK Parliament required Scottish ministers to put a marine plan in place in the offshore region once the MPS (DEFRA, 2011) came into effect. In practice, inshore waters are governed by the Marine (Scotland) Act 2010. Taken together, the two Acts (referred to as the 'Marine Acts') provide the legislative and management framework for all of Scotland's seas. The preparation of Scotland's *National Marine Plan* (Scottish Government, 2015) effectively comprises two plans under two pieces of legislation passed at different levels. Scottish Government Circular 1/2015 sets out the relationship between marine and terrestrial planning and emphasises the need for close collaboration and formal consultation. In stressing the importance of liaison, the circular highlights that different lead roles will be necessary if appropriate priorities, policies and proposals are to be identified with respect to terrestrial and marine planning matters. As part of an aligned framework, reference to both the National Marine Plan, the NPF and SPP are thus required.

The implications of the Marine and Coastal Access Act 2009 for Northern Ireland are similar in that there is one plan for its inshore region under the Marine Act (Northern Ireland) 2013 (legislation passed by the Northern Ireland Assembly) and a second plan for its offshore region (as required by the Marine and Coastal Access Act 2009). As at January 2016, and following a period of engagement with departments and agencies at both Northern Ireland and UK level, the latest version of the draft Marine Plan was undergoing a Sustainability Appraisal. The legislative provisions of the Marine and Coastal Access Act 2009 cover English and Welsh inshore and offshore waters. An initial pre-consultation draft of the Welsh National Marine Plan was published in November 2015 and was out for comment until January 2016.

Operation of marine planning

In terms of prioritisation and allocation of the sea for specific uses or development, such as identifying where energy infrastructure should go, it is acknowledged that a full range of interests must be involved, including industry-based stakeholders, marine scientists, local communities, as well as landowners and advocacy groups such as the National Trust or RSPB.

In terms of what a marine plan should contain, advice in England is that it should encourage local communities to be involved in planning; make the most of growth and job opportunities; consider the environment from the start; enable sustainable development in the marine area; integrate with terrestrial planning; save time and money for investors and developers by giving clear guidance on things to consider or avoid; encourage shared use of busy areas to benefit as many industries as possible; and encourage developments that consider wildlife and the natural environment (MMO, 2016). Each of the 11 marine plan areas for England will have a long-term (20 years) horizon of activities and be reviewed every three years. All marine plan areas are scheduled to have a plan by 2021. To date, two sets of marine plans have been prepared: the East Inshore and East Offshore marine plan areas (MMO, 2014a) and the South Inshore and South Offshore marine plan areas (MMO, 2014b).

To support its first *National Marine Plan* (Scottish Government, 2015), Marine Scotland has created 11 marine regions that cover sea areas extending out to 12 nautical miles. Regional Marine Plans will be developed in turn by Marine Planning Partnerships (Scottish Government, 2016), thereby enabling more local ownership and decision-making in relation to specific sub-regional and local issues within an area. There has been a phased approach to putting the regional marine plans in place, with two regions particularly important in sharing learning. First, Shetland Islands Council has developed considerable experience, having already adopted the fourth edition of the Shetland Islands' Marine Spatial Plan as supplementary guidance to the Shetland Local Development Plan in 2015 (Shetland Islands Council, 2015). Importantly, in March 2016 the Shetland Isles Marine Planning Partnership, comprising Shetland Fisheries Training Centre Trust and Shetland Island Council, gained delegated powers under a ministerial delegation of powers direction in relation to the regional marine plan for the Scottish marine plan for the Shetland Isles. Second, a pilot exercise involving the preparation of the Firth of Clyde Marine Spatial Plan (Donnelly et al, 2010) subsequently led to the establishment of the Clyde Marine Planning Partnership, which will also have authority to create a regional marine plan under delegated powers.

Chapter summary

This chapter has illustrated the evolving and dynamic nature of planning law. We have outlined the statutory basis for planning in terms of primary and secondary legislation, and highlighted the hierarchical policy framework that exists and that provides the decision-making context for development management. We have also drawn attention to the wider agenda of planning reform and modernisation that is driving various changes, such as the streamlining of national policy through consolidating previously separate and sector-specific policy statements. Moreover, across the devolved UK experimentation is taking place with respect to finding the appropriate scale for development plan making and creating locally relevant and sensitive policies. There is evidence that an interest in further devolution and a broader concern with decentralising plan-making is leading to new thinking, both at the level of the city-region and at the level of the community or neighbourhood. Both Northern Ireland and Wales have new primary planning legislation in place (2011 and 2016, respectively) that has yet to be tested in practice, while Scotland, as a consequence of its 2016 root-and-branch review, may be on the point of introducing further statutory reforms. Meanwhile, England's neighbourhood plans are the subject of evaluation. We are learning by doing. Moreover, as developments in marine planning evolve, ideas from terrestrial planning seem to be having an influence on the sea.

Recommended reading

For a general overview, see:

Davoudi, S. (2015) 'The framework of plans', in B. Cullingworth et al (eds), *Town and country planning in the UK*, 15th edn, Abingdon-on-Thames: Routledge, pp 85–136.

For an applied discussion of devolution and policy development, see:

Peel, D., Lloyd, M.G. and Ritchie, H. (2010) 'An introduction to land use planning and business in Northern Ireland', in H. Browne (ed) *Aspects of law relating to business*, Harlow: Pearson Education Limited, pp 55–78.
Peel, D. and Lloyd, M.G. (2007) 'Improving policy effectiveness: land use planning in a devolved polity?' *Australian Journal of Public Administration*, vol 66, no 2, pp 174–84.

For a discussion of regionalism and regional development, and the city-region idea under devolution, see:

Bradbury, J. (ed) (2008) *Devolution, regionalism and regional development: The UK experience*, London: Routledge, pp 166–82.
Tewdwr-Jones, M. and Allmendinger, P. (eds) *Territory, identity and spatial planning: Spatial governance in a fragmented nation*, London: Routledge.

Recommended websites

Aspects of devolution can be followed up here: https://devolutionmatters. wordpress.com

The NPPG merits review, given its importance to both practice and process. It is extensive and covers matters previously covered by a number of circulars and guidance documents. The NPPG can be found here: http://planningguidance.planningportal.gov.uk/blog/guidance/

Information on infrastructure planning in England and Wales can be found on the Planning Inspectorate's National Infrastructure Planning website: http://infrastructure.planninginspectorate.gov.uk/

Information on neighbourhood planning is available at: https://www. planningportal.co.uk/info/200130/common_projects/42/neighbourhood_ planning

FIVE

Core elements of planning law

Chapter contents

- Development
- Operational development
- Material change of use
- Planning units
- Ancillary and incidental uses
- Intensification
- Abandonment
- Lawful Development Certificates
- Chapter summary

Introduction

In this chapter we explore the basic legal building blocks of statutory land-use planning. In the first instance we outline the scope of planning – the matters planning can and cannot influence. We then consider the core legal underpinnings of the planning process, including how planning conceptualises the land resource and views activities taking place on it, under it, or indeed over it. In particular we examine the meaning of 'development'. Where relevant, we highlight nation-specific legislation, but we focus on certain shared concepts, and these transcend the individual planning systems of the four UK administrations. We conclude by briefly considering certificates of lawfulness, which provide a point of comparison with the approach adopted when determining a planning application.

Development

Our starting point is the concept of 'development'. The term 'development' may be considered the essential building block of the British planning system. Development has a legal definition, which has been interpreted through the Courts. At a very basic level, if something is held to constitute 'development', some form of control through the planning system exists. If something is not development, then the planning system has no influence. The concept of development is therefore fundamental because it effectively determines the scope and reach of the planning system. As we have noted, planning cannot and indeed need not or should not control all change in the built and natural environment.

Through the interpretations of a single word the limitations of planning controls are defined. Thus, according to Moore and Purdue (2014), the term 'development' lies at the heart of the legal powers the state has to manage the built and natural environment.

The definitions of development are set out in the different legislation for England and Wales, Scotland and Northern Ireland:

- England and Wales: Section 55 of the Town and Country Planning Act 1990, as amended by Section 49 of the Planning and Compulsory Purchase Act 2004
- Scotland: Section 26 of the Town and Country Planning (Scotland) Act 1997, as amended by Section 3 of the Planning etc. (Scotland) Act 2006
- Northern Ireland: Article 11 of The Planning (Northern Ireland) Order 1991, as amended by Article 18 of the Planning (Amendment) (Northern Ireland) Order 2003 and Article 7 of the Planning Reform (Northern Ireland) Order 2006 and Section 23 of the Planning Act (Northern Ireland) 2011.

Irrespective of the precise legislation, however, the definition across the UK is the same. Development consists of the carrying out of building, engineering, mining or other operations in, on, over or under land, or the making of any material change in the use of any buildings or other land.

When thinking about the definition of development we can point to two 'limbs'; that is to say, development covers two distinct activities (Figure 5.1). The first limb relates to 'operational' development and effectively covers physical change taking place with respect to land: building, engineering, mining or other operations. The second limb relates to the manner in which land and buildings are used. Thus, while no physical change may have taken place to the land or associated buildings, development may nevertheless have taken place because of the change in the nature of the use. Here, it is worth noting that one activity can involve both elements of development.

Figure 5.1: The two 'limbs' of development

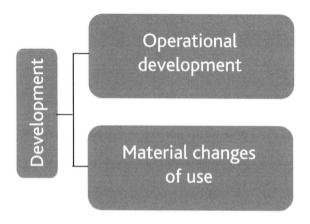

Moreover, the scope of development is not limited to what takes place on the land: it also extends to and provides for control of activities taking place over the land or within or under the land. The control of development is thus more extensive than one might at first think.

Interestingly, and in parallel with defining what development is, considerable attention has also been paid to identifying matters that are *not* development. Here, the Courts also play a useful role in developing this understanding. In terms of the legislation, the following are generally *not* deemed to constitute development, and we reflect on why this might be:

1. the maintenance, improvement or other alteration of any building, being works which affect only the interior of the building or do not materially affect the external appearance of the building (but later we will look at listed buildings, for example, and what might constitute a material change);
2. the carrying out by a local roads authority, on land within the boundaries of a road, of any works required for the maintenance or improvement of the road (a practical example of where controls would be disproportionate, perhaps);
3. the carrying out by a local authority or statutory undertakers of any works for the purpose of inspecting, repairing or renewing any sewers, mains, pipes, cables or other apparatus, including the breaking open of any road or other land for that purpose (again, there would be no advantage in controlling this);
4. the use of any buildings or other land within the curtilage of a dwelling-house for any purpose 'incidental' to the enjoyment of the dwelling-house, as such (here it is worth thinking about what 'incidental' might mean, and the earlier discussion of private property rights);
5. the use of any land for the purposes of agriculture or forestry (including afforestation) and the use for any of those purposes of any building occupied together with land so used (perhaps recognising this as the 'baseline' use of land in some respects);
6. a change of use within the same use class (discussed further below).

Demolition constitutes 'building operations' and as such is a form of development. There is an exemption of some very minor forms of demolition from the definition of development through a Direction by the Secretary of State however, and most other forms constitute Permitted Development.

Box 5.1: Demolition, 'development' and 'projects': The Mitchell's Brewery Complex

The judgment delivered by the Court of Appeal in 2011 is key to it being held that demolition constitutes a project under the terms of the EU Environmental Impact Assessment (EIA) Directive, when it allowed a pressure group, SAVE Britain's Heritage, the right to pursue Judicial Review (JR) against the proposed demolition of a former brewery site in Lancaster. The application for redevelopment was refused, but the developers wished to demolish the brewery in any event. The developers proceeded on the basis that planning permission was not needed, as it was covered by the Secretary of State's Demolition Direction. This Direction provided that certain buildings did not amount to 'development' in the legal sense of the definition. Buildings covered by the Town and Country Planning (Demolition – Description of Buildings) Direction 1995 contained at Appendix A to Circular 10/95 included listed buildings, buildings in conservation areas, scheduled ancient monuments and buildings other than dwellings or buildings adjoining a dwelling-house, any building not exceeding 50m, and fences and gates.

SAVE Britain's Heritage commenced a JR seeking a declaration that the Demolition Directive was unlawful as it contravened the EIA. SAVE argued that the demolition should be considered as a 'project' under the Directive, potentially requiring an EIA to be carried out. The problem, however, was that, since demolition did not constitute development, no planning permission was needed for demolition and, since EIA can be required only where planning permission is needed, this results in demolition 'escaping' from the requirement of EIA. The effect of the judgment on developers is that they should expressly consider including demolition as part of the development that is to be subject to planning permission, as well as the necessity for an EIA, and the scope of any required EIA.

Case law has defined certain matters as not constituting development. Of particular note are:

1. de minimis matters
2. ancillary uses.

'De minimis' is a Latin expression meaning that something is a minimal thing. If something is very minor in nature, for example a small alarm box on the front of a house, or a television aerial (not necessarily a satellite dish), then it may be considered to be de minimis and therefore not constituting development. The concept of ancillary uses is discussed later in this chapter.

The definition of development is important to us because it is linked to a core principle associated with the planning system: proportionality. Accepting the necessity of state intervention through planning is only the first step in the philosophy behind the manner in which the planning system is realised in practice. The state exercises planning controls to protect or derive certain social or environmental benefits, such as public health and well-being, but how much the state intervenes, in what ways and to what extent, must be proportionate to ensure that the form of state intervention can be justified when considered against the reason why the intervention is taking place.

Defining an activity or structure as development is the first stage. It means that society recognises that allowing an activity, such as waste incineration, or a structure, such as a mobile phone mast, could have an impact. Over time, developments have been brought into the scope of planning. The question is then how planning intervenes — which we discuss further in the next chapter. First, however, we discuss operational development.

Operational development

Figure 5.2: Operational development

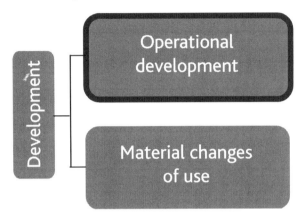

'Operational' development relates to building, engineering, mining and 'other' operations. We consider each in turn.

Building operations

Building operations is an inclusive term covering building, rebuilding, alterations and additions to existing buildings, demolition and other operations normally carried out by a builder. Key to the understanding of building operations is what constitutes a 'building' and a 'builder'. In planning law a building is defined as any structure or erection. As with many legal definitions, the legal meaning is much wider than any popular sense of the term might initially imply.

Box 5.2: What is a building?

To understand what we mean by a 'building' for the purposes of planning controls, it is helpful to look at case law. Typically, multiple cases allow us to establish a clear understanding and basis for decision-making. In terms of defining 'building', the two most significant cases are *Cheshire CC v Woodward (1962) 2 QB 126* and *Barvis Ltd v Secretary of State for the Environment (1971) 22 P&CR 710*.

The Cheshire County Council case concerned a coal-hopper mounted on wheels and associated equipment. The judgment, made at the High Court by Chief Justice (CJ) Lord Parker was that the coal-hopper did not constitute development and that the Act should be considered to be referring to any structure, or erection, that is effectively part of the real estate and changes its character. Lord Parker CJ noted that it is important to look at the whole circumstance, and particularly the degree of permanency, as part of the question of whether or not any structure or erection is part of the real estate.

In the Barvis case, further clarity and definition was provided. The question in this case was whether a large crane (approximately 90 feet) that ran on a permanent steel track was a building. Significantly, the crane could be dismantled and re-erected over a period of several days. In this case, the key 'tests' of what constitutes a building emerged, specifically, size, permanence and physical attachment to the ground. By considering these matters, it was found in the Barvis case that the crane was a 'building'.

What constitutes a 'building' is not as easy to define as might at first appear. Certainly we can be clear that it extends beyond what might normally be considered a building in the common usage of the word. The importance of recognising that structures and erections may be considered to be buildings is stated clearly in the definition. Planning case law is very valuable, with the tests that emerged from the Woodward and Barvis cases of size, permanence and physical attachment to the land forming the basis of this judgment.

Box 5.3: Models, marquees, swing-boats and sheds

It is important to remember that the tests of what constitutes a building are a matter of professional judgement and must form the basis of a balanced interpretation of the situation. For example, in *Buckinghamshire CC v Callingham (1952) 2 QB 515* a model village and railway were under consideration. Here, despite the structures and erections being modest in size, they were still considered to be a building. Conversely, a quite substantial battery of six swing-boats was found not to be a building because the battery could be taken down quickly. As such, the degree of permanence was considered to be slight (*James v Brecon CC (1963) 15 P & CR 20*).

Other useful case law includes: *Skerrits of Nottingham Ltd v Secretary of State for the Environment, Transport, and the Regions (2000) JPL 1025.* This case concerned the annual siting of a marquee from February to October. *Tewkesbury Borough Council v Keeley (2004) EWHC 2594 (QB)* addressed the matter of a mobile shed. In the Skerrits case the marquee was found to be a building, despite it being removed each winter. The crux of the issue was the degree of permanence when considered in its totality. In the Tewkesbury case, in contrast, the structure was determined not to be a building because of the degree of the shed's mobility.

Engineering operations

There is less guidance on what constitutes an 'engineering operation'. What we do know from the legislation in place across the devolved UK is that engineering includes the formation or laying out of means of access to highways. Clearly, this definition is far too limited to represent the full extent of the scope of engineering operations. Given the limited definition and clarity that exists in relation to engineering operations, the importance of professional judgement and reasonableness is critical. So, for example, it is very unlikely that a resident digging a hole with a spade in their garden for a small pond would reasonably be considered as undertaking engineering operations under the law. As the extent of the excavation works increase, however, we may find that we move along a spectrum to a point where the nature of the activity, the scale of the task, the equipment in use and the people involved would take us into the realms of engineering operations.

Box 5.4: Engineering common sense?

From English case law we can find a little more clarity. Of particular note is the decision in *Fayrewood Fish Farms Ltd v Secretary of State for the Environment [1984] JPL 267*, where it was stated that engineering operations must be given their ordinary meaning in the English language; that is, engineering must include operations of the kind usually undertaken by engineers, or operations calling for the skills of an engineer. It appears that a degree of common sense must apply.

Mining operations

A little more clarity exists in the various planning legislation in place across the devolved UK as to what constitutes a mining operation (see: England and Wales: Town and Country Planning (Minerals) Act 1981; Scotland: Town and Country Planning (Scotland) Act 1997; and Northern Ireland: Planning (Northern Ireland) Order 1991). The legal definition specifies mining operations as including the removal of any material of any description from a mineral-working deposit, from a deposit of pulverised fuel ash or other furnace ash or clinker, or from a deposit of iron, steel or other metallic slags. The definition also includes the extraction of minerals from a disused railway embankment.

Other operations

The inclusion of 'other operations' within the definition of development is a classic example of how planning legislation allows a certain vagueness. Situations change over time and this catch-all term provides for a degree of flexibility that a series of precise definitions would not allow. Moreover, this approach supports the use of the Courts in providing clarity and definition as circumstances evolve (in line with the common law tradition discussed above). There is no real definition of what constitutes an 'other operation', but it needs to relate to a clear activity that has taken place that is similar to a building, mining or engineering operation. Case law has provided us with some examples, including: the creation of a new golf-tee, the installation of shop security-grills, free-standing parasols with sunken bases and extensive 'staking out' of a development site.

Box 5.5: Staking out: development?

As with other forms of building and engineering activity, judgement is required when considering whether an 'other' operation constitutes development. It is often a matter of the degree of the activity. Using a dozen stakes to show where an extension is to be built, for example, would be very unlikely to trigger confirmation of development. In the case of *R (on the application of Beronstone Ltd) v First Secretary of State and Chiltern DC (2006) EWHC 2391 Admin*), however, some 554 stakes were involved over 40 plots of land. This staking-out was held to constitute operational development. The judgment of the planning professional and of the Courts are therefore particularly important in determining whether or not a specific activity constitutes an 'other' operational development.

Material change of use

Figure 5.3: Material change of use

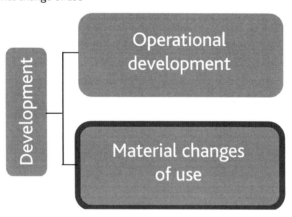

Thus far we have been concerned with some of the physical dimensions of planning. We now consider aspects of use. Clearly, how we use land and buildings has different implications for the environment, adjoining neighbours, the local community and wider society. For example, certain activities, such as pubs and restaurants, may create noise or cooking smells, or may generate heavy pedestrian and traffic movements at different times during the day or evening. Contrast these activities with, say, those relating to a primary school or a church or cinema. The various comings and goings associated with these physical buildings differ over the course of the year. If you live above an office that is generally open from 9 to 5, the nature of the use of that unit will affect your amenity in very different ways than if you live above a hot food takeaway that is open until late in the evening, preparing food on the premises and perhaps receiving customers in large groups. What controls, if any, exist to regulate such types of change?

Unlike operational development, material change of use is not defined in the respective planning acts; it is therefore left to case law to provide definition and clarity. To begin with, two aspects concern us: the meaning of 'use', and the meaning of 'material'.

Box 5.6: Differentiating between use and operational development

In differentiating between use and operational development a particularly useful comment came from *Parkes v Secretary of State for the Environment (1978) 1 WLR 1308 CA*. In this case Lord Denning MR (Master of the Rolls) stated that, while operational development may be considered to be concerned with a physical alteration to land, involving some permanence, use was something which is done in, on, or alongside the land, but which did not affect its characteristics physically.

Box 5.7: Selling eggs at a garage: a material change of use?

Another important case is *Bendles Motors Ltd v Bristol Corporation (1963) 1 WLR 247*. This case concerned an egg-vending machine at a garage, which the local authority considered to represent a material change of use, since the vending machine could be considered to be a shop use distinct from the garage operations. Lord Parker CJ disagreed with the LPA and reaffirmed his position previously stated in *East Barnet UDC v British Transport Commission (1962) 2 QB 484* Divisional Court in which he had stated that it was 'a question of fact and degree'. Here, then, we can see the importance of the word 'material' and the importance of exercising judgement. A change of use will constitute development only when there is something of note about it, something material.

Classification of uses

Clearly, identifying and then listing individually all the different 'uses' to which land and buildings could be put would be an impossible (if not inefficient) task. To enable the effective control and management of uses and material changes of use, planning therefore needs an organisational construct. In a similar way to the use of 'other' with respect to operational development, a degree of openness is desirable. As the title of this sub-section indicates, the solution has firstly been to categorise similar uses through certain groupings, creating a body of 'use classes' (Table 5.1).

A material change of use is deemed to occur when the use of a building or piece of land changes from one use class to another. Given that the grouping of uses is deliberately designed to comprise similar types of activity, changes falling within a use class do not constitute development. In practice, changing a clothes shop to a shoe shop and then to a mobile phone shop does not involve development as no material change has occurred. In contrast, changing a clothes shop to an office would involve a material change of use. As we shall see, however, not all changes between use classes require planning permission, as the impacts of the change may be relatively negligible.

One way to think about the classification system is to imagine that uses are put together into boxes; if you stay within your box you are not undertaking development, but if you move between boxes you may have undertaken a material change of use requiring planning permission. It is also important to note that some uses are identified as sui generis (of its own kind), that is, they are excluded uses. These uses tend to be rather distinctive in practice (for example a scrap-yard or amusement arcade) and likely to cause particular impacts on the surrounding area, so they are kept separate. Given their rather unique status, applications to use a building for a sui generis use (or to change the use to something else) are almost always held to constitute development. Although the detail of the use classification and sui generis definition vary across the devolved UK, there are fundamental similarities in thought and approach. A simplified summary of the use classifications is set out below in Table 5.1.

Use Classes Order

The Use Classes Order is a very useful and necessary tool to enable the management of uses and material changes of use. The most recent versions of the legislation are:

- England: Town and Country Planning (Use Classes) Order 1987 (as amended);
- Wales: Town and Country Planning (Use Classes) Order 1987 (as amended);
- Scotland: Town and Country Planning (Use Classes) (Scotland) Act 1997;
- Northern Ireland: The Planning (Use Classes) Order (Northern Ireland) 2015.

Table 5.1: The classification of uses (as at 2016)

England	Wales	Northern Ireland	Scotland
A1 Shops	A1 Shops	A1 Shops	Class 1 Shops
A2 Financial and Professional Services	A2 Financial and Professional Services	A2 Financial, Professional and other services	Class 2 Financial, professional and other services
A3 Food and Drink Restaurants and cafes	A3 Food and Drink Restaurants and cafes	B1 Business	Class 3 Food and drink
A4 Drinking Establishments	B1 Business	B2 Light Industrial	Class 4 Business
A5 Hot Food Takeaways	B2 General Industry Industrial process other than that falling within B1	B3 General Industrial, B4 Storage or Distribution	Class 5 General industrial
B1 Business		C1 Dwellinghouses,	Class 6 Storage or distribution
B2 General Industry Industrial process other than that falling within B1	B8 Storage or Distribution	C2 Guest Houses,	Class 7 Hotels and hostels
B8 Storage or Distribution	C1 Hotels	C3 Residential Institutions	Class 8 Residential institutions
C1 Hotels	C2 Residential Institutions	C4 Secure Residential Institutions	Class 9 Houses
C2 Residential Institutions	C3 Dwellinghouses	D1 Community and Cultural Uses,	Class 10 Non-residential institutions
C2a Secure Residential Institutions	C4 Houses in multiple occupation	D2 Assembly and Leisure uses	Class 11 Assembly and leisure
C3 Dwellinghouses	D1 Non-residential institutions		
C4 Houses in multiple occupation	D2 Assembly and leisure		
D1 Non-residential institutions			
D2 Assembly and leisure			

There is a strong degree of commonality between the systems but it is important to look out for the differences. In England, for example, fast food takeaways are given a specific use class (A5), whereas they are excluded uses (sui generis) in Scotland and Northern Ireland. There is probably no perfect model, but the use classes change regularly to try to find the best way of grouping and managing different uses and their impacts. Finally, it is worth noting the importance of professional judgement and the decisions of the Courts when trying to assess use and material change of use, as is not always evident which 'box' a given use can be said to fit into. Establishing use can be particularly testing, especially when more than one use takes place in a given unit.

The planning unit

The relationship between planning and land is a special one; development rights in the UK are nationalised and planning permission does not relate to an individual but, rather, is carried with the land. Planning also has a very particular way of viewing land. Landownership is not irrelevant to planning, but planning does not 'see' land based upon ownership alone. Planning considers land in an abstract way, in the sense that distinctly different uses with different impacts can coexist on land within the same ownership; indeed, multiple uses can exist within the site of a single company. The idea of planning 'units' is therefore important because it allows us to understand and manage land and the impacts associated with the uses taking place on it. The idea of the planning unit is vital to how uses are managed. A material change of use that causes an impact may occur within a single site, and the system needs the ability to respond to this.

Box 5.8: Planning unit

There is no legislative detail for identifying a planning unit, and so it is from case law that clarity is derived. In this instance, the most significant case is that of *Burdle v Secretary of State for the Environment (1972) 1 WLR 1207 Divisional Court.*

Justice Bridge presented the following three criteria:

1. Whenever it is possible to recognise a single main purpose use of land to which secondary activities are incidental or ancillary, the whole unit of occupation should be considered.
2. It is also appropriate to consider the whole unit of occupation, even though the occupier carries on a variety of activities, but it is not possible to say that one is incidental, or ancillary, to another.
3. Where a single unit of occupation has two or more distinct and separate areas occupied by substantially different and unrelated purposes, however, each should be considered a distinct planning unit.

Consideration of the 'planning unit', however, requires interpretation and judgement. Moreover, it is of note that in the Burdle case Justice Bridge commented that sometimes it is difficult to define the planning unit, stating that it must be 'a question of fact and degree'. Nevertheless, the nuances teased out in the Burdle case are helpful in providing guidance on how land should be mapped and viewed for planning purposes and, in turn, how we can then establish material changes of use.

Ancillary and incidental uses

Part of the assessment of a planning unit includes whether activities are 'ancillary' to the primary use. The accepted principle of having 'incidental' or 'ancillary' uses associated with a primary use is based upon the necessity of planning being functional within the real world. In other words, we need to acknowledge that a primary (or main) use will often have other associated uses connected with it. A planning system that did not accommodate such operational realities would not be reasonable, proportionate or practical. For example, a large factory, or a university campus, would typically include a cafe facility. Ancillary uses can therefore be seen as associated and secondary to the operation of the primary use.

Box 5.9: An ancillary helicopter-pad

The case of *Harrods v Secretary of State for the Environment, Transport and the Regions and the Royal Borough of Kensington and Chelsea (2002) JPL 1258* is often cited when considering what can be considered an ancillary use. In this case, it was contended that the use of the roof of the London-based Harrods store as a helicopter-pad by Mohamed Al Fayed was an ancillary use because of his daily involvement in the store's operations as chairman. The decision, however, was that this was not an ancillary activity because it was not ordinary, normal or reasonable practice in connection with running a shop.

In relation to matters not constituting development, the idea of ancillary uses is also significant. The use of land and buildings for purposes that are ancillary to a primary use will not constitute development. When this ceases to be the case and where, for example, an ancillary use becomes a primary use, then a material change of use may have taken place and development may have occurred.

Box 5.10: Quarrying, quarry waste and a refuse tip

A helpful example in considering ancillary can be found in Scotland from *Alexandra Transport Company Ltd v Secretary of State for Scotland 1974 SLT 81*, where a quarry ceased operating for quarrying and began to be used as a refuse tip. In this case, it was suggested that no development had occurred because quarry waste had always been disposed of in the quarry. It was found, however, that this refuse activity had been an ancillary activity and had then become a primary one, thus a material change of use had taken place and development had occurred.

The difference between the terms 'ancillary' and 'incidental' activity is not specifically defined in planning law, but the term incidental is applied in consideration of another matter that has been stated as not constituting development, specifically the use of any buildings or other land within the curtilage of a dwelling-house for any purpose 'incidental to the enjoyment of the dwelling-house as such'. The extent of the 'curtilage' is a judgement based upon matters such as physical layout, ownership, function and relationship to the dwelling itself (*James v Secretary of State for the Environment (1990) 61 P&CR 234 Divisional Court*). *Sinclair-Lockhart's Trustees v Central Land Board (1950) 1 P&CR 195* in Scotland is also helpful because it states that the curtilage must be land that is 'used for the comfortable enjoyment of the house'. Within the curtilage of a dwelling, it is therefore possible to undertake activities that can reasonably be considered to be associated with a person's enjoyment of their own property, for example, using a space as a workshop or small home office.

Intensification

Uses can change to the extent that a material change of use can be said to have taken place. The term 'intensification' is potentially a misleading one, though, because it suggests, in the common usage of the word, that something is happening at a larger scale. In fact, where intensification is said to have taken place in planning terms, it actually means that a change has resulted in a material change of use.

Box 5.11: Intensification of car reparation in a domestic garage

In *Peake v Secretary of State for Wales (1971) 22 P&CR 889 Divisional Court* a residential property owner used his own garage for car repairs. He also occasionally repaired his friends' cars. The owner was made redundant and decided to do more work from his garage, repairing cars on a full-time and billed basis. Here, intensification had occurred because a material change of use had taken place, from the use of a garage for activities 'incidental' to the enjoyment of a dwelling-house to a parcel used as a dwelling-house and commercial garage.

Abandonment

Determining whether a particular use has been 'abandoned' is important because any subsequent attempt to return the unit to use may constitute development. For example, if a former dwelling-house is considered to have been abandoned, then an attempt to return it to residential use will constitute development and require planning permission. In the open countryside, where strong planning controls exist, this could be a significant interpretation. As with many matters already discussed, whether abandonment has occurred is a matter of interpretation, based upon the individual circumstances of the case.

Box 5.12: Determining whether abandonment has occurred

It is again through the Courts that we find some clarity on when 'abandonment' might have occurred. Perhaps, the most useful case is *Trustees of the Council-y-Mynach Estate v Secretary of State for Wales (1985) JPL 40* because this included a judicial acknowledgement of a submission by Counsel that the decision on whether something has been abandoned should consider the following:

1. the period of time that there has been a non-use
2. if there has been an intervening use
3. what the intentions of the owner were.

Lawful Development Certificates

The approach of certain activities within the broad field of planning may be considered more or less legalistic. In this chapter we have highlighted some of the complexities surrounding the legal definition of 'development'. It is thus possible to imagine situations in which a developer or property owner is unsure as to the need for formal planning permission. In the sale or purchase of premises, for example, a question may arise as to whether or not a development or use is authorised. Formal documentation could prove useful in such circumstances.

Lawful Development Certificates (LDCs), which apply in England and Wales, provide such confirmation. The time-limit for an LPA to issue a certificate is eight weeks. The relevant legislation is the Town and Country Planning Act 1990 (S191), as amended by S10 of the Planning and Compensation Act 1991; and the Town and Country Planning (General Development Procedure) Order (England) 2015 (Planning Portal, 2016). The procedures also cover operations or activities in breach of a planning condition (see Chapter Seven). In Scotland and in Northern Ireland the term used is Certificate of Lawfulness and separate legislation applies. There is a right of appeal in cases where the LPA fails to issue the certificate within eight weeks, or where the LPA refuses or partially refuses to issue a certificate.

Proving the lawfulness of an existing use or development rests with the applicant. The relevant test is on the 'balance of probability'. The Courts have held that the applicant's own evidence (such as photographs, addressed utility bills) does not need to be corroborated by independent evidence. If the applicant can satisfy the LPA of the lawfulness of the development or activity, a certificate will be issued. Importantly, then, the LPA has no discretion when processing the application, as it is making a determination of law, based on the facts and information provided. As we shall see, this legalistic context is in contrast to the discretionary approach adopted when determining a planning application.

Chapter summary

In this chapter we have explored some of the fundamental legal definitions and concepts underpinning the control of development. In exploring the meaning of development as comprising both operational and use dimensions, we have illustrated how the scope of planning seeks to manage the impacts of both physical development and activity. We have also seen that legislation alone is often insufficient. Case law in the form of judges' various pronouncements on the interpretation, intention and spirit of the law is thus all important in building up a shared understanding of what can and cannot be controlled. Throughout this chapter we have highlighted that in practice planning is not a formulaic activity, since professional judgement needs to be exercised on a case-by-case basis. Often, whether or not something constitutes development is a matter of fact and degree; this requires weighing up the evidence. Principles of reasonableness and functionality also need to be applied. In the next chapter we will look in more detail at how the planning system operates and some of the key principles underpinning the administration processes involved.

Recommended reading

Hart, T. (2015) 'The management of development', in B. Cullingworth et al (eds), *Town and country planning in the UK*, 15th edn, Abingdon-on-Thames: Routledge, pp 137–94.

For more legalistic discussion concerning the matters covered in this chapter, the following are recommended:

Duxbury, R. (2012) *Telling & Duxbury's planning law and procedure*, 15th edn, Oxford: Oxford University Press, chapter 6.
McMaster, R. and Smith, G. (2013) *Scottish planning law*, London: Bloomsbury Publishing, chapter 4.
Moore, V. and Purdue, M. (2014) *A practical approach to planning law*, 13th edn, Oxford: Oxford University Press, chapters 5 and 6.

For the most current materials on planning legislation you are advised to consult online. A good starting point is:

England: Planning Portal (remembering to identify 'England' as your location): http://www.planningportal.gov.uk
Northern Ireland: Planning Portal: https://www.planningni.gov.uk/
Scotland: ePlanning Scotland: https://eplanning.scotland.gov.uk/WAM/
Wales: Town Planning Portal (remembering to identify 'Wales' as your location): http://www.planningportal.gov.uk

---

SIX

Development management: permissions, applications and permitted development

Chapter contents

- Development management approaches
- The proportionality principle
- Types of application
- Application processes and requirements
- Major projects
- Varying the system and facilitating development
- Other forms of control and implementation
- Chapter summary

Introduction

This chapter is concerned with process. Specifically, we explore how the planning system deals with those matters that constitute development. Where the ability exists to exercise control, it is intended that the planning system should operate in a manner that is proportionate and fair, seeking to balance private and public interests and having regard to social justice. The chapter will consider how planning attempts to operate proportionately and will explore how the different systems work when 'express planning permission', that is, formal approval, from the LPA is required.

Development management approaches

Before we explore the nature of planning decision-making in the devolved UK, brief mention should be made of the manner in which development proposals and associated planning applications are intended to be approached. A fundamental principle underpinning planning in the UK is that it should be positive and constructive. Planning not only acts to serve the public interest by restricting, limiting and preventing; it must also be proactive, facilitative and enabling. Planning has a key role in supporting economic, environmental and social progression; it is at the heart of our ability to pursue sustainable development and to promote quality of life and creative place-making.

The branch of planning activity associated with processing planning applications can be seen as a restrictive one. True, planning (rightly) says 'no' to certain developments that will have significant adverse impacts, but some people may actively wish to see that development happen. Planning may also be seen to be reactive and rather narrow, in the sense that it tends to be seen as responding to the submission of development proposals, rather than proactively leading and delivering development and actively engaging communities in shaping the places where they live.

The present development management approach across the devolved UK emerged in the early 2000s as an overt representation of a constructive and positive model of planning where the state actively enables development and change. Associated with a broader culture change, a development management approach was advocated to counter arguments that the existing planning arrangements and behaviours in some locations were too restrictive, time consuming and costly. An important contrast was made between the development control functions of the planning system – effectively the decision-making end – and the policy or development planning aspects. Development control was portrayed as slow, reactive and limited in scope and aspiration.

The term, and the philosophy of and approach to development management tend to be presented as more than development control. Development management goes beyond a focus on the planning application process only and engages with the wider project more holistically, notably encouraging early involvement by all stakeholders in the realisation of change. The emphasised focus of development management is outcomes and quality delivered; this is in contrast to the suggested process orientation of development control. This approach to mediating potential goal-conflicts means robust 'pre-application' arrangements, active involvement in ideas by a full range of sectors and actors, a comprehensive project management approach and a focus on delivery rather than on the procedural and administrative aspects.

For development management to work as an approach, it requires everyone to be 'signed up', from the applicant to the agent and developer, the community, politicians, other sectors and the LPA and its officers. This logic lies at the heart of development management thinking. The new development management approach has gained traction to differing degrees across the devolved UK. Nevertheless, some would argue that development management does not necessarily represent anything new; positive and proactive planning approaches already existed in some LPA areas. We would also suggest that underlying the contemporary development management discourse is a concern with identifying and using better practices to regulate development in the public interest and, ultimately, with creating better places.

The proportionality principle

Modelled on the basis of increased state intervention, and set against the likelihood of impact or harm, a 'proportionality hierarchy' differentiates a spectrum of planning controls. This notion is a very important part of the philosophy of the planning approach in the UK; state controls are based on a need for intervention. The type of intervention must be justifiable and proportionate to the perceived need.

Figure 6.1 differentiates between development permitted by the state and development requiring express permission. The distinctions are based on the perceived extent of the potential impact arising from a proposed development. Whether or not a physical operation or a use constitutes 'development' is therefore the first question to address. The bottom step of the hierarchy designates that the activity is development and establishes state legitimacy potentially to intervene. Not all development, however, is subject to state control. It is the impact-based nature of the proportionality hierarchy that gives the planning system its sophistication (Sheppard, 2015). Each step up the proportionality hierarchy, from 'permitted development' to 'prior approval' to 'express planning permission', is accompanied by greater state control.

Figure 6.1: The proportionality hierarchy

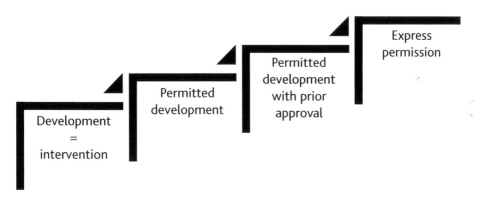

Put simply, where a matter is permitted development, it may be undertaken, subject to compliance with set conditions and limitations, without any formal approval from the LPA. Prior approval represents an intermediate position, giving the LPA limited discretionary decision-making powers. These are linked to specific areas of consideration associated with some forms of permitted development. Finally, express planning permission is where the LPA has full control over whether a development is approved (with or without conditions) or refused. We consider each of these 'steps' individually.

Permitted development

Permitted development rights allow development to take place through pre-approved planning permission. Permission is effectively granted in three ways:

1. through an express planning application
2. by a deemed grant of planning permission
3. by means of a development order.

Development orders are made at the national level and can be 'special', that is, covering specific locations, or 'general'. The most significant orders, for our purposes, are the various Permitted Development Orders in place. These orders grant planning permission for relatively minor forms of development, so-called 'permitted development rights'. The current orders are:

- *England*: Town and County Planning (General Permitted Development) Order 2015 (as amended)
- *Wales*: Town and County Planning (General Permitted Development) Order 1995 (as amended)
- *Scotland*: Town and County Planning (General Permitted Development) (Scotland) Order 1992 as amended (most notably by Town and County Planning (General Permitted Development) (Scotland) Order 2011)
- *Northern Ireland*: Planning (General Development) Order 2015.

The legislative orders variously set out the permitted development rights under 'Parts' and 'Classes', effectively grouping particular forms of development. For example, development within the curtilage of a dwelling-house enjoys permitted development rights with respect to minor development, such as small extensions, alterations and out-buildings. Moreover, the state specifies the parameters and circumstances of the development allowed. The individual orders are thus very specific and prescribe the restrictions and conditions that apply. Typically, the extent of operational development, for example, will be specified in terms of dimensions or volume and with reference to distances from boundaries.

Permitted development rights are not limited to operational development. Changes of use within the same 'use class' do not constitute development. A change of use, even though it represents a material change (that is, it moves between the boxes) may also constitute permitted development. For example, a change of use class from 'Storage and Distribution' (B8 in England and Wales, B4 in Northern Ireland and Class 6 in Scotland) to 'Business' (B1 in England and Wales, B1 in Northern Ireland and Class 4 in Scotland) can be considered permitted development, subject to limitations.

Certain national restrictions exist alongside the general conditions that change the development allowed in certain geographical areas. Such restrictions cover areas with increased sensitivity, such as National Parks, or Article 4 Directions (see below). On the one hand, the restriction of permitted development rights in defined areas reinforces the proportionality principle; it reduces what might otherwise be deemed unnecessary or excessive control. On the other hand, the overall coherence of a development may benefit from stronger controls. Planning permission may therefore impose a condition limiting permitted development rights. Development in certain places, such as conservation areas, may have a more significant impact than in a new housing settlement. The impacts of the development merit further consideration, and thus the state reserves the right to intervene to prevent, control, limit and/or condition the proposed change. In other words, such developments are pushed up the hierarchy.

Temporary buildings and land use allowances

The question of temporary development raises an interesting set of questions for managing land and buildings in the public interest. Certain temporary activities may have an adverse impact on the local community or environment; others may be relatively innocuous. In seeking to provide reasonable and proportionate controls, certain development is permitted by the state. Notably, these permitted developments may be time specific:

1. buildings, such as builders' huts, used on a construction site during the course of building operations
2. use of any land for any purpose for not more than 28 days in total.

The 28-day period applies to a temporary use and does not allow the land to be used for the entire period on a permanent basis. Temporary use is 'measured' differently – temporary, casual or permanent intermittent use. Examples include clay-pigeon shooting, recreational events, markets and car-boot sales. This provision does not apply to land within the curtilage of a building, or to caravan sites.

Box 6.1: The 28-day period

In *Ramsay v Secretary of State for the Environment and Suffolk DC [1998] JPL 60*, a Certificate of Lawful Use was sought to use land for a vehicular sports and leisure track for not more than 28 days in any calendar year. In between events, the land was returned to grazing land for sheep. It was concluded that the use was permanent, intermittent use, since the track retained permanent features, such as ropes, around the track and involved the collection of entry-fees. The certificate was refused on the ground that the proposed use was a permanent use falling outside of the permitted types of activity. The temporary use was *not* permitted under the General Permitted Development Order.

A form of temporary usage that has recently become quite widespread involves 'meanwhile uses'. Empty units in a town centre, for example, may be used for specialist retail, such as hand-crafted goods, or to test out particular products. The so-called 'pop-up' phenomenon is helping to rejuvenate high streets by making creative use of otherwise empty spaces and is encouraged as a way to enable entrepreneurs to trial their ideas. Although planning permission is required if there is a change of use from one use class to another under the Use Classes Orders, planners have been encouraged to look favourably on community usage of such units, for example if for less than six months.

Where development complies with the restrictions and conditions, and constitutes permitted development, no formal approval is required from the LPA. Informal advice as to whether something constitutes permitted development may be sought from the LPA, although often for a fee. There may be situations, however, where a developer considers it desirable to have legal confirmation that a development is permitted. Certificates of Lawfulness exist for this purpose and cover: (i) proposed use or development; (ii) existing use or development. These certificates are considered further in Chapter Nine. The key point, however, is that, in contrast to 'express planning applications', which consider acceptability and material considerations, certificates of lawfulness are simply concerned with whether or not the use or operation constitutes development in legal terms.

Box 6.2: PD or not PD? That is the question

Permitted development (PD) rights are an area of planning law that is particularly subject to change (some might say 'erosion'). It is thus always important to check the status of the relevant legislation. The recent Independent Review of the Planning System in Scotland (Beveridge et al, 2016), for example, highlighted a view that the scope of PD rights could be broadened. One argument is that reducing planning control over relatively minor development (for example bike sheds, telecommunication masts) could potentially free up (limited) resources to allow planning officers to focus their professional skills on other planning matters. A similar line of argument with respect to PD relates to 'reducing the administrative burden of the planning system, to support growth and improve the supply of housing' (DCLG, 2016, p 4). Permitted development questions are raised in relation to an expanding catalogue of issues, from film and TV production to equipment housings for sewerage undertakers, so it is a topic to follow.

We would suggest checking the following websites:

England: Planning Portal (remembering to identify 'England' as your location): http://www.planningportal.gov.uk
Northern Ireland: Planning Portal: https://www.planningni.gov.uk/
Scotland: ePlanning Scotland: https://eplanning.scotland.gov.uk/WAM/
Wales: Town Planning Portal (remembering to identify 'Wales' as your location): http://www.planningportal.gov.uk

Box 6.3: Deemed grant of planning permission

Although deemed grant is not explicitly presented in the proportionality hierarchy, it needs to be mentioned. The concept of deemed grant of planning permission is primarily the means to avoid duplication in planning law and involves planning permission being realised without any formal action taking place. A helpful example is advertisement consent. Advertisements are covered by separate legislation (see also Chapter Nine), but the works involved in erecting signage could be development. However, it is considered that it would be inappropriate for planning controls to be duplicated for the same activity, so any development associated with the advertisement benefits from deemed grant, provided that advertisement consent is forthcoming. A deemed grant may, in certain circumstances, also be attained through the prior approval route.

Permitted development with prior approval

Prior approval is a form of permitted development right, but provides scope for the LPA firstly to consider whether any controls (such as requiring further information) should be exercised. In effect, before (permitted) development can commence a prior approval application must be submitted to and considered by the LPA. Prior approval differs from express permission because the LPA is limited in the matters it may consider. Development is allowed to commence only once approval is given or is determined as not required, or after a set number of days without a decision being made. In the latter case, approval is granted by default, under the deemed grant process described above.

The LPA may refuse a prior approval application or require the submission of an express planning application. The principle behind prior approval is that it is a balanced approach to providing additional flexibility and reduced state intervention, but in a controlled manner. Historically, the use of prior approval was very limited, for example, covering certain forms of agricultural development. More recently it has been used more often, including for small-scale wind turbines, as in Scotland. In England the use of prior approval has been expanded since 2010, to include matters as diverse as residential extensions, and offices, warehouses and agricultural buildings being converted to residential accommodation.

Box 6.4: Expanding prior approval: for better or worse?

Prior approval as a form of control is not without criticism. The expanded reliance on prior approval in England, for example, has prompted questions with respect to the potential undermining of the proportionality hierarchy and an associated weakening of the powers of the LPA effectively to control development. Permitted development through the prior approval route for the conversion of office buildings into residential use, or for the conversion of agricultural buildings into a diversity of uses, including residential, is arguably the most sensitive and contentious.

It has been argued that, in attempting to reduce the burden of state intervention, there is a risk that LPAs will lose the necessary powers to exercise control. Moreover, there is an interesting tension in the use of prior approval. On the one hand, it appears that this step is designed to simplify the planning system (by minimising the amount of information required under a formal planning application). On the other hand, prior approval may be seen as introducing an additional step in the process (since further information, or a formal planning application, may be required). Furthermore, the interpretive and judgement-based nature of UK planning may result in different LPAs coming to different conclusions, leading to inconsistency.

Express permission

Express permission, the final step in the proportionality hierarchy, is the formal process of applying for planning permission. This process involves completing and submitting a planning application to the LPA for consideration. The documentation includes plans and supporting information. The LPA is able either to grant, with conditions, or to refuse the application. In certain circumstances, usually involving major developments, the decision will be taken at a higher (for example, national) scale. The processes are broadly similar across the devolved UK and we generalise some of the steps involved.

Types of application

There are two types of planning application, depending on whether 'full' or 'outline' permission is required. As the nomenclature suggests, a full application involves the majority of (if not all) matters being considered at the same time. If permission is granted, development can commence, subject to the requirements of any attached planning conditions. An outline application is effectively the first part of a two-stage approach and involves only certain details being submitted to the LPA. If permission is granted, another application (or applications) will need to be submitted to the LPA, covering 'reserved matters'. There is no requirement for the applicant to be the same, so this staged process could, for example, first involve a landowner seeking 'outline' planning permission for a house on a piece of land. A developer could then come forward with the precise design and layout. The first stage establishes that a house can be built. The second stage involves the creative aspects, but also the costs of drawing up the design of the building and floorplans in line with the relevant policies.

The amount of detail submitted with an outline application may include: layout, access, design, landscaping and scale. Relevant matters for the development that are not submitted are 'reserved' until a later stage. These aspects form the subject of the subsequent reserved matters application. The outline approval constitutes the planning permission, the reserved matters applications are then associated with this permission.

The concept behind the outline approach is that it allows the principle of development to be established. With all matters reserved it may, indeed, only be the principle that is being considered. The advantage of establishing the principle of development is that it allows the fundamental planning decision to be made without producing a detailed design scheme. This approach minimises the resource and work requirements in the first instance, thereby reducing losses or risk in the event of an unsuccessful application. Moreover, if the application is successful, securing outline planning permission has the potential to significantly increase the land's value and allow investor confidence in pursuit of the reserved matters. Nevertheless, the LPA's decision letter will impose a condition limiting the time horizon of the outline permission, since it is in the interest of society that land with the benefit of planning permission should come forward for development and not remain development on paper.

Application processes and requirements

Regardless of the type of application, the LPA process for determining planning applications is broadly the same. In this section we address the stages set out in Figure 6.2 under three broad phases that we call preparation, submission and decision-making. This allows us to illustrate the front-loading of the system and to highlight the application of the plan-led approach in practice. We pay attention to other important aspects related to the content of the application, including any environmental information to be included (EIA process) and the nature of material considerations.

Phase 1: Preparation

Two aspects are important in relation to development management: pre-application and pre-submission.

Pre-application

Under the development management style of planning, pre-application has become a very important step involving active engagement and discussion between applicants and agents, and developer-led consultation. Pre-application is intended to extend to all stakeholders, including the local community, the LPA and relevant infrastructure or heritage bodies, for example. Pre-application should be appropriate to the application. While ideas about the design and content of a scheme will likely have been started before the pre-application consultation and engagement process is commenced, based upon the landowner's/developer's intentions, it is anticipated that the scheme should evolve in response to the discussions and feedback. Pre-application discussions are intended to improve the outcomes of a project by obtaining other views, perspectives and information relevant to the proposed development.

Figure 6.2: The stages of the application process

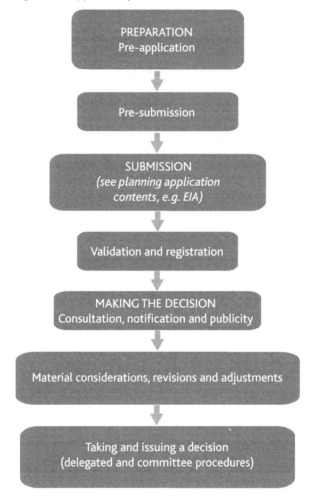

Pre-submission

The decision when precisely to submit a planning application will be based on timing factors associated with the wider processes of land and property development. Land assembly, availability of finance and the status of the development plan may all be relevant considerations. When the decision to submit is made the landowner (if not the applicant) must be notified of the intention to apply for planning permission. Interestingly, in the UK anyone can apply for planning permission on any piece of land they choose, whether or not they have ownership or an interest in that land. Securing planning permission does not necessarily mean a right to build, however.

Phase 2: Submission

Planning applications, including of all of the necessary material, are generally submitted to the LPA. In instances involving major infrastructure, applications are required to be made to the national level of government. Submissions are accompanied by the required fee, which is fixed in light of the scale of the scheme being undertaken. Technological improvements have enabled LPAs to develop electronic (e-)planning facilities, which has substantially improved the submission, consultation and administrative processes.

Planning application contents

A planning application will vary in its content and appearance. For 'minor matters' there may be little more than a completed standard planning application form; ownership and/or agricultural holding certificate; a location plan that identifies the land to which the application relates, usually a red line outlining the development on an up-to-date Ordnance Survey map; a site plan, which should be drawn at an identified metric scale; and any other plans, drawings and information necessary to describe the development that is the subject of the application. Depending on the application, information may include: elevation plans, roof plans, floorplans, for example.

More complex schemes require further elements to be submitted. Such information may variously include:

- an environmental statement
- a supporting planning statement
- a design and access statement
- transport assessment, and potentially an associated draft travel plan
- heads of terms for planning obligations
- statement(s)/appraisal(s) covering relevant matters, such as flood risk, drainage, heritage, retail and sustainability.

It is worth noting that an application could potentially be 'retrospective'. Here, development has already been undertaken, but without obtaining the required planning permission. (We will look at enforcement in detail in Chapter Seven, as retrospective applications may be the result of the LPA taking enforcement action). Such applications are treated in exactly the same manner, with the decision taken on the merits of the scheme, irrespective of the fact that the development is already in place.

Environmental assessments

Environmental assessments are an established feature of international planning systems. Originating in Europe in the early 1970s, the Environmental Impact

Assessment (EIA) process must be followed for certain types of development. The objective is to ensure that the environmental impacts of a given scheme are given full consideration.

The EIA process requires the developer to submit an environmental statement (ES). The ES presents the implications of the proposed development, the options considered for addressing these implications and the mitigation associated with the preferred option. The requirement for an EIA is provided for under the EU Directive 85/337/EEC (as amended). While the full consequences of the result of the UK's EU 'Brexit' referendum are unknown at this stage, we should anticipate that forms of environmental assessment will remain, since EIA and the goals of sustainability are promoted internationally, such as by the World Bank.

There is no single route associated with the EIA process; some forms of development always require an ES, others do so only in some circumstances. In the first instance the EIA process identifies two categories of development: Schedule 1 schemes (which always require an ES), and Schedule 2 schemes (which may require an ES, depending upon the scale and nature of the proposal). Schedule 1 schemes can include certain forms of power station, nuclear processing plants, chemical plants, smelting works for cast-iron and steel, metal production, and major infrastructure, including certain road, rail, airport, water and sewerage schemes. Some Schedule 2 schemes may be similar in type to those under Schedule 1 but smaller in scale; the environmental implications may thus be less extensive. Schedule 2 schemes are relatively more diverse in nature, but include proposals associated with intensive agriculture, mining, energy production, manufacturing plants, some infrastructure projects and certain types of industrial activity, involving, for example, food, textile, leather, wood, paper and rubber. Whether or not Schedule 2 schemes require an ES is determined through a screening process. Projects listed in Schedule 2 that are located in or partly in a sensitive area such as a National Park, SSSI or AONB also need to be screened, even if they are below the thresholds or do not meet the criteria.

Screening

An LPA needs sufficient information to decide whether a scheme is Schedule 1 or Schedule 2 and whether or not an ES is required. The EIA process requires a developer first to submit the requisite information to the LPA in order to obtain a 'screening opinion'.

Scoping

Alongside or following the screening process is the scoping stage. Scoping utilises the same information that is required for the screening process but addresses the requirements for the ES. This step identifies the information necessary for the LPA to judge the effects of the proposed development on the environment. The

LPA is required to give the developer a 'scoping opinion' within five weeks to allow them to prepare the ES as part of the planning application.

In England, the Secretary of State is sometimes called upon within the EIA process if there is disagreement over the screening decision, or if the LPA fails to provide the required screening or scoping opinion within the time period. In Northern Ireland, this would be the PAC.

Environmental Statements

The ES should include a description of the proposed development, the data and analysis of the impact of the proposed scheme, the options considered, the justification for the proposed option and a non-technical summary. Given the additional sensitivities and complications associated with planning applications that have an ES, as well as the additional consultation and publicity requirements necessary, the LPA has 16 weeks in which to determine the planning application. Apart from this longer time period, in procedural terms the application process is otherwise similar to any other planning application type, including the right to appeal.

Validation

The LPA's validation process involves checking that all of the required elements for assessing the planning application have been submitted prior to the submission being formally accepted. Once validated, the application becomes live and the clock starts ticking on the statutory time-scale for determination. Planning applications may be more or less complex, and in order to provide certainty and consistency in the development process and to minimise the financial and time costs involved in seeking permission, planning laws set out the minimum time frames for dealing with applications: 8 weeks for a 'minor' application; 13 weeks for a 'major' application; or 16 weeks where an EIA is required in accordance with European law.

Registration

In parallel with the validation process, LPAs are required to maintain a public register (record) of all planning applications received.

Phase 3: Making the decision

Publicity, notification and consultation

It is important that neighbours and local communities are made aware of development proposals as they have a right to input their views into the decision-making process. The nature of the publicity undertaken for an application will vary depending upon the scale and sensitivity of the scheme. Around the UK approaches may vary a little, including between local authorities in terms of precise practise. All development proposals are made publicly available on the LPA's website though, and their respective websites will explain their approach to consultation.

Notification is where there is a requirement to notify particular people that an application is being made for planning permission. For example, parish or community councils may ask to be notified of applications. There is a requirement for a newspaper advertisement in relation to development affecting the setting of a listed building and/or the character or appearance of a conservation area.

Consultation refers to seeking the views of specialists. Land-use planning decisions often rely on the skills or knowledge of other statutory bodies and consultation must be undertaken with the appropriate authority so that the necessary information and expertise can inform the decision-making process. The range of consultees that are required to be consulted may extend to infrastructure, heritage, environmental health, flooding, safety or aviation. A consultee must be given 14 days to respond to the consultation. These views are 'material considerations' in the decision-making process.

Applying the plan–led approach

In this book we have emphasised the discretionary nature and plan-led basis of the UK planning tradition. When an application is received the process is not simply an administrative one of checking the scheme against a plan for conformity; rather, each decision is based on interpretation and judgement in the light of the development plan and other material considerations. Specifically, we are concerned with the 'merits' (or otherwise) of each proposal.

Although the precise wording of the various planning laws, regulations and guidance varies across the UK, the plan-led approach is shared and a planning decision must be made in accordance with the development plan unless material considerations indicate otherwise. In short, the development plan is given primacy in planning decision-making. Assessing a proposal against the development plan will partly be a question of conformity with quantifiable matters, but it will also include interpretation of conformity; for example, whether a scheme represents 'good' design. Regard must be had to development plans that have been formally adopted, although plans in preparation (emerging) also carry weight and will constitute an 'other' material consideration. The extent of what constitutes the development plan requires some care. In England, the Localism Act 2011 also allows for a recognised neighbourhood plan to be considered part of the development plan where this plan has been formally approved. In Scotland, the development plan can comprise up to three parts: the local plan prepared by one of the 32 LPAs, the strategic development plan (prepared by Scotland's four city-regions) and supplementary planning guidance.

Material considerations

Material considerations are extremely important in UK planning. They are nonetheless quite difficult to define, since the use and development of land can vary and therefore what is material at any given point in time or place will fluctuate. Anything can be considered material if it is deemed to be relevant to the specific development – and, importantly, relevant to what can be controlled by planning law. Building on practice and case law, material considerations can include: national planning policy and circulars; emerging local policy; previous decisions; written parliamentary answers; consultation responses from statutory and non-statutory bodies; planning history (including previous decisions); statements, letters and guidance notes; surrounding uses; conservation issues; design and appearance; access, traffic generation or parking; environmental, social, economic or sustainability factors; negotiations for off-site works; amenity; creation of a 'precedent'; or indeed, in some cases, after-dinner and conference speeches (by government ministers). Planning decision-making involves exercising judgement and weighing up the relative weight of the matters at hand. The amount of weight to be afforded to a material consideration is a judgement in itself.

Box 6.5: What is a material consideration?

The open-ended nature of what may constitute a material consideration is captured in relation to Justice Cooke's comment in *Stringer v Minister of Housing and Local Government [1970] 1 WLR 1281.* The case concerned a development which would have interfered with the operation of the Jodrell Bank telescope. Justice Cooke stated:

> it seems to me that any consideration which relates to the use and development of land is capable of being a material consideration.

Revisions and adjustments

A degree of flexibility within the planning system allows for revisions and adjustments to submitted schemes, within reason, during the statutory period for determining applications. As such, planning proposals are not necessarily subject to a single review and decision at a single point in time; rather, in certain circumstances they may be considered 'live' and subject to review. The importance of this flexibility is to enable negotiation and revision in order to ensure that an acceptable scheme is produced and the best outcome for an area is delivered. At the same time as enabling possible revisions and improvements, care must be taken to ensure that interested parties are aware of the changes occurring mid-stream. Moreover, statutory time periods within which decisions must be made constrain the amount of time available for negotiation. For these reasons, emphasis is placed on early discussions between developers, neighbours, communities and the LPA. Front-loading effectively means making the best use of pre-application stages, in particular ensuring early community engagement.

The decision

In most cases, it is the LPA that makes decisions on planning applications. Who in the LPA makes the decision will depend upon the nature of the application. Certain arrangements also exist that mean that decisions can be made at the national level, for example by the Planning Inspectorate in England and Wales (see 'Major projects' below).

Delegated powers

Arrangements within individual LPAs vary. An important aspect of ensuring that there is an efficient, effective and democratic planning system in place turns on the concept of delegated powers. As a core function of local government, planning and development decisions are fundamental to the economic base, environmental quality and social well-being of individual places. Ultimately, locally elected councillors (elected members) exercise political control over the policy direction of their particular council area. While local development plans are clearly shaped by national priorities and policies, local place-making agendas are the responsibility of councillors. In terms of local democracy, elected members exercise a political role, while officers provide professional advice and perform the administrative functions supporting the planning process. Given the number of planning applications received by individual LPAs, and that many of the development proposals may be relatively minor or uncontentious in nature, local councils have the power to put 'schemes of delegation' in place that dictate whether the decision is made by a planning committee or delegated to a senior officer. Based on the principle that planning should be proportionate, this approach allows for effective use of resources and means that relatively more sensitive or important developments can be given fuller attention by the locally elected members.

Planning committee meetings

Precise arrangements vary, but, typically, each planning application is presented to elected members by the LPA's planning team. A recommendation is presented, based on an accompanying committee report, setting out the relevant details, policies and material considerations. As part of the collation of evidence, the applicant and/or their representatives, supporters and objectors will be given some opportunity to address the committee. Members then discuss the scheme, taking into account advice as necessary. The decision, including in the case of a refusal the policy basis for that decision, is then subject to a vote. While such public meetings may be politically charged, with party politics perhaps in evidence over the relative weight to be given to particular policy or material considerations, the decision to approve or refuse a planning application must be well reasoned and based on sound planning considerations. Regardless of whether the decision is taken by a professional planning officer under delegated powers or by a councillor as an elected representative sitting on a planning committee, decisions must give primacy to the development plan (that is, be plan led) and other material considerations. The materiality of and weight given to these considerations will be on a case-by-case basis. Moreover, as we discuss in the next chapter, an approval will likely include planning conditions and may, in some instances, be associated with a planning agreement.

Issuing the decision

A planning decision letter is an important legal document. Not only does it set out the decision in relation to a specific piece or parcel of land and describe the precise nature of the development, but it provides the detail of any conditions attached and the accompanying reason for each of these. In some circumstances an advisory note informing the developer of other important issues, such as the need for another form of consent, is also attached. In the case of a refusal, the decision letter or notice states the reason(s), referring where appropriate to the relevant development plan policies. The date of the decision is all important as it represents (i) the point at which development may commence, subject to any conditions requiring further information or detail having been agreed; (ii) the starting point for the time frame for considering any appeal; and (iii) the end of the statutory time period for determining a planning application.

Major projects

Distinct regulations and procedures exist across the UK for dealing with major projects, and particularly for infrastructure projects. In Northern Ireland major development matters tend to be considered by central government, rather than to be delegated to local councils.

In England and Wales nationally significant infrastructure projects are similarly not determined by the LPA but are instead considered by the Planning Inspectorate (the national tier), with a recommendation being made to the Secretary of State. Here, approval of a scheme constitutes a development consent rather than a planning permission. Development consents are a form of integrated permission, which removes the requirement for individual permissions such as LBC. These major applications are considered in relation to the National Policy Statements (see Chapter Four).

Additionally, in England, under Clause 1 of the Growth and Infrastructure Act 2013, applicants have the option to apply directly to the Planning Inspectorate for the determination of a major planning application in cases where the LPA is judged to be a 'failing' authority. A council is considered to be 'failing' where the LPA determines fewer than 50% of major applications within 13 weeks over a two-year period. On the one hand, this route enables a developer to secure a decision on their development proposal in a timely way. On the other hand, by-passing the local council undermines the LPA, potentially reducing local input and community confidence in the system.

Box 6.6: Dundee Waterfront

Scotland's National Planning Framework 3 lists a number of nationally significant developments, including the Dundee Waterfront, part of a £1 billion investment and major regeneration scheme extending along the River Tay. A central element of the broader project involves building the first V&A Museum of Design outside London, due to open in 2018. In terms of development management, the LPA was responsible for assessing the full planning application of the Kengo Kuma-designed building and extension to the Riverside Walk. As a major scheme in an estuarine location, the application provides an interesting example of the content of a planning application, the decision-making process and the type of information taken into account. The submission included the need to obtain an EIA screening opinion. The report to committee explains the various actions undertaken, including pre-application consultation with the community and consultation with various bodies. The proposal was considered in the light of policies in TayPlan (strategic level) as well as the local plan, and took into account a number of material considerations, including a short discussion of what is not a material consideration. The decision to grant the application had conditions attached.

(https://www.dundeewaterfront.com/ Details of the application, accompanying documentation and permission (13/00224/FULM) are available through Dundee City Council's e-planning online simple search tool.)

Varying the system and facilitating development

This final section briefly explores the potential for variance in the decision-making process. The planning system is set up with a recognition that a one-size-fits-all arrangement may not be the most suitable in all situations; sometimes greater control may be necessary, sometimes less. For example, it may be deemed desirable that in certain areas and at certain times, such as the need for economic regeneration of a former industrial area, special forms of development management, or indeed fewer controls, should be put in place.

Enterprise Zones and Simplified Planning Zones

Enterprise Zones and Simplified Planning Zones are examples of where the same procedures for express planning permission discussed above do not apply. An

Enterprise Zone is a designated area within which governments tend to adopt a deregulatory stance. Governments may also introduce special tax arrangements to incentivise investment and speed up development. From a planning perspective, a particular sort of permitted development rights regime may be put in place. In effect, and following the logic of regulatory planning approaches discussed in Chapter Two, identified forms of development are allowed to come forward without the requirement for express planning permission: the planning system is simplified. As with permitted development rights, certain conditions and restrictions will nonetheless apply to ensure that only desired forms of new development come forward and that they are delivered in an acceptable manner. Such zoning and compliance-oriented approaches represent a way of granting planning permission in advance.

Removal of permitted development rights

Permitted development rights may be extended or increased within a defined geographical area. Typically, stronger controls are used to restrict even minor development in sensitive locations, such as conservation areas or certain housing developments with a particular layout. The reason is because the uncontrolled exercise of otherwise given permitted development rights would be harmful.

In England, Article 4 of the General Permitted Development Order 2015 is used. Here, the boundaries and restricted development provisions of Article 4 Directions can be made by the LPA through the relevant Secretary of State (or by the latter alone). A key principle is that the imposed limitations must be impact based and proportionate. Importantly, it is possible to seek compensation in some instances where an Article 4 Direction has been introduced. This arrangement, which is time limited in practice, reflects an on–going concern with securing a balance between private interests and state intervention in the public interest. The general principle underpinning the idea of permitted development rights may be understood as providing an acceptable 'baseline'. Any attempts to restrict these private rights necessitates balancing the potential benefits in the public interest. Where the existence of an Article 4 Direction means that what, elsewhere, would have constituted permitted development requires submission of an application for express planning permission, compensation may be sought. This is in recognition of the costs (for example, time or money) involved and the potential of permission being refused. Similar arrangements for the removal of permitted development rights exist in all of the nations of the UK.

Local and Neighbourhood Development Orders

In England and Wales, a Local Development Order (LDO) is able to provide additional flexibility within a defined geographical area. An LDO is effectively the opposite of an Article 4 Direction and allows for the expansion of permitted development rights. In contrast to Enterprise Zones and Simplified Planning

Zones, LDOs are not as business focused. They are also used in residential areas or retail centres to provide greater flexibility where this is deemed desirable. An LDO can also be imposed on a very specific site to facilitate a particular objective. Arguably, this means that an LDO can be more targeted. For example, the Honda car plant in Swindon has a bespoke LDO in place to support the growth and evolution of this facility.

Neighbourhood Development Orders (NDOs) work in the same manner as LDOs. An important difference is that they originate at the neighbourhood, not local, scale of government. Arising from the Localism Act 2011 and applying in England, NDOs may be proposed by the neighbourhood planning body and implemented with the support of the LPA. In practice, NDOs perform a similar function to LDOs in that, when in place, they provide for a permissive planning context in identified areas and for prescribed uses.

Permission in principle (PiP)

The Planning and Housing Act 2016 introduced a new concept in England in the form of planning permission delivered through a plan document, rather than a decision on a planning application. The 2016 legislation creates the potential for a plan to designate an area of land as having planning permission in principle (PiP), effectively granting outline planning permission via the plan document in some senses. The technical details, akin to reserved matters, would then be pursued via an application to the LPA. This application would be determined in line with the 'normal' plan–led decision-making process. The underlying intention behind this arrangement is to enhance the certainty of a full development proposal receiving planning permission by side-stepping the need for the outline application stage. This development may be seen as supporting the Westminster government's aspirations to create a more regulatory based planning system within the context of a discretionary planning framework.

The attempt intellectually to further merge these two distinct approaches is an interesting concept. The benefits of the PiP approach will be tested over time, but it is interesting to note that the Independent Review of Planning in Scotland has similarly identified PiP as a way to improve certainty (Beveridge et al, 2016). In this instance, it is suggested that the PiP would again set the principle for the type of development allowed on a particular site, with more detailed consent required through an application for Approval of Matters Specified as a Condition (AMSC) before work could begin (Beveridge et al, 2016).

While the reasoning is presented as strengthening the status of allocated sites in the development plan, in practice, proposals will still be subject to the need for planning permission as they come forward and thus a core discretionary model retained in reality.

Other forms of control and implementation

Planning does not operate in isolation. The process of development is a complex series of systems, actors and processes acting (ideally) together in the delivery of change. From the perspective of state intervention, a number of related forms of regulatory systems operate in parallel to planning. These controls include environmental health, licensing and building control. Together, they form a body of public administration concerned with the effective management of the built and natural environment. Planning therefore forms part of a 'system of systems' and has a key role to play in managing space and place. All forms of state intervention operate within a market capitalist economy. As such, related functions such as the arrangements for land assembly, availability of development finance and powers of taxation are also central to the occurrence of change. The extent to which the LPA can influence these dynamics in the UK is relatively weak when compared, for example, with the powers enjoyed by local government in the Netherlands.

Compulsory Purchase Orders (CPOs)

Under circumstances of market failure, where, for example, derelict land remains under-used or undeveloped, or where strategic infrastructure needs are required to be met, such as the provision of a school, social housing or road infrastructure, the state can intervene as a means to realising the ambitions of communities and local authorities. Compulsory Purchase Orders (CPOs), for example, are powers enabling a local authority to acquire land for development that is demonstrated as being necessary for the economic, social or environmental well-being of an area. In practice, CPOs can be very sensitive because they represent one of the more extreme and powerful forms of state intervention because in exercising CPO powers the state is 'taking' land from a private individual. Given the potential sensitivity of this process, acquiring land in this way can be a very involved and expensive process, including addressing issues of the appropriate compensation for the landowner. Nevertheless, CPOs can also be a very useful tool, given the importance of effective land assembly to realise major projects, and where there are several landowners involved. Interestingly, the Neighbourhood Planning and Infrastructure Bill 2016 in England proposes to rationalise a hundred years of (sometimes conflicting) statutes and case law in relation to CPO with a view to speeding up the system and making it clearer and fairer.

There are other ways that the planning system can be part of wider, area-based change initiatives, where a range of forms of intervention (for example taxation, zoning, regeneration) need to be in alignment in order to address specific local needs. Key examples include Urban Development Corporations, Urban Regeneration Companies and Local Delivery Vehicles. These are methods of adapting systems of urban governance and creating partnerships to deliver comprehensive change within a given geographical space. The delivery vehicles vary in their powers, institutional form and approach.

For instance, under the Urban Development Corporation arrangements the LPA effectively loses a degree of control of the designated area, with a separate body being specifically created as part of a Quasi-Autonomous Non-Governmental Organisation to oversee change within a defined time-scale. Urban Development Corporations benefit from both plan-making and CPO powers and are intended to enable financial and physical change in the areas over which they have control. These corporations have gained a degree of prominence since 2015, although they may be controversial for reasons associated with public participation and local democratic control. Such measures illustrate some of the ways in which planning controls over land and buildings continue to change since the 1947 legislation.

Chapter summary

In this chapter we have deepened our understanding of the essentials of planning law by examining development management approaches and practices in more detail. With reference to experience across the UK, we have identified a number of core terms. The aim has been to generalise, in so far as this is possible and helpful, for those seeking to work, live or invest in the UK or to learn from the different systems evolving in England, Wales, Scotland and Northern Ireland. Despite certain differences, key principles and terminology are sufficiently similar to allow an understanding of how development management is intended to work. We have stressed the role of the Courts in elaborating the meaning of 'development' as comprising both use and operational dimensions. The chapter has also set out how the proportionality principle usefully identifies different types of control and illustrated how planning is intended to provide a proportionate system. Specifically, the discussion has differentiated between minor and major forms of development and highlighted the role of permitted development rights in relation to small-scale change. We have also illustrated how related tools, such as EIA or CPO, may be used in advancing better places and have mentioned some alternative methods of control. In pointing to emerging measures, such as LDOs and NDOs, we have shown that innovation in forms of control continues apace. It is evident that control over development does not lie with the LPA alone. Having established the key building blocks and outlined the basic process for making planning applications, in the next chapter we look in more detail at how planning seeks to improve the quality of development.

Recommended reading

Hart, T. (2015) 'The management of development', in B. Cullingworth et al (eds), *Town and country planning in the UK*, 15th edn, Abingdon-on-Thames: Routledge, pp 137–94.

Duxbury, R. (2012) *Telling & Duxbury's planning law and procedure*, 15th edn, Oxford: Oxford University Press, chapters 7, 8 and 9.

McMaster, R. and Smith, G. (2013) *Scottish planning law*, London: Bloomsbury Publishing, chapters 5 and 6.

Moore, V. and Purdue, M. (2014) *A practical approach to planning law*, 13th edn, Oxford: Oxford University Press, chapters 9, 11 and 12.

You should also consult up-to-date information online:

England: Planning Portal (remembering to identify 'England' as your location): http://www.planningportal.gov.uk
Northern Ireland: Planning Portal: https://www.planningni.gov.uk/
Scotland: ePlanning Scotland: https://eplanning.scotland.gov.uk/WAM/
Wales: Town Planning Portal (remembering to identify 'Wales' as your location): http://www.planningportal.gov.uk

SEVEN

Planning conditions, agreements and obligations

Chapter contents

- Management of 'delivery' and 'in perpetuity'
- The power to impose conditions
- The six legal tests for planning conditions
- Other considerations with conditions
- Planning gain
- Planning agreements
- Planning gain and conditions
- The Community Infrastructure Levy
- Chapter summary

Introduction

This chapter considers two positive and constructive ways in which planning helps to ensure that developments come forward to create 'great places' (Beveridge et al, 2016):

1. the use of planning conditions attached to a planning permission or consent issued by the LPA, or through development orders in relation to permitted development rights
2. planning gain.

We examine the legal principles underpinning the use of conditions arising from case law, such as the powers to impose conditions and discuss the six legal tests needed to ensure the validity of conditions and the approaches available for removing them. We then consider the different models of planning gain available, distinguishing these tools from planning conditions and considering their effects. Simply stated, planning gain relates to monies received in association with an approved development proposal to offset any development implications. The funds are held by the LPA to enable it both to mitigate against impact(s) and to support the appropriate realisation of change on the development site and in the wider area. Both measures are core to development management and serve to improve development proposals so that they become more acceptable.

Management of 'delivery' and 'in perpetuity'

In Chapter Six we characterised the development management approach as different from development control. Specifically, we suggested that planning performs a role in delivering sustainable development that involves much more than the processing of a planning application and issuing of a decision. Planning must be understood as the on-going management of change to improve societal and environmental outcomes. It has a critical role to play in the shared activity of making great places.

An often overlooked aspect of planning control relates to the management of development after planning permission has been granted. *How* should the development be undertaken? And how should the development be managed in the *longer-term*? These are the questions that explain the purpose of planning conditions. It is very rare to have a permission with no conditions attached. Conditions improve the acceptability of a development in the wider public interest. For example, conditions may control the hours of construction to erect a building in the first place; they can be used to ensure that appropriate building materials or landscaping are used so that the new development fits in with the wider street-scene; or they may be imposed to control the opening- and closing-times of a restaurant so that local residents' quality of life is protected. Without the imposition of conditions a development could have unacceptable impacts. In short, a conditional approval to ensure wider benefits is preferable to a refusal notice.

Before physical construction even begins, planning conditions can play an important role. An area with sensitivities around matters such as heritage, ecology, wildlife, flooding or archaeology may require investigation before a development commences. Investigations and monitoring may well continue during the construction phase. Planning conditions can be used to require particular information, including details of mitigation measures, to be provided in a particular way. The construction phase of a new scheme can lead to a number of environmental issues such as noise, dust, traffic and smell. To contain and ameliorate the potential disruption to neighbours and wildlife for the duration of the build, planning conditions may be used to limit not only days and times of operation but how the construction work is undertaken.

Once a development is complete, further restrictions may be necessary to ensure that the building (or land) remains in a particular use type; or that a certain named person resides at the development for a certain time-period; or that certain species of trees or hedgerows are replanted, if they have been removed or destroyed during the construction phase. The imposition of conditions is designed to ensure that the development is acceptable not only on the date when planning permission was granted, but continues to be acceptable in perpetuity. Planning conditions are thus an extremely important planning tool for the state in managing development and its potential impacts on the built and natural environment.

Box 7.1: Reasonable and necessary: missing evidence

In an appeal against the conditional grant of outline permission for a replacement dwelling-house and garage in Northern Ireland, the principal issue turned on whether the conditions were reasonable in relation to the positioning of the site and development within the curtilage. The Commissioner found that the conditions were not, then removed them and provided new conditions. The original decision maker (the former DOE) had imposed the conditions in order to prevent the proposed development from marring the distinction between the existing settlement and the surrounding countryside, or resulting in urban sprawl.

The onus was on the (former) DOE to justify the imposition of the conditions. The DOE did not explain why it attached weight to a new proposed development limit to a town in the relevant draft development plan. Since this vital piece of evidence (reason) was missing, the Commissioner concluded that the DOE had failed to demonstrate that the conditions were reasonable and necessary.

The power to impose conditions

In determining planning applications, an LPA has three options. These are:

1. to refuse planning permission
2. to grant planning permission unconditionally
3. to grant planning permission with conditions.

The relevant planning legislation for each country allows the LPA to grant planning permission subject to such conditions as it thinks fit. Although this remit may seem very wide ranging, conditions may be imposed on the grant of planning permission to regulate the development, to regulate the use of any land under the control of the applicant or to require the carrying out of works on any such land in connection with the development authorised by the permission or to require the removal of any buildings.

Conditions are often restrictive in nature. They are designed to control some aspect of the development delivery, occupation or use. These conditions – or restrictions – may be what makes the scheme acceptable; they represent a form of continuing control. Without the conditions the development might not be delivered at all, or planning permission might be refused.

Box 7.2: Primary roles of planning conditions

The purpose of the LPA imposing conditions on a planning permission is to enhance the quality of developments or to ameliorate adverse effects. The purpose of conditions in regulating land may be summarised as follows.

1. Planning conditions are a mechanism to improve the function of development management to realise better outcomes and to enhance confidence in the planning system.
2. Planning conditions enable the approval of a development proposal where it would otherwise be necessary to make a refusal.

The six legal tests for planning conditions

Across the four administrations the relevant legislation states that it is essential for planning conditions to be used sensitively. Conditions should be tailored to address specific issues, rather than used to impose unjustified controls. Moreover, if they are applied in an unreasonable way it may be impracticable or inexpedient to enforce them.

The power to impose conditions when granting permission is very wide. The legislation associated with the use of planning conditions is explained in the Planning Practice Guidance in England, Circular 11/95 in Wales and Northern Ireland and Circular 4/98 in Scotland. The circulars contain guidance on when conditions should or should not be used and their appendices provide a non-exhaustive list of model conditions for LPAs to use. Although they derive their basis from different legislation, the provisions pertaining to conditions are very similar across the devolved UK and revolve around six key legal tests.

The so-called 'six tests' have emerged through case law. A condition must satisfy all the tests if it is to be valid. Although the tests have now all been clarified through legislation and policy, the case law remains important to both their definition and interpretation. In general, conditions should be imposed only when they are:

(i)   necessary
(ii)   relevant to planning
(iii)   relevant to the development to be permitted
(iv)   enforceable
(v)   precise
(vi)   reasonable in all other respects.

Conditions that do not meet one of these tests should not be used.

These conditions elaborate an earlier three-strand test laid down in *Newbury DC v Secretary of State for the Environment [1981] AC 578* that was later restated and clarified as six tests across the devolved UK. Given the importance of the six tests and case law in teasing out the use of planning conditions, we consider each one individually and make reference to key cases that are particularly helpful in providing clarity and definition.

(i) Necessary

A key test in deciding if a condition is necessary turns on whether or not planning permission would have been refused if the condition were not imposed. If planning permission would have been granted without the condition, then the condition needs special and precise justification. Similarly, if a condition is too wide ranging it will fail the test of necessity. The reasoning underlying this test can be related to one of the fundamental principles of the planning system: it must operate proportionately and appropriately as a form of state intervention. Planning conditions must conform to the wider operating remit of the system and, as such, it is important that they do not go beyond the reach that is appropriate. If a condition is not necessary, then planning should not seek to impose that control, for to do so would go beyond the spirit of planning. This idea relates to the second test.

(ii) Relevant to planning

It is established that statutory powers can be exercised only in line with the purpose for which they were given. If a condition has no relevance to planning, then it has no place being imposed by planning. Such an action would be deemed unreasonable (often referred to as 'ultra vires' ['beyond the powers']). The main principles to emerge from case law are that:

1. a condition imposed solely or primarily to serve some non-planning purposes is invalid: for example *R v Hillingdon LBC ex p Royco Homes Ltd [1974] QB 720* where the planning permission was quashed in this instance;
2. conditions should not be used for ulterior objectives, no matter how desirable that might be in the public interest: for example *MJ Shanley Ltd v Secretary of State for the Environment [1982] JPL 380*, where the condition was declared invalid and unenforceable.

(iii) Relevant to the development to be permitted

A condition will not be relevant to the development to be permitted if it seeks to control something unconnected to the development. To pass this test, the condition must seek to control something that is directly associated with the realisation of the development. The main principles to emerge from case law are that there needs to be a clear connection between the condition and the development to be permitted: for example *British Airports Authority v Secretary of State for Scotland [1980] JPL 260*; and later in the 'Newbury' case and subsequently in *Tarmac Heavy Building Materials Ltd UK v Secretary of State for Environment, Transport and the Regions [2000] PLCR 157*, where it was found that the condition could not be said to be fairly and reasonably related to the planning permission originally granted and the condition was therefore quashed.

(iv) Enforceable

The Courts can declare a condition invalid on the grounds that it is unenforceable. For example, such a declaration may occur because an infringement of the condition may be undetectable. If a condition cannot be enforced, then it becomes meaningless and worthless. The legal challenge to this is based on the grounds of 'Wednesbury' 'reasonableness' (*Associated Provincial Picture Houses Ltd v Wednesbury Corp [1947] 2 All ER 680* – relating to perversity and irrationality). A condition will be invalid if it is clear that no reasonable person or authority (e.g. LPA) could have imposed it. A condition may be unenforceable on the grounds that the LPA has no power to ensure compliance with a condition: for example, *British Airports Authority v Secretary of State for Scotland, [1980] JPL 260*. The condition attached to the grant of planning permission for development at Aberdeen Airport restricted the hours of aircraft take-off and landing. This was found to be reasonably related to the development permitted, and therefore was enforceable. A condition must be precise enough to ensure that its requirements are carried out. Finally, a condition that does not conform with this rule is ultra vires: for example *R v Ealing LBC, ex p Zainuddin [1995] JPL 925*, where planning permission was granted for a mosque, with a condition that worship should take place solely within buildings. Only a frame of the building was built, however, with no roof or sides, and worship took place within the frame. It was held that this had not been within breach of the condition.

(v) Precise

It is essential that conditions are carefully worded if they are to be effective for the purposes intended. A condition will be invalid if it can be given no meaning, or no sensible or ascertainable meaning. The main principles emerging from the case law are that conditions can be declared invalid on the basis that their wording makes them virtually meaningless: for example *Fisher v Wychavon DC [2001] JPL 964*, where a condition regarding the length of time for the temporary use of a caravan was unclear and, as such, the condition was of no effect. Vague conditions cannot be made acceptable by requiring something to be done by a certain time, or to a certain standard: for example *Newbury DC v Secretary of State for the Environment [1981] AC 578*.

(vi) Reasonable

A condition is not reasonable if it is unduly restrictive. If it appears that a permission could be given only subject to conditions that would be likely to be held unreasonable by the Courts, then it will be necessary to refuse the application altogether. Again, with this final test, it can be seen that the fundamental principles of proportionality and appropriateness of state intervention are being reaffirmed. The planning system must behave in a way that is reasonable in all of its manifestations, including the use of planning conditions. The state's intervention in private rights and the market is argued as being necessary, but also sensitive. It is therefore essential that the intervention that occurs is reasonable. Therefore conditions may be declared ultra vires even if the applicant agrees to the conditions: for example *Hall & Co Ltd v Shoreham-by-sea UDC [1964] 1WLR 240 (CA)*, where a company agreed to constructing a public road at its own expense; and *City of Bradford Metropolitan Council v Secretary of State for the Environment [1986] JPL 598 (CA)*, where it was held that a condition that required a highway to be widened by the applicant was unreasonable.

Other considerations with conditions

LPAs can usually impose conditions only over land which is in the control of the applicant. However, it is possible for conditions to consider other land. Two points are of note: the so-called 'Grampian' conditions and validity.

In *Grampian Regional Council v City of Aberdeen DC (1984) P&CR 633*, the imposition of negative conditions requiring that no development should be carried out until 'X' happens was highlighted as enforceable. Grampian-type conditions are mostly used in relation to highway works where development needs to be completed on other land before development takes place on the application land. Grampian conditions can be attached to planning permission only if there is a reasonable prospect of their being fulfilled, as demonstrated in *British Railways Board v Secretary of State for the Environment [1994] JPL 32*.

The 'validity' of a condition may be challenged following an appeal. This can have a potentially serious impact that could extend beyond the mere revision or removal of a given condition. For example, from case law we have seen that if a planning condition is found to be invalid it can mean that the entire permission is deemed invalid: for example, *Hall & Co Ltd v Shoreham-by-Sea UDC [1964] 1 WLR 240 (CA)*. Additionally, if the invalid condition was fundamental to the planning permission or to part of the structure, the whole planning permission will fail. If the invalid condition was trivial, incidental or superimposed on the permission, then it can be severed from the permission: for example, *Kent CC v Kingsway Investments (Kent) Ltd [1970] 1 ALL ER 70*.

Due to the nature of most conditions being time limited, it is often the case that conditions expire naturally. Furthermore, once a condition is fulfilled it will cease to be applicable. If a condition is incapable of being fulfilled, it will cease to apply: for example, *R Bell & Co (Estates) Ltd v Department of the Environment for Northern Ireland [198] NI 332*.

Finally, it is also possible to apply for a condition to be varied or removed through a process akin to the normal planning application process. In such cases, the LPA must consider only the question of the conditions. The LPA can grant the permission subject to the same conditions, or can impose new or different conditions, so long as they do not amount to a fundamental alteration to the original proposal put forward: for example *R v Coventry City Council, ex p Arrowcroft Group plc [2001] PLCR 113.*

Planning gain

We now focus on the nature and structure of planning gain. As noted, the purpose of planning gain is to enhance the quality of a development and to enable developments to go ahead that might ordinarily be refused, provided that they are relevant to planning. Planning gain goes beyond conditions. Conceptually, it goes to the core of the philosophy of the planning system. As discussed by Greed (2014), the result of granting a planning permission is that land values increase and various stakeholders participating in the process of development are able to make a profit. The community within which a project is situated and will be realised facilitates this profit, but may also be adversely impacted on by the development. Having regard to important matters such as social justice and the public interest is all important. It is necessary to mitigate any negative impacts on the community. An important tool is planning gain, which at its simplest is the provision of monies or goods in kind by the developer to mitigate against the impacts of the proposed development.

Across the devolved UK the standard form of securing planning gain is through planning agreements. The Community Infrastructure Levy (CIL) also exists in England and Wales, and this is dealt with separately.

Planning agreements

We start with a very basic example of a planning agreement. If a new supermarket is built, then some of the community may benefit from the goods and services offered by this new facility. At the same time, however, congestion, pollution or issues of highway safety could result, due to increased traffic on the transport network. Others may be disadvantaged. The payment of monies to the LPA through the planning gain system would enable it to invest in the local highway infrastructure to ensure that the new store did not adversely impact on transport and movement in the local area.

Planning agreements are therefore directly linked to the impact caused by the proposed development and are intended to make the scheme acceptable from the perspective of the development itself, but also from the perspective of the implications on and needs of the wider community. A planning agreement can thus cover payments or benefits in kind for a diverse range of matters. For example, a large housing scheme could have planning gain–derived benefits associated with transport and movement, education and schools, libraries, parks and open spaces, ecology, flood management, public art, the emergency services and health services. Each of these matters could be placed under additional pressure due to a major housing scheme coming forward. As such, it is considered appropriate for the developer to mitigate against the impact. This is another example of the planning system acting in the interests of social justice and the public interest.

Mechanisms for enabling planning gain actually pre-date the modern planning systems formulated in 1947. Current provisions for planning agreements can be found in: section 106 of the Town and Country Planning Act 1990 for England and Wales; article 76 of the Planning Act (Northern Ireland) 2011; and section 75 of the Town and Country Planning (Scotland) Act 1997. The legislative reference is often used in common parlance when discussing planning agreements, as in Section 106 Agreements in an English context.

An interesting and subtle distinction exists between planning gain and conditions. Positive change in an area may be facilitated through planning gain, from which the applicant may also benefit. Conditions, on the other hand, tend to be restrictive. While the wider community may benefit, the applicant may feel constrained. Planning gain is not universally supported. However, it can be argued that it is a positive mechanism for delivering positive change and shows planning as constructive and enabling place-shaping, rather than merely a servant of state regulation.

The LPA may enter into a planning agreement with any person who has an estate in land for the purpose of facilitating, regulating or restricting the development or use of the land. Established by way of a deed, the agreement could restrict the development or use of the land in a specified way. Examples of planning gain include: the provision of open space; bus-shelters; park-and-ride schemes; provision of social, recreational or educational facilities; installation of public art; improvement of flood-defences; provision of traffic-calming measures; or payment of a sum of money to the LPA that relates to the land or to the development. Other examples involve providing social housing or compensation for loss of open space, or otherwise mitigating the impact of a development. Negotiations between the developer and the LPA can take place before the grant of planning permission. However, the obligation will come into operation only after planning permission has been granted. The agreement may be subject to a time limit or expiration. Obligations can be modified, amended or discharged by application to the LPA if the obligation no longer serves a useful purpose, namely to meet a planning objective. It is possible for obligations to be appealed to a higher authority, for example the relevant Secretary of State in England.

Planning agreements come in two basic forms. In addition to the planning obligations route that we have just considered, there is also the 'unilateral undertakings' route. The difference between these two forms can be assigned based upon the nature of the contract. Planning obligations are negotiated agreements between the LPA and the developer or landowner. In contrast, a unilateral undertaking is a pre-drafted proposal submitted to the LPA for its express agreement. Both approaches are essentially contracts between the LPA and the developer or landowner. Planning agreements are entirely separate from the planning application, although they will be cross-referenced.

You may be wondering about the consequences of monies being paid to an LPA in relation to the pursuit of planning permission. A fundamental point is that planning permissions cannot be bought or sold. Voluntarily entering into a planning agreement or unilateral undertaking with an LPA in anticipation of the grant of planning permission certainly does not mean that planning permission will be forthcoming, and while it is true that a planning agreement is a key part of a positive and constructive planning negotiation, an agreement is not always necessary. Where planning gain is used, it is because it ensures that a scheme that would otherwise be refused can be realised.

Box 7.3: Reasonableness in planning agreements

Case law has played an important part in defining the operations of planning gain through Section 106 agreements (England). Such cases highlight the challenges associated with using the system effectively. In *Tesco Stores Ltd v Secretary of State for the Environment [1995] 1 WLR 759*, a new road was proposed by Tesco to the west of a town, as requested by the LPA. It was found in Court that the link between the road and the supermarket was tenuous and unreasonable. Here, the limitations of planning gain 'offers' can be seen.

Planning gain and conditions

In terms of the relationship between planning gain and conditions, planning agreements go beyond what could be required of a condition. A requirement by the LPA for the developer to make a monetary payment is a case in point. As we have already suggested, in some respects planning conditions can be seen as a relatively restrictive mechanism, whereas planning gain is held to be a constructive and positive enabling tool. Planning conditions are also part of a planning permission, whereas a planning agreement or obligation is a parallel matter.

In some other respects, however, there are parallels between these tools. First, both conditions and planning gain must be in accordance with the general principles of planning with regard to proportionality and appropriateness. In *R v Wealden DC, ex p Charles Church (South East) Ltd [1989] JPL 837*, it was held that one of the six tests for conditions, that of being 'fair and reasonable' does not apply to the making of planning agreements. Nevertheless, there are tests of 'reasonableness' that should be afforded to planning gain that can be viewed as not entirely dissimilar to the tests of conditions. A condition cannot require monetary payments to be made by a developer, whereas a planning agreement can.

The relevant legal tests in relation to planning obligations can be found in Planning Practice Guidance in England, Circular 05/2005 in Wales and Northern Ireland and Circular 1/2010 in Scotland. These tests can be summarised as follows: be relevant to planning; be necessary to make the proposed development acceptable in planning terms; be directly related to the proposed development; be fairly and reasonably related in scale and in kind to the proposed development; and be reasonable in all other aspects.

Developers tend to be in favour of planning conditions, as they are considered less onerous than planning agreements and are easier to have removed by the various appeal bodies, similar to breach of condition notices (see Chapter Ten). On the other hand, the LPA may favour planning agreements because they are perceived to be a relatively more secure means of obtaining safeguards on development. As we have seen, unlike conditions, planning agreements can deal with matters that do not relate to the development for which planning permission is sought.

Box 7.4: Appropriate use of planning agreements

Planning agreements can be quite sensitive and controversial. As noted, not everyone supports their use. Numerous cases exist that have generated debate concerning whether the planning gain system is being used appropriately. In *R v Plymouth City Council ex p Plymouth and South Devon Co-operative Society [1993] JPL 1099*, Tesco Stores Ltd and Sainsbury plc applied separately for planning permission to Plymouth Council in 1992 for the erection of a superstore on the outskirts of the city. Both permissions were dependent on the companies entering into an agreement under Section 106 of the Town and Country Planning Act 1990. Each company covenanted to provide projects that did not form part of the development, namely a tourist information centre, an art-gallery and bird-watching hide. The Co-operative Society, a third retailer, challenged the Council's decision, stating that it had to compete against two rivals where previously there was one. Both companies stated that the Council had acted unlawfully by taking into account immaterial considerations, namely the community benefits. They stated that they were not 'necessary'. The Court of Appeal held that the benefits offered by Sainsbury's and Tesco did serve a purpose, and did fairly and reasonably relate to the development permitted. If we consider this against the example in Box 7.3, we can see the challenges associated with determining 'reasonableness' in planning agreements.

As with conditions, case law is important for purposes of clarification and use. Some key principles merit mention:

- Planning agreements are usually seen as a way of securing planning ends that are beyond the scope of a condition. This does not mean they will override other statutory powers however: *Windsor & Maidstone BC v Brandrose Investment [1983] 1WLR 509*, where it was held that a planning agreement could not be used to prevent the carrying out of other statutory powers, in this case a legal agreement was entered into that included matters concerning demolition that were subsequently impacted upon by the designation of a Conservation Area.

- Planning agreements cannot be used to validate what would be an invalid condition: *Bradford City Council v Secretary of State & McClean Homes [1986] JPL 598 (CA).*
- Planning agreements must satisfy the first and the third requirements for the imposition of valid conditions (as found in the Newbury case): *R v Gillingham BC ex p Parham Ltd [1988] JPL 336;* there is no requirement, as with conditions, for the test of a fair and reasonable relationship to the development proposed: *R v Wealden DC ex p Charles Church (South East) Ltd [1989] JPL 837, Good v Epping Forest DC [1994] JPL 372,* where it was accepted that planning agreements could be valid even if they went beyond what could be dealt with by a condition.
- A planning agreement is less at risk of JR (as it should have been mutually discussed at a pre-application stage) and the remedy of an agreement is an injunction (damages or specific performance are also used as remedies), which is easier to enforce than an enforcement notice for a condition: *R v Westminster CC ex p Monahan [1989] 2 All ER 74.*

The Community Infrastructure Levy (CIL)

There are a number of controversial aspects to the use of planning agreements. Concerns tend to relate to aspects of accountability, consistency, democracy, clarity and integrity. Such debate has generated regular discussion about finding a more effective model of enabling planning gain. In England and Wales this deliberation ultimately led to the emergence of the CIL, a levy that local authorities in England and Wales can choose to charge on new developments in their area. The mechanism does not replace planning agreements but is intended to become the principal planning gain tool. The aim is to make planning charge setting more straightforward; to provide a fairer means of securing contributions from developers; and to encourage regions and local authorities to plan positively for housing and economic growth. The CIL is not compulsory but, with increasing restrictions on how planning agreements may be used, it has become an important route for securing cost recovery.

The CIL allows an LPA to set a charge for potentially all new development taking place within its area. It can be used to finance infrastructure, the definition of which is wide and includes transport, flood defences, schools, healthcare, open space, sport, police stations and district heating. It also includes a 5% administration fee to enable the delivery of the model.

The CIL may be levied on any form of new building, excepting those not designed for people to enter, such as a machinery-building. It is based on the development created, either by floorspace or number of units, and is a fixed flat-rate charge. It includes both new buildings and extensions to existing buildings over 100 square metres or more of gross internal floor space and is charged on the basis of the square metres of any new floorspace created. This means that any floorspace already existing on the site is discounted from the final levied amount.

The CIL can also be levied where the proposal involves the creation of a new dwelling, regardless of the size.

It is argued that the CIL has a number of important features that differentiate it from planning agreements. A planning agreement is designed to directly off-set the impact and implications of a proposed new development and is therefore primarily focused on the area broadly local to the site. In contrast, the CIL goes into one large LPA pot to be spent on infrastructure demands across the local government area. Importantly, then, the CIL breaks the direct link between the development and the planning gain – a significant and potentially quite controversial step. The amount charged by the CIL must be based on infrastructure needs resulting from all new development within the LPA area, and from this perspective it may be seen as more akin to a development tax.

The CIL is directly linked to the local development plan and the rate is set against the anticipated infrastructure needs resulting from all the planned growth identified within the plan. Based upon the anticipated growth, the 'charging authority' will publish a list of the infrastructure that it believes will be required. These requirements form the 'Regulation 123 List', which is effectively the list of infrastructure spending priorities that the CIL will be used to fund. The Regulation 123 List is subject to full public consultation in much the same way as a local development plan would be and is examined through an independent examiner at public inquiry. The public inquiry is important because it tests the soundness of the spending list and charging schedule. This test of soundness underpins the accountability and integrity of the system. The CIL is intended directly to address some of the concerns levelled at planning agreements, and the use of a public inquiry as part of the process of identifying spending requirements is key. When the negotiated basis of planning gain is set against the fixed and non-negotiable flat-rate fee associated with the CIL, it is easy to see some of the advantages that it potentially provides: namely, clarity, certainty, transparency and rigour.

The level of CIL to be levied by the charging authority is presented in a 'charging schedule', which details the precise amount to be paid. The rate is not necessarily fixed across the whole authority area but is based on development viability on a geographical basis. On a national basis some forms of development are specifically excluded from the CIL, including some self-build projects, development under 100 square metres that is not a whole house, social housing and charitable development and buildings that people do not normally enter, such as machinery buildings. Local variation is also available; thus each LPA is able to establish different rates for different developments and for different areas. The basis of the rate to be set is intended to be a balance between the desire and need to fund infrastructure within an LPA area and the need to levy a rate that is not so high that it could impact upon the viability of development within the council's boundaries.

In some LPA areas the CIL rate could be set at zero for some or all forms of development, due to the circumstances found in that location. In some cases particular forms of development might be set at a zero CIL rate across the entire LPA area, due to issues of viability. Given this fact, and despite some restrictions on how they can be used, planning agreements remain an important mechanism for delivering planning gain on a site-by-site basis. More widely, from the perspective of the relationship between the CIL and planning agreements, the latter remain important for delivering the site requirements. Essentially they are used for affordable housing contributions and development-specific on-site requirements, whereas the CIL is used for wider infrastructure needs.

To conclude, the CIL has many positives attributes, but it is suggested that its introduction represents a missed opportunity for deeper reform. First, planning agreements are still in place, with all of their real and perceived issues. Second, the non-negotiable nature of the CIL means that the nature and form of the resulting development, as well as the remaining planning agreement matters, including affordable housing, can potentially be changed or 'squeezed', due to development viability concerns. The fixed nature of the CIL may be seen as important to the certainty and consistency of the system, but it may also be considered a potential weakness. Planning agreements have the advantage of flexibility and can be negotiated (although this brings its own challenges and perceived limitations), while the CIL is fixed and the system is thus not responsive to circumstance. It remains to be seen how issues of planning gain will be resolved. Perhaps the solution lies in a planning agreement model that is reformed to provide more transparency and integrity so as to create a system with both rigour and flexibility.

Chapter summary

This chapter has contrasted the use of planning conditions and planning gain as ways to facilitate and enable development by mitigating any associated adverse impacts. We have shown how case law has, over time, elaborated tests that qualify and restrict the controls the state may impose on developers through the use of planning conditions. We have noted once again how the principles of proportionality and reasonableness underpin the workings of the planning system. While both planning conditions and planning gain serve the wider, public interest, planning gain may also directly benefit the developer. In contrast, planning conditions tend to be restrictive on the developer in the way that they mitigate impacts. Finally, we contrasted the design and use of individually negotiated planning agreements with the relatively more formulaic and standardised CIL and highlighted the benefits in terms of flexibility versus certainty, private negotiation versus published transparency and development-site relation versus de facto development tax. Most importantly, perhaps, we have reiterated the constructive role that the planning system plays in enhancing societal and environmental outcomes through the development management process.

Further reading

For more legal and technical detail concerning the matters discussed in this chapter, see:

Duxbury, R. (2012) *Telling & Duxbury's planning law and procedure*, 15th edn, Oxford: Oxford University Press, chapter 10.

McMaster, R. and Smith, G. (2013) *Scottish planning law*, London: Bloomsbury Publishing, chapter 6.

Moore, V. and Purdue, M. (2014) *A practical approach to planning law*, 13th edn, Oxford: Oxford University Press, chapter 14.

Some matters discussed in this chapter change regularly. For example, the CIL regulations have been regularly updated since first published. To ensure you have the most up-to-date information, you should consult:

England: Planning Portal (remembering to identify 'England' as your location): http://www.planningportal.gov.uk

Northern Ireland: Planning Portal: https://www.planningni.gov.uk/

Scotland: ePlanning Scotland: https://eplanning.scotland.gov.uk/WAM/

Wales: Town Planning Portal (remembering to identify 'Wales' as your location): http://www.planningportal.gov.uk

EIGHT

Specialist planning arrangements

Chapter contents

- Minerals planning
- Waste planning
- Marine planning
- Chapter summary

Introduction

Thus far we have primarily been concerned with the evolution of statutory planning controls over land and buildings. We have focused on urban development and the built form and related aspects of environmental protection, emphasising the need for proportionate state controls over private interests, based on need (necessity) and improved outcomes. The planning system is intended to serve the wider public interest, including future generations, and development management has a constructive role to play in the design and making of successful places in the immediate and longer term.

This chapter considers the nature of the planning controls exercised over three very particular areas: minerals, waste and the marine environment. Here, bespoke systems have evolved with separate guidance, policy and, in some cases, legislation. Given the specialist nature of these activities, the specific planning law frameworks that exist and the different issues raised, we discuss each of these three areas separately. While this may be seen as adopting a sector-specific approach to addressing particular activities in society, we wish also to show that these activities have become intrinsic to an established way of life and are fundamentally interrelated with how we plan and manage land (and marine) resources.

Society's use of raw materials and marine and coastal environments is an established feature of how we manage and organise our economy in social, cultural and political terms. The UK's particular geology has afforded many opportunities to mine and extract a range of materials, involving both surface and underground activities that can have harsh consequences for the natural environment and landscape quality. Minerals are non-renewable resources and, as we will discuss, minerals planning is a crucial activity if we are to control the extraction of minerals in the public interest. The legacy of mined land also needs to be controlled and managed.

While minerals are critical to the production of many items that we use and consume, the waste created by society is something that is often characterised as requiring means of disposal. Out of sight is out of mind, perhaps, but where should waste-management facilities be sited? How should 'waste' be used? A wider body of environmental law promotes reusing and recycling materials so as to reduce the amount of waste sent to landfill. The concept of the 'circular economy' involves thinking about the production and use of items in terms of a circular process. For example, instead of being thought of as a problem, waste is being socially reconstructed as a potentially valuable resource that can help to serve our energy needs. The planning system plays a fundamental role in supporting innovative ways to better manage finite environmental resources and to protect and improve the land that supports this activity. Moreover, the non-renewable nature of minerals means that it is important to make best use of them. For example, rather than disposing of inert waste construction materials to landfill it is often cheaper and more environmentally sustainable to re-use or recycle them wherever possible. As advocates of the necessity for creating an 'industrial symbiosis criterion' in planning argue (Climate-KIC, 2016), planners also need to think about how best to co-locate compatible industrial uses to make the best use of circular-economy principles.

Finally, by way of introduction, each of the four UK administrations has an extensive coastline, with fishing and coastal communities that rely on the marine environment for their livelihoods. As already discussed, national planning policy guidelines in Scotland were initially introduced to deal with offshore oil and gas extraction and the impacts of landward development. Substantial sand and gravel deposits offshore also provide important sites for mineral extraction. The economic importance of shellfish- and fish-farming has also increased development activity in coastal and marine locations. Competing development pressures and new technologies, for example relating to tidal-power, potentially compromise traditional economic and leisure activities such as fishing. While an offshore wind farm is located out at sea, the physical infrastructure required for the necessary grid connections is land based. The physical development of marinas and growth in cruise tourism bring different socioeconomic impacts, this time in relation to port-related development and the intermittent but substantial consequences of cruise-liner visits to coastal locations McCarthy (2008). How such pressures are managed raises an important set of questions with respect to the effects of new forms of development impact.

Minerals planning

Raw materials are vital to our economy. Over time, and for various reasons, society has extended its use of raw materials such as coal, rock, sand, peat and, more recently, shale gas. These materials form the basis of certain core activities, including the building industry; physical infrastructure needs, including roads; the wider manufacturing industry; and energy. However, the associated extraction works can have severe impacts on our landscapes and natural heritage if not carried out in a controlled manner.

In planning law terms, extracting minerals normally involves an 'invasive' mining, quarrying and or drilling process, although pumping and other mechanical means are sometimes employed. Minerals operations therefore comprise 'development'. As such, planning permission is required before any development takes place. The 'resources' identified on geological maps become 'reserves' once they benefit from planning permission. The controls extend over extraction and related processing activities.

Planning applications for mineral extraction are generally accompanied by an EIA so that the LPA can make an informed decision on the environmental impacts before any development takes place. Dedicated Mineral Planning Authorities (MPAs) are usually based within a county council or unitary authority.

Mineral operations tend to have a precise geography, and mineral planning may be considered relatively unique within the planning system family. Minerals have become central to our way of life and essential to the production of a vast array of goods and to maintaining our style of living and business needs. Mineral 'aggregate' deposits, including sand, gravel and stone, are important and supply identification and management is required. Aggregates form the basis of the bricks, windows and roofing we use for our shelter, with around 60 tonnes of aggregate needed to build an average house (BGS 2016). The metals used in vehicle manufacture and railway tracks and the aggregates forming the roads we drive on support our travel needs. To support our consumption of minerals two factors are important: the fixed location of metals and minerals; and how they are distributed across the country to serve particular market areas. Most minerals are transported to their respective markets via road (railways carry around 11% percent, waterways less than 1%). Due to their bulk and weight they are expensive to haul long distances and so they are generally used within 38 kilometres of their source (CBI, 2011).

Detailed geological maps show where different types of minerals can be found in the UK (British Geological Survey, 2016). The specific locations of different raw resources vary and are often in what are held to be attractive landscapes, such as upland areas for hard rock or lowland river valleys for sand and gravel).

The amounts of aggregates that are required each year are based on *Local Aggregates Assessments* based on 10-year historic sales data. These amounts are then further refined between each MPA by Regional Aggregate Working Parties (RAWP) and the national coordinating group. Each MPA then prepares a statutory development plan, called a Minerals Local Plan, identifying locations for specific types of future mineral working to provide land banks of reserves.

Extracting minerals normally involves an invasive mining, quarrying and or drilling process, although pumping and other mechanical means are sometimes employed. The duration of operations varies from borrow–pits dug for a few months to supply specific development needs close to the point of use, to more extensive workings over many decades supplying a wider market. Minerals development is not just limited to the extractive processes, but also includes the processing and refining of the minerals on site (where these activities are undertaken at the point of extraction), and the subsequent restoration and aftercare of the site.

The removal of mineral deposits, while time limited, is an inherently destructive process that can have significant impacts on the environment and host communities, both human and natural. On the one hand, impacts include noise, dust, vibration, blasting, landscape impact, machinery and/or plant, vehicles, stockpiling, loss of agricultural or forestry land, loss of habitats, flood risk and change of groundwater quality. On the other hand, regulating minerals development has the potential to encourage what may be seen as positive 'new' impacts, for example by creating alternative habitats. The restoration of former gravel pits or quarries may involve the creation of an SSSI. Minerals planning plays an important role in managing this form of development so as to minimise the impacts and improve the outcomes.

Planning for minerals is complex, and research findings and scientific evidence, new technology and evolving environmental protection provide fresh understanding of the issues. In practice, the restrictions placed on older sites may no longer be considered adequate in relation to issues such as noise levels, vibration, dust and hours of working.

Given its likely environmental effects, minerals development is subject to 'special' planning controls, specifically in relation to the need for restoration of the land to a required standard and aftercare condition. In England and Wales it is controlled under the Planning and Compensation Act 1990; in Northern Ireland it is controlled under the Planning Act 2011. In Scotland it was controlled first under the Environment Act 1995; then the Town and Country Planning (Scotland) Act 1997 introduced new procedures to deal with old mining procedures and the problems associated with them, such as their validity and the adequacy of planning controls.

In the late 1990s planning authorities were required (and continue to be required) to review old mineral planning permissions (euphemistically termed 'ROMPs'). The aim was to address the weak levels of control that could be exerted over these permissions. Indeed, certain permissions had been granted under Interim Development Orders in the aftermath of the Second World War, when there was a need for a quick and substantial supply of building materials. The review process makes it possible to apply new conditions to activities ongoing. Reviews can also be used to distinguish active sites from those considered to be dormant. In the latter cases, no further works may be commenced until any required new planning conditions are attached to the site.

Box 8.1: Northern Ireland: extraction of sand and gravel and proximity to a designated AONB

An appeal against the refusal of full planning permission for the extraction of sand and gravel was allowed after the (former) DOE had refused a quarry on the basis of six reasons for refusal. Although the DOE withdrew its objection to the principle of the proposal and the six reasons for refusal, the appeal considered third party objections relating to the effects on rural character, residential amenity, road safety and impact on tourism. It was noted that the site lay within the designated Mourne AONB and within a proposed 'Area of Constraint on Mineral Development' (ACMN) in the draft area plan. The draft designation had already been objected to, however, and could not be applied in advance of the adoption of the emerging plan. The appeal was allowed as it was found that the need for mineral resources greatly outweighed the concerns raised. It was found that the site was not conspicuous from public viewpoints; stockpile levels were to be controlled and less than 10 metres high; and any impacts on visual amenity would be short term (less than two years).

Waste planning

An important goal of planning, alongside other environmental and environmental health legislation, is to control pollution of the air, land and water and to avoid adverse public health impacts. Over time, local and international concerns in relation to waste have led to priority being given to: reducing waste at source; its re-use and recovery by recycling; and its potential as a source of energy. Everyone produces waste as part of daily activities, and waste needs to be managed. An increase in the number of waste-management facilities has focused attention on the need for this work to be carried out in a safe and environmentally acceptable manner. Importantly, then, where planning permission is granted for such developments, planning conditions tend to be attached. The use of conditions is intended to mitigate or compensate for any adverse environmental effects. Here, sustainability principles are key.

Waste management is planned for on the basis of the 'waste hierarchy' (see Box 8.1). In England, the following messages are conveyed:

- don't produce it in the first place ...!
- re-use it (in its current form – repair)
- recycle or compost it (by changing its characteristics)
- recover value from it (energy generation)
- bury or burn it (as a last resort).

Figure 8.1: Guidance on applying the waste hierarchy

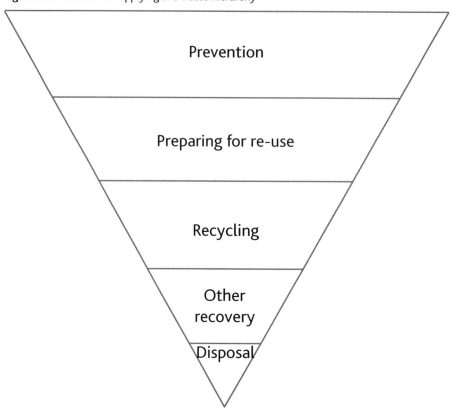

Source: Defra. Contains public sector information licensed under the Open Government Licence v3.0.

The role of the land-use planning system in waste planning is largely to discourage the production of waste; to provide suitable locations for the facilities to manage that waste where it does arise; and to determine planning applications for waste facilities where proposals are put forward by the waste industry.

Planning policy for minerals matters is dealt with slightly differently across the UK, partly as a result of attempts to consolidate guidance. In England, the key national planning policies for minerals are set out in the NPPF (DCLG, 2012) alongside other national policy areas. Similarly, in Wales, PPW (Welsh Government, 2016) includes overarching policy guidance for minerals, supported by dedicated MTANs. In Scotland, the SPP (Scottish Government, 2014b) is the principal source of policy in relation to resource extraction and site restoration, together with the NPF (Scottish Government, 2014a), dedicated statements, supporting guidance and advice. In Northern Ireland, policy and guidance are provided through the SPPS (DOE, 2015), with the Planning Service serving as the Minerals Planning Authority. A Minerals Resources Map of Northern Ireland was published in 2012 to aid developers and investors, inform local development plan preparation and improve the efficiency of processing planning applications.

Waste planning is generally undertaken by county councils in two-tier local government areas or by unitary authorities in single-tier areas. Waste Planning Authorities (WPA) prepare a Waste Local Plan (WLP) for their area, identifying suitable locations for different types of waste-management facility. The WPA also determines planning applications for waste facilities, although there are some specific instances where the LPA in a district council will determine waste-related planning applications. Historically, waste planning is a function that has been undertaken alongside mineral planning, as the impacts of the two forms of development are relatively similar. Moreover, the two activities have potential linkages: for example, the void created by digging minerals out of the ground may be used for the disposal of waste materials. Although international practice varies, alternatives to land-filling are now actively sought in the UK, due to the 'costs' of disposal in economic, environmental and social terms.

Local councils are responsible for the collection of household waste, comprising around 14% of the total waste that is produced annually in the UK (DEFRA, 2015), while the actual disposal and/or recycling of waste is undertaken by the waste industry. Other waste 'streams' include commercial/industrial waste (24%), construction/demolition waste (50%) and hazardous waste. There are overlaps between these streams. In addition, there are agricultural wastes and mining or quarry wastes, although these forms of waste are usually handled onsite and therefore often do not enter the waste-management process and planning for specific off-site processing facilities tends not to be required.

Around 44% of the household waste that arises in the UK is recycled (DEFRA, 2012). Under EU Waste Framework Directive (2008/98/EC) it is intended that this figure be increased. Such thinking seeks to ensure the provision of facilities that are capable of diverting waste from disposal, including materials-recovery operations and anaerobic digestion plants. The haulage of waste is relatively costly, so there need to be a range of facilities close to the source. Bulking-up and transfer stations may also be required in the management of waste

To reduce the amount of waste entering the waste-management process, LPAs (that is, not just those responsible for waste planning) can place conditions on planning permissions requiring waste management to be undertaken on site during construction or demolition phases. Other conditions may relate to the provision of waste recycling boxes and composting bin storage during the period of the building's occupation.

Detailed advice may be provided in dedicated guidance. For example, Gloucestershire County Council's (2006) supplementary planning document *Waste minimisation in development* (incorporating reduction, re-use and recycling requirements) was endorsed by the six district council planning authorities within its administrative area. The document instructs that waste is to be managed in accordance with the waste hierarchy unless it can be demonstrated that an alternative approach is more environmentally sound. It defines waste minimisation as not producing waste in the first place and reducing the quantity of waste that needs processing or disposal. The document sets out a two-level approach.

Applicants for planning permission for major development (for example 10+ dwellings) must prepare and submit a Waste Minimisation Statement to accompany the application. Planning applications for all other developments need to abide by the principles of waste management.

Box 8.2: A pile of old poultry rubbish?

In 2013 the (former) DOE refused a very high-profile and long-running planning application for a major chicken-litter incinerator near Glenavy on the shores of Lough Neagh in Northern Ireland. Rose Energy wanted to build a £100 million biomass burner that would use poultry litter and meat- and bone-meal as fuel. This would produce a 30MW capacity of electricity as an output of the incineration process, and would create a number of jobs. The poultry industry lobbied strongly in favour of the project, but locals fought a campaign against it. After a long legal battle the DOE issued its planning decision, refusing approval. The Environment Minister said it had been a 'complex planning application' but that environmental and other impacts had outweighed the economic arguments.

In terms of development management, the decision notice provided the following reasons for refusal under four different Planning Policy Statements (PPS) (that is, prior to the creation of the SPPS):

- PPS21 'Sustainable Development in the Countryside': if permitted the proposal would result in detrimental change to the rural character of the area and would be unduly prominent, creating an unacceptable visual impact in the landscape.
- PPS11 'Planning and Waste Management': the proposal would be incompatible with the character of the area and would harm the living conditions of the residents by its visual impact and increasing heavy goods vehicular movements.
- PPS18 'Renewable Energy', the proposal would create an unacceptable impact on visual amenity.
- PPS1 'General Principles': the proposal would cause demonstrable harm and would be incompatible with existing industry in the area.

Interestingly, none of the refusal reasons was linked to the environmental grounds on which most objectors had lobbied.

Marine planning

Experience from land-based (terrestrial) planning is helping to inform the design of emerging marine planning processes. Indeed, some argue that planning and managing the marine resource can be undertaken in similar ways to land-use planning. For example, particular emphasis is placed on promoting sustainable development; facilitating appropriate stakeholders and public engagement; and devising a plan-led approach to inform individual development decisions in a coordinated, coherent, integrated and consistent way. However, similarities between the land and marine environments are contested. In contrast to land, the marine environment is relatively more dynamic and offers different types of goods and services that are not fixed. When thinking about the multi-dimensional nature of the marine resource, we need to consider the sea bed (for mineral extraction or pipe-lines, for example), the water column (in relation to the marine ecosystem and potential pharmaceutical opportunities, for instance); and the surface (in terms of supporting activities, such as different means of transportation or floating security devices). Marine wildlife and seabirds often combine use of the sea and its associated air space. Taking these factors together, it is thus necessary to balance development, protection and conservation in an integrated way, taking account of interrelated spaces and media.

The introduction of statutory powers to create marine plans at different scales is an important development for the ability to manage the very different marine environments and coastal areas around the UK (see Chapter Four). Marine activities are principal contributors to the UK and global economy in terms of culture, employment and quality of life (DEFRA, 2007). In 2013 the combined direct contribution to GDP of the UK's maritime services sector (ports, shipping and maritime commercial businesses) alone totalled some £9.9 billion gross value added, with some 219,400 people directly employed (Oxford Economics, 2015). These figures were considered 'conservative', as they 'excluded North Sea oil and gas extraction, the manufacture of marine equipment and the naval defence industry' (Oxford Economics, 2015, p 2). Moreover, while they are significant for trade and commerce, the UK seas are also unique in terms of rare and declining species (Claydon, 2006). The requirements of migratory birds and fish add a further dynamic. However, devising a single integrated regulatory and governance system poses a significant challenge (Kidd and Shaw, 2014), since the volume, nature and range of sectors and temporal patterns of marine activities vary significantly. As with air, the management of water involves transboundary issues, since the seas are a fluid medium: marine planning demands cross-jurisdictional cooperation.

Natural processes of coastal erosion and sediment accretion may be more or less discernible. On occasion, coastal settlements are subject to environmental degradation from pollution and oil spills. The threats of severe infrastructure damage in relation to railway lines or nuclear power facilities situated on the coastal plain, or the managed retreat of homeowners from certain coastal-edge locations, have drawn attention to the need for appropriate development management at the coast (Duck, 2011). Previously the sea was less well understood and there was a sense in which we planned for the marine environment with our backs to the sea (GAUFRE, 2006). Today, planning needs to be more sensitive to climate change, sea-level rise, more intensive storms and coastal flooding and to consider these aspects as material in new regeneration masterplans, for example (Peel and

Lloyd, 2013). Taking a social–ecological approach effectively means integrating different systems such as river basin management, coastal regeneration and coastal defence with a view to improving the resilience of places (Lloyd et al, 2013).

In Chapter Four we set out the UK–wide, national and regional plan–making arrangements for marine planning. Deriving their legal basis from the Marine and Coastal Access Act 2009 and the respective marine legislation in Scotland and Northern Ireland, the new plans provide the context for the exercise of a range of controls, including licensing and the operation of particular sectors such as offshore energy. Here, we focus on the landward implications of offshore development, since most operational or use developments in the marine environment also have an onshore impact and alignment between marine and terrestrial planning is therefore key. Efforts are needed to ensure that a proactive and reciprocal relationship, based on cooperation, is developed whereby local (land-based) development plans and marine plans have a mutual regard. Marine planning is at a relatively early stage and changes are imminent; it is perhaps one of the most exciting areas to watch for new developments in planning law.

Box 8.3: Development of a new mussel farm

In 2016 Shetland Islands Council received an application to develop a new mussel-farm comprising six 220-metre twin-headed longlines. The site address was given as North of Papa, Little Swarbacks, Minn.

The application was duly advertised as part of the statutory procedure in the *Shetland Times*. Consultations were undertaken with Environmental Health, Ports and Harbours Operations, the community council, the RSPB, Crown Estate, Marine Scotland Science, Northern Lighthouse Board, Scottish Natural Heritage, Shetland Amenity Trust, Shetland Shellfish Management Organisation and the Shetland Fishermen's Association. The latter raised an objection to the location of the proposed mussel farm, since the site was heavily fished for lobsters and velvet crabs. Negotiation with the developer led to the site being moved 20 metres north of the original development location within the red box boundary. This overcame the objection.

The plan-led system demands that determination of planning applications should take into account relevant policy and other material considerations. The proposed development was considered in the light of the Shetland Local Development Plan 2014; Shetland Council's Interim Policy for Marine Aquaculture 2007; Supplementary Guidance Shetland Islands' Marine Spatial Plan 2015; and Scotland's National Marine Plan 2015. The application was dealt with under delegated powers.

The proposal complied with the relevant policies. It was considered that the mussel farm could be accommodated without having an unacceptable detrimental impact on the built and natural environments. The proposed development was therefore granted permission, subject to conditions and reasons. These may be summarised as relating to (i) development in accordance with the approved plans (unless otherwise approved) for the avoidance of doubt; (ii) submission of the Notice of Initiation of Development to comply with pre-commencement procedures; (iii) the site being clearly marked with buoys and lights to ensure safe navigation; (iv) colouring surface buoys and floats black, blue or grey (other than those required for navigational safety) to minimise the visual impact of the development; (v) where necessary, the use of non-lethal and non-destructive predator control measures in the interest of protecting wildlife in the area; (vi) a requirement to repair, make good, move or destroy any parts of the development that might become damaged or redundant, for reasons of navigational safety; and (vi) where operational use ceased (that is, for a period exceeding three years), the removal of the longlines, anchors and associated apparatus for the growing of shellfish and restoration of the site to the satisfaction of the LPA, to ensure the site does not become a navigational hazard or cause marine litter.

We have seen that conditions are subject to six tests. Other important and relevant guidance to assist the developer may be given in the form of advisory information. The decision letter included a number of notes in relation to the commencement of works; the use of anti-predator netting; disease control; marine licensing; seabed lease; the equipment deployed; and completion of the development.

Details of the application, accompanying documentation and permission (2016/014/MAR) are available through Shetland Islands Council's e-planning online simple search tool.

Chapter summary

In discussing three specialist areas of planning we have seen how the exercise of controls over development has expanded. Controls may be considered necessary as the precise impacts of development are recognised, or be driven by the effects of cumulative development. Despite the particular intricacies of these areas, the basic principles of planning law apply and a similar process is followed. For instance, interest in marine planning is expanding, requiring a range of specialist expertise to be synthesised and balanced. The above example of the mussel farm usefully illustrates some of the development management aspects of planning in inshore areas, where terrestrial controls over the marine environment exist. The case highlights the widening remit of the development plan context, since it was determined in the light of land and marine plans at various scales, and the proposed development was considered following the plan-led approach. The range of conditions imposed on the planning permission highlights the different types of consideration to be taken into account by terrestrial planners in marine contexts. As new forms of technological development come forward, in relation to communications and energy, for example, other material considerations will likely come to the fore, necessitating a wider range of professionals and interests to engage with the planning system.

Recommended reading

For more on minerals, see, for example:

Moore, V. and Purdue, M. (2014) *A practical approach to planning law*, 13th edn, Oxford: Oxford University Press, chapter 17.

For an overview of planning issues in relation to fracking, see:

Department for Energy and Climate Change (2014) *Fracking UK shale: Planning permission and communities*, London: DECC. Available at: https://www.gov.uk/government/uploads/system/uploads/attachment_data/file/283832/Planning_v3.pdf [Accessed: 27 July 2016]

For more on England's national waste policy, see:

DCLG (2014) *National planning policy for waste*, London: DCLG. Available at: https://www.gov.uk/government/uploads/system/uploads/attachment_data/file/364759/141015_National_Planning_Policy_for_Waste.pdf [Accessed: 27 July 2016]

For further information on marine planning in the UK, see:

Ritchie, H. and Ellis, G. (2009) *Across the waters. Implementation of the UK Marine and Coastal Access Act and devolved marine legislation, cross-border case studies: The North Channel*, Belfast: Queen's University Belfast for WWF, pp 1–14.

The following websites are relevant:

England: https://www.gov.uk/government/collections/marine-planning-in-england
Northern Ireland: https://www.daera-ni.gov.uk/articles/marine-plan-northern-ireland
Scotland: http://www.gov.scot/Topics/marine/seamanagement
Wales: http://gov.wales/topics/environmentcountryside/marineandfisheries/marine-planning/?lang=en

NINE

Other forms of planning control and consent

<table>
<tr><td>

Chapter contents

- Listed buildings
- Conservation areas
- Ancient monuments and areas of archaeological importance
- Outdoor advertisements
- Trees and hedges
- Chapter summary

</td></tr>
</table>

Introduction

We have noted so far that planning is one regulatory tool, among others, used to manage urban, rural and, more recently, marine developments, while other statutory controls enable related professions to address issues of environmental health or building standards, traffic or navigational safety. Our primary focus in this book is the legal controls over development as defined in legislation and through case law. Certain forms of development, such as waste, minerals and marine planning are controlled by specific legislation. Here we turn our attention to other development management aspects of the built heritage and examine controls over listed buildings, conservation areas, ancient monuments and advertisements. Looking at the wider environment, we also consider development controls over trees and hedges.

Listed buildings

Specific planning controls exist for buildings of special architectural or historic interest. Listed Building Consent (LBC) prevents the unrestricted demolition, alteration or extension of a listed building without consent from the LPA (Moore, 2010). By their very nature, buildings and structures that are listed are considered very valuable and sensitive. They may be of national or local significance. If they are demolished, they are lost forever. In earlier discussion of what does and does not constitute development we noted that internal alterations and some types of demolition do not require the formal submission of a planning application. In the case of listed buildings, however, such actions could be harmful. With this in mind, LBC allows for the comprehensive management of a fuller range of controls. Stated very simply, any alteration beyond 'like-for-like replacement' or 'care and repair' requires LBC.

In England and Wales the legislation relating to LBC is the Planning (Listed Buildings and Conservation Areas) Act 1990. Elsewhere in the UK it is the Planning (Listed Buildings) Regulations (Northern Ireland) 2015 and the Planning (Listed Buildings and Conservation Areas) (Scotland) Act 1997. Certain differences apply in relation to terminology, notably in Scotland, but the broad principles are very similar.

Listing

The overarching basis upon which buildings are identified for listing is the architectural and historical interest of the building, and the selection of buildings to be listed is based upon set criteria. These criteria vary marginally across the devolved UK. In Scotland, the *Historic Environment Scotland Policy Statement* (HES, 2016) stipulates:

- age and rarity
- architectural or historic interest
- close historical association.

In England, Wales and Northern Ireland the criteria are grouped and phrased a little differently. Below we also highlight some of the thinking behind the criteria:

- age and rarity – the older a building is, the fewer surviving examples of its kind and the more likely its special interest;
- aesthetic merits – the appearance of the building: its intrinsic and architectural merit;
- selectivity – listing can be a comparative exercise and needs to be selective where a substantial number of buildings of a similar type and quality survive;
- national interest – the most significant or distinctive buildings regionally that contribute to the national historic stock;
- state of repair – this is *not* a relevant consideration.

Buildings are classified in three grades. In England and Wales the following distinctions exist:

- Grade I buildings are of exceptional interest
- Grade II* buildings are particularly important buildings of more than special interest
- Grade II buildings are of special interest, warranting every effort to preserve them (most listed buildings fall within this grade).

In Northern Ireland, and similar to England and Wales, the following three categories apply:

- Grade A: special buildings of national importance including both outstanding grand buildings and the fine, little-altered examples of some important style or date;
- Grade B+: special buildings that might have merited A status, but for relatively minor detracting features such as impurities of design or lower-quality additions or alterations;
- Grade B1 and B2: special buildings of more local importance or good examples of some period or style. Some degree of alteration or imperfection may be acceptable.

In Scotland, again three categories exist:

- Category A: buildings of national or international importance or representing little-altered examples of some particular period, style or building type;
- Category B: buildings of more than local importance, or examples of some particular period, style or building type which may have been altered;
- Category C: buildings of local importance and constituting lesser examples of any period, style, or building type.

The grading or categorisation does not reflect a difference in the degree of protection that exists legally but it does denote the status (and perceived value) of the building and, as such, there will be a difference in how alterations may be pursued by a developer. A higher grading may affect the difficulty, or likelihood, of obtaining LBC, or the finance available to carry out works to the building. Listed buildings may have their listed status withdrawn, for example following a fire or through discovery of new evidence that demonstrates that the original listing decision can no longer be supported, but it is rare for a Grade I or Category A structure to be granted consent for demolition.

What can be listed

In thinking about listing, we need to return to our discussion of the definition of a 'building' from the Town and Country Planning Act 1990 (1997 in Scotland). This definition refers to: any structure, erection, and any part of a building. In practice, then, the term 'building' as defined in the legislation may include lamp-posts, water-troughs, bridges, tunnels, urinals – that is, every 'part of a building'. In other words, both internal and external 'parts' of the building may be listed.

Furthermore, the qualification of the meaning of 'building' means that any object or structure that is fixed to the building or any object or structure within the curtilage of a building or that forms part of the land can be controlled as development. A two-fold legal test has been laid down to determine whether an article may be considered a fixture. This involves considering first, the degree to which the fixture has been annexed to the building, and second, the purpose of its attachment. A building that is listed is therefore protected in quite an extensive way.

It is a criminal offence to demolish or alter a listed building or any part of it without LPA authorisation, unless it can be proved that the works to the building were urgently needed in the interests of health and safety or for the preservation of the building, in which case the demolition would be only partial. Even in the case of urgent minimal works or measures, however, one must be able to show that it was not otherwise practicable to secure public safety or health, or to preserve the building by repair works. Large fines, and potentially imprisonment, may result from undertaking works without consent, since such action is a criminal offence. Moreover, the offence is one of strict liability, meaning that the prosecution does not have to prove that the defendant was aware that the building was listed in order to establish criminal liability.

Box 9.1: The Schimizu case

With the definition of 'development' in mind, under the Town and Country Planning Acts across the UK the issue of demolition or alteration is not always clear. It is important to consider the whole of the building, as demonstrated in *Schimizu UK Ltd v Westminster City Council [1997] JPL 523*. Here it was held that partial demolition will be regarded as an alteration rather than demolition. Despite this decision, substantive demolition of a listed building should be treated as total demolition of the building. In addition, it is important to look not only at the physical scale but also at the quality of the building to be demolished and the part's contribution to the listed building as a whole.

Across the UK, Authorities have the power to Grant LBC. If you plan to demolish, make alterations or to change anything that may affect the special character of a listed building, it is generally advisable to consult the following national amenity bodies, which can provide expert advice in relation to that part of the UK, namely: in England, Historic England; in Wales, Cadw, the Welsh Government's historic environment service; in Scotland, Historic Environment Scotland; in Northern Ireland, the Historic Environment within the (new) DfC.

Box 9.2: The Georgians didn't have uPVC

An appeal was dismissed against a refusal of LBC for the installation of white uPVC double-glazed windows in a listed building in County Fermanagh. The main issue of the appeal was whether the proposed alteration was sympathetic to the essential character of the listed building. PPS6, *Planning, Archaeology and the Built Heritage* (that is, prior to the SPPS) stated that listed building consent would be granted for alterations only where three criteria were all met: (i) the essential character would remain intact and unimpaired; (ii) sympathetic building materials were used; and (iii) the architectural details matched or were in keeping with the building. The Commissioner stated that the windows of this particular property were an intrinsic part of the character of the building and that the loss of double-hung Georgian windows represented an unacceptable loss of a special feature and the appearance would not be in keeping with the architectural integrity and character and appearance of the listed building. The proposal failed to meet all three of the essential criteria. The proposed works were found to be unacceptable and contrary to planning policy in that they would have had an unacceptable impact on the listed building.

Obtaining LBC

Applications for LBC are made to the LPA. It is not possible to obtain outline LBC, so it is important for a sufficient degree of detail to be included in the application. A higher-level planning authority also has call-in powers; in England, for example, the Secretary of State can make a decision on an application. The right to appeal is available for non-determination of an application within eight weeks. In determining an application the LPA must have regard to the desirability of preserving the building, or its setting, or any features of special architectural or historic interest.

The use of conditions

As with other forms of planning permission, LBC can be granted subject to conditions. These may require the preservation of particular features of the building; or involve making good any damage caused to the building; or require the reconstruction of the building following the execution of any works. Time limits may also be imposed. An LBC may be associated with another planning application, for example where a change of use is involved. In order to prevent a 'building' (understood in its widest sense) being demolished prematurely, planning permission has to be granted for the proposed redevelopment before demolition can take place. Appeals on the refusal of LBC, or on conditions attached to an approval, can be made to the various appeals bodies: PINS or, on rare occasions, the Secretary of State (England and Wales); the PAC (Northern Ireland); or the Planning and Environmental Appeals Division of the Scottish Government. (See also Chapter Ten regarding appeals).

Due to the criminal nature of carrying out unauthorised works to a listed building, the LPA may issue a listed building enforcement notice, without the related stop-notice that is usually required if works are on-going. Enforcement action can be taken irrespective of who carried out the works. There is no time limitation for the serving of a Listed Building Enforcement Notice (see Chapter Ten).

If a non-listed building appears to be in danger of demolition, or of alteration that could affect its special architectural or historic interest, a Building Preservation Notice (BPN) may be served by an LPA (or national park authority), which acts as a temporary listing. Once a BPN has been issued it becomes a criminal offence to carry out alterations or demolition without obtaining LBC. The BPN protects the building for six months, which is intended to provide sufficient time to assess the building more fully. Separate to a BPN is 'spot listing', where a building can be added directly to the public register.

Conservation areas

Certain areas within a council area may be identified as having special architectural or historic interest, or an appearance that it is considered desirable to preserve or enhance. The LPA can therefore pursue a statutory process to delineate a 'conservation area'. A conservation area is not afforded the same degree of legal protection as listed buildings, but this status does provide an additional layer of protection with respect to particularly sensitive areas where development may be proposed. Within a conservation area additional protection also exists in relation to matters such as permitted development rights.

Central to the management of conservation areas is the need to preserve or enhance the character of the area. In *Steinberg v Secretary of State for the Environment (1988) 58 P&CR 453* the initial decision of the Inspector was quashed, due to the precise wording used in relation to the purpose and intention of conservation areas. The rephrasing was relatively subtle. Nevertheless, the High Court made it clear that the duty imposed by the Listed Building and Conservation Area Act 1990 was 'to pay special attention to the desirability of preserving or enhancing the character or appearance of the Conservation Area'. Any deviation from this is unacceptable. The view expressed in this case turned on the desirability of taking a positive step in preserving or enhancing a conservation area. The case was about whether the proposed development would 'harm' the character of the conservation area.

Conservation area status gives the LPA considerable powers over use and development. Moreover, the LPA has broad discretion to determine which parts should be preserved or enhanced. Nonetheless, conservation area status cannot be used to protect one individual building from demolition (see *R (on the application of Arndale Properties Ltd) v Worcester City Council [2008] JPL 1583*). It was noted that the Court will strike down a decision to designate a conservation area if this is simply a pretext to prevent the demolition of a specific building.)

Preserving or enhancing the character or appearance of a conservation area is the crux of development management decisions. Proposals for change must demonstrate either a positive contribution to preservation or that development leaves the character or appearance unharmed.

Where the demolition of an unlisted building is proposed in a conservation area, the LPA will require the redevelopment of the site so as to prevent the site lying vacant and detracting from the general character and appearance of the area. Demolition will not be allowed to take place until a contract for redevelopment has been entered into and planning permission received. The landmark Schimizu case (see Box 9.1) established that consent is required only for the total or substantial demolition of an unlisted building in a conservation area, and not for minor alternations.

Given the sensitivity of certain conservation areas, it is sometimes the case that Article 4 Directions are put in place in addition to conservation areas status. This allows the LPA to exercise controls over very minor development. For example, an LDO may be used to prevent the replacement of wooden windows with plastic (something that might otherwise be possible through permitted development rights even in a conservation area), in the interests of preserving the character and appearance of the area.(See also Chapter Six for further information on Article 4 Directions and LDOs).

In Scotland, Wales and Northern Ireland an additional layer of control to that in England exists through conservation area consents. Such consent is required in order to undertake some works of demolition. This power existed historically in England but has since been removed and was replaced in 2013 with a requirement for planning permission for demolition of a building. This measure was intended to reduce duplication and simplify the system.

Ancient monuments and areas of archaeological importance

Since 1882 statutory protection has been awarded to ancient monuments. For England, Scotland and Wales, the Ancient Monument and Archaeological Areas Act 1979 S. 61(7), and for Northern Ireland section 2(6)(a) of the Historic Monuments and Archaeological Objects (NI) Order 1995, define a monument as: 'any building, structure or work, whether above or below the surface of the land, and any cave or excavation'. Under the legislation monuments are to be added to a schedule. This involves compiling a list, the schedule, of monuments which were deemed to be of national importance. Although the majority of scheduled monuments are on land, some are under the sea.

Scheduled ancient monuments are considered to be of public interest by reason of their historic, architectural, traditional, artistic or archaeological interest. Well-known scheduled monuments include Stonehenge, the Tower of London and Hadrian's Wall. In England, the Secretary of State maintains a 'schedule of monuments' setting out what is included and if it is of national importance. In Scotland the criteria are set out by Scottish ministers in Scottish Historic Environment Policy. Historic Environment Scotland then compiles and maintains the schedule, assessing which monuments are of national importance and identifying any buildings that should be added.

It is a criminal offence to execute works to a scheduled monument without gaining scheduled monument consent. Works refers to demolition, destruction, damage, alterations, flooding or tipping operations, such as tipping soil or spoil or depositing building or other materials or matter (including waste materials or refuse) on any land.

The Secretary of State has the power compulsorily to acquire any ancient monument for the purpose of securing its preservation. In addition, s/he is given power to acquire an ancient monument by agreement or gift. Alternatively, an ancient monument can be taken into guardianship for control and management by the Secretary of State without disturbing the ownership of the monument.

The 1979 Act also designates five city-centre areas of archaeological importance, namely: Canterbury, Chester, Exeter, Hereford and York. Although no form of specific consent is required, these historic city centres are afforded extra protection. For example, utility companies usually benefit from permitted development rights, but in areas of archaeological importance even work that would likely result in ground disturbance, such as pipe laying, is controlled. The controls mean that investigation and recording can take place prior to and during such works.

More generally, archaeological remains are an important part of our cultural heritage. The redevelopment of brownfield sites offers the potential for excavation, therefore in specific cases , development may be refused or a condition or legal agreement may be imposed to enable investigations to be carried out prior to the development itself being undertaken, or certain protective measures may be put in place. This may include a watching brief. The *Neighbourhood Planning and Infrastructure Bill* 2016 identifies changing pre-commencement planning conditions. The argument for this is that such conditions can potentially hold up development. In the case of archaeological investigations in advance of new building work, however, the use of archaeological conditions is of paramount importance. The ideas set out in the proposed Bill illustrate how efforts designed to improve the planning system can have unintended potentially negative consequences, further justifying the need for professional judgement and discretion to be exercised on a case-by-case basis. Marine archaeology, such as wrecks, benefits from separate protection.

Outdoor advertisements

Outdoor advertisements have a bespoke planning system, but it is one with strong parallels to the conceptual approach employed in 'mainstream' planning. There are similar arrangements in place across the devolved UK in relation to this consent-based system. Though amended in some cases, the main legislation is as follows:

- England: Town and Country Planning (Control of Advertisements) (England) Regulations 2007
- Wales: The Town and Country Planning (Control of Advertisements) Regulations 1992
- Scotland: Town and Country Planning (Control of Advertisements) (Scotland) Regulations 1984
- Northern Ireland: Planning (Control of Advertisements) Regulations. (Northern Ireland) 2015.

Some forms of advertisement are 'excluded from control', others benefit from 'deemed consent' and yet others require 'express consent'. In dealing with express consent the LPA may refuse or grant consent, in whole or in part, subject to certain standard conditions and any other conditions as deemed necessary. Although this consent process is slightly different to the system for obtaining planning permission, it is not as complicated as one might think. In some ways, it mirrors the proportionality hierarchy discussed in Chapter Six (see Figure 6.1). Although the two systems are legally different, conceptually they are similar in some respects (Figure 9.1).

Figure 9.1: Advertisement consent: parallels with the planning system

The display of advertisements is controlled on the basis of two considerations: the potential danger to public safety; and amenity. It is not the aim of the legislation to censor other matters, such as the content of the advertisement.

Factors relating to public safety include aspects such as the safety of persons using any highway, railway, waterway or aerodrome; or whether the display of the advertisement is likely to obscure the interpretation of any traffic sign or aid to navigation, or the operation of any device used for the purpose of security or surveillance or for measuring the speed of a vehicle.

Factors relating to amenity include matters such as the presence of any feature of historic, architectural, cultural or similar interest.

The term 'advertisement' has a very wide definition, covering words, letters, models, signs, placards, notices, awnings and blinds. Advertisements can be illuminated or not. The definition also extends to hoardings and similar structures, such as rotating poster panels designed for advertisements and other devices principally used or designed for use for advertisements. As such, advertisement controls also cover objects such as gantries, pylons or free-standing drums used in shopping-centres.

Fly-posting is not defined in planning law, but posters relating to events or market produce that are pasted onto buildings and street furniture without the consent of the owner are considered to be advertisements. The activity is difficult to control, due to the need to collect the necessary evidence, and prosecutions are thus problematic. More recently, fly-tipping has been included under the Anti-Social Behaviour Act 2003 in England and Wales, Anti-Social Behaviour etc (Scotland) Act 2004, and Anti-social Behaviour (Northern Ireland) Order 2004, where the LPA can issue a penalty notice.

Area-based controls can also be applied in relation to advertisements. In the same way that conservation areas or AONBs can enable additional protection for an area, so, too, can Special Protection Areas (SPAs). An SPA classification has a similar effect to the removal of permitted development rights. Drawing again on the parallels with the hierarchy of proportionality, matters that would otherwise have 'deemed consent' require 'express consent'. Table 9.1 differentiates between those advertisements that are excluded from control and those that benefit from deemed consent.

Three final points merit highlighting in relation to outdoor advertisements. First, advertisement consents are time limited. Given the dynamic nature of environments, they are fixed to expire after five years (or some other time period prescribed by the LPA), so as to allow for review. After the time period has lapsed, advertisements benefit from 'deemed consent' for continued display in the absence of the LPA's intervention. This arrangement ensures that neither developers nor those operating the system are hampered by unnecessary applications.

Second, as with listed buildings and conservation areas, the process involves obtaining consent, rather than permission. This distinction reflects the legal status of advertisement controls. Failure to obtain consent to display an advertisement constitutes an offence. As we discuss in Chapter Ten on enforcement, this differs from other forms of planning, where it is only the failure to comply with enforcement action that results in an offence being committed.

Finally, in relation to enforcement, the LPA can require the removal of any advertisement displayed that contravenes the regulations in force (with the advertiser effectively being guilty of an offence). Care needs to be taken. For example, it was found in *Kingston upon Thames RBC v National Solus Sites Ltd [1994] JPL 251* that where different posters were displayed on hoardings located in different sites without consent, each display constituted a separate and different offence. The fines imposed for illegal advertisements vary, and the LPA may decide not to prosecute. However, it may decide to take remedial action, as in the case of fly-posting.

Table 9.1: Arrangements for advertisement control

Excluded from control	Deemed consent	Express consent
• Advert on a vehicle normally used as a vehicle • Advert incorporated into the fabric of a building • An advert on something for sale • Elections • Traffic signage • Some flags • Advert inside a building	• Adverts by government departments • Notices advertising that a profession, business or trade is being carried out at a premise (e.g. doctor's, dentist's) • Adverts relating to religious or educational facilities; hotels, inns, public houses, B&Bs • Some temporary advertisements • Certain illuminated adverts on business premises • Certain (other) adverts on business premises • Some (other) flags	• Other forms of advertisement

---

Box 9.3: Display of signage on a listed building in a conservation area

An application for advertisement consent on a Category B listed building within the Dundee Central Conservation Area comprised a number of individual elements, including illuminated façade-mounted and glass-mounted signs, as well as menu-boxes, a brass plaque and lettering incorporated into a canopy to be displayed above the main entrance. The signage comprised the company's corporate lettering, using a uniform design and a variety of sizes. The lettering was to be illuminated individually. The site history was relevant in terms of related alterations undertaken as part of the hotel's refurbishment. Moreover, the application for advertisement consent was in parallel with an application to the LPA for listed building consent for the display of signage and installation of external lighting and closed-circuit television (under the separate planning arrangements).

The relevant development plan policies to be considered concerned design issues in relation not only to the advertisements, but to the building's listed status and siting in a conservation area. The application was subject to a statutory advertisement in the *Evening Telegraph* as a development affecting a conservation area. In line with the advertisement regulations, controls could be exercised only in the interests of (i) amenity and (ii) public safety. The scheme was also considered under the Planning (Listed Buildings and Conservation Areas) (Scotland) Act 1997. The application was granted because it was considered that the proposed signage would not adversely impact on the level of amenity and the special interest of the surrounding historic environment, or on the level of safety afforded to pedestrians and road users.

Details of the application, accompanying documentation and permission (13/00136/ADV) are available through Dundee City Council's e-planning online simple search tool.

Trees and hedges

Why we need to be concerned about trees

Trees can have high amenity value and make an important contribution to the environment around us by creating a varied and interesting landscape. They help to define the character of an area and can help create a sense of place. They can also help to screen and integrate development. They also provide a habitat for wildlife and contribute to the health and well-being of humans (DOE, 2011).

Tree Preservation Orders

The planning system seeks to protect and encourage the planting of 'trees' by placing a duty on LPAs to give provision to the preservation or planting of trees by way of condition(s) on planning permissions. There is no statutory definition of a tree but, as helpfully pointed out by Justice Philips in *Bullock v Secretary of State for the Environment (1980) P & CR 246 at 251*, anything that might reasonably be called a tree is a tree.

Other case law provides some further clarification on this matter, such as in *Kent CC v Batchelor (1976) 33 P & CR 185 (CA)*, where Lord Denning states that a tree should be over 7 or 8 inches in bole diameter. This comment, however, was *obiter* (said in passing) and a common-sense approach is generally applied.

Tree Preservation Orders (TPOs) are a key tool to manage trees considered to be of value. The TPO system is used as a means of control in the interests of amenity in relation to either particular trees or areas of woodland. A TPO can specify the prohibition of cutting down, topping, lopping, uprooting, wilful damage or wilful destruction of trees, except with consent of the LPA.

The law on trees and TPOs

LPAs encourage good tree management. TPO legislation is contained in Part VIII of the Town and Country Planning (Tree Preservation) (England) Regulations 2012 and Part 6 of the Localism Act 2011, which concerns the law on time limits for proceedings into non-compliance with TPOs. In Wales, the legislation to make provision for a TPO is set out in the Town and Country Planning (Trees) (Regulations) 1999. This has been amended by the Town and Country Planning (Tree) (Amendment) (Wales) Regulations 2012, to make changes to the form and content of the application for a TPO. In Scotland, S. 160(1) of the Town and Country Planning (Scotland) Act 1997 gives powers to the LPA to make TPOs. The Town and Country Planning (Tree Preservation Orders and Trees in Conservation Areas) (Scotland) Regulations 2010 make provisions for the form of a TPO, and other stipulations such as a requirement for the submission of a map with the position of the tree. In Northern Ireland all of the legislation is contained within Chapter 3 S. 121–S. 128 of the Planning Act (Northern Ireland) 2011, which sets out the powers afforded to councils to make TPOs.

TPOs are imposed in order to protect selected trees or woodland if their removal is likely to have a significant impact on the local environment and its enjoyment by the public. A TPO cannot prohibit the cutting down or uprooting of trees where they have become dangerous, or where actions are considered necessary for the abatement of a nuisance or the carrying out of development for which full planning permission has been granted. Moreover, there must be imminent damage, not pure encroachment of roots and branches into adjoining land.

The process for putting a TPO in place can be initiated by the LPA or by a member of the public. It is a criminal offence to cut down, lop, top, uproot or wilfully damage a protected tree in a manner likely to destroy it, without consent. On summary conviction, significant fines can be levied.

The following criteria are important when assessing the merits of a TPO:

- *Potential threat* – priority will be given to the protection of those trees deemed to be at immediate risk from active felling, or damage from development on site.
- *Visibility* – the extent to which the trees or woodlands can be seen by the general public will inform the assessment of whether the impact on the local environment is significant.
- *Individual impact* – the mere fact that a tree is publicly visible will not itself be sufficient to warrant a TPO. The tree's particular importance will be assessed by reference to its size and form. Its future potential as an amenity should also be assessed, taking into account any special factors, such as its screening value or contribution to the character or appearance of an area.
- *Wider impact* – the trees in their local surroundings will also be assessed, taking into account how suitable they are to their particular setting, as well as the presence of other trees in the vicinity.
- *Historical importance* – this may also be relevant for certain trees because of their age and association with the setting of listed buildings, or the contribution they make to the special character of a conservation area.
- *Rarity* – this may be important where a tree or trees require protection, although priority will reflect the rarity of the species.

At the time that a TPO is served on the owner a copy of the order will be attached to a protected tree in an obvious location. Neighbours will also be notified by letter.

Importantly, trees in a conservation area benefit from the same protection as if a TPO were in place. In a conservation area anyone proposing to carry out works to trees must apply to the LPA, which has six weeks to consider the proposal and respond. Work cannot proceed until the LPA has responded or the six-week period has expired.

Box 9.4: Uninterrupted views of Purbeck Hills and harbour from hot-tub

The felling of a 12-metre maritime pine that was protected by a TPO led to both the owner of the property and the neighbour, who had axed the tree, being found guilty of causing the wilful destruction of a tree. In addition to a fine of £75,000, the property owner was required to pay the Council £50,000, the estimated rise in value of the house as a consequence of the (uninterrupted) view. The neighbour was fined £2,500. Both men were required to pay costs to Poole Council totalling £17,500. The local residents' association welcomed the outcome as an important deterrent to chopping down trees. (Winter, 2012)

Hedges

Occasionally neighbourhood disputes have arisen with respect to how high hedges on private property have been managed. In particular, Leylandii trees, for example, can grow up to one metre per year. Nuisance can then be caused where light is lost or maintenance issues result for neighbours.

The respective High Hedges Acts (England 2005; Wales 2004; Scotland 2013; Northern Ireland 2011) were introduced to provide a legal basis for the LPA to take action over a problem high hedge. The controls deal with evergreen and semi-evergreen hedges that are more than two metres in height and affecting light reaching a neighbouring domestic property. The legislation provides for a formal complaints system, but one that should be used only as a 'last resort', as neighbours are encouraged to resolve the problem themselves.

The legislation does not mean that all hedges above two metres in height should be cut down, or that people need permission to grow or retain a hedge along the boundary of their property. Rather, the legislation can be utilised where nuisance is considered to be occurring. Action may be taken only where a complaint is made. Further, it must be demonstrated that the individuals concerned have tried to resolve the issue with the owner of the hedge before making a formal complaint. Mediation is also recommended. The legislation does not extend to single trees or single shrubs, whatever their size. Where a council decides to take action, a high hedge (remedial) notice can be served, which can state the initial action to be taken and any preventative action that should be considered. If a hedge owner fails to comply with the notice this constitutes an offence and a fine may be levied.

Chapter summary

There is sometimes a tendency in discussions about planning to focus only on the mainstream system involving planning permission for development. This chapter has shown, that a diversity of regulatory arrangements exist to manage the built and natural environment. The scope of the planning 'family' includes listed building, advertisement and conservation area consent, and less frequently, scheduled monuments and areas of archaeological importance, as well as TPOs and hedges. The chapter has presented issues in the round, commenting on some of the practical implications of acting in an unauthorised way. Importantly, this chapter has highlighted those areas of planning control where failure to obtain prior consent constitutes a criminal offence. This discussion leads us neatly into the next chapter, on enforcement.

Recommended reading

Historic England (2015) *Building Preservation Notice* (BPN), December. Available online: https://content.historicengland.org.uk/content/docs/listing/bpn-guidance-2015.pdf

Pendlebury, J. (2015) 'Conservation of the historic environment', Chapter 8 in Cullingworth et al, *Town and country planning in the UK*, 15th edn, Abingdon-on-Thames: Routledge, pp 317–49.

For a more legalistic and technical exploration of these planning family systems, you should consider:

Duxbury, R. (2012) *Telling & Duxbury's planning law and procedure*, 15th edn, Oxford: Oxford University Press, chapter 16.

McMaster, R. and Smith, G. (2013) *Scottish planning law*, London: Bloomsbury Publishing.

Moore, V. and Purdue, M. (2014) *A practical approach to planning law*, 13th edn, Oxford: Oxford University Press, chapters 21 and 22.

As with the 'mainstream' planning arrangements, regulations and legislation change relatively regularly in these planning family areas and case law is, of course, always evolving. You should also consult with the information that is available for you online:

England: Planning Portal (remembering to identify 'England' as your location): http://www.planningportal.gov.uk

Northern Ireland: Planning Portal: https://www.planningni.gov.uk/

Scotland: ePlanning Scotland: https://eplanning.scotland.gov.uk/WAM/

Wales: Town Planning Portal (remembering to identify 'Wales' as your location): http://www.planningportal.gov.uk

TEN

Enforcement

Chapter contents

- What is a breach of planning control?
- Legislation
- Other powers
- Chapter summary

Introduction

An important principle of the planning enforcement system in the UK is that it is not focused on punishing those who have fallen foul of planning legislation. Rather, enforcement seeks to achieve appropriate development in the right location, with appropriate control. Negotiation comes first. This is not to say that there is no penalty for those who do not comply with enforcement action taken against them. A system of criminal convictions and fines exist for those found guilty of offences under the relevant Acts. This distinction is important. It is not an offence to carry out a breach of planning control. It is an offence when enforcement action is not complied with. Nonetheless, as we saw in the previous chapter, unauthorised works that affect the character of a listed building are an immediate offence.

The UK's enforcement system has been honed by High Court appeals that have established certain legal principles that shape the way enforcement is conducted. Local appeal decisions may also influence the manner and extent to which the LPA may choose to enforce against a particular type of breach of planning control. Enforcement is a very particular and potentially costly type of planning activity and alternative approaches are available to tackle unauthorised development. These other routes may be pursued in preference to enforcement, which some see as adversarial. Given the strict manner in which the relevant legislation must be complied with on a day-to-day basis, planning enforcement assumes a more legalistic character than the planning activities we have looked at thus far. As a consequence, this chapter is rather more legalistic in style, although we focus on how the legislation is utilised in practice.

Expediency

The consideration of 'expediency' plays a significant role in whether or not enforcement action is taken. The decision whether or not to take action is taken at the discretion of the LPA, taking into account appeal decisions that may have gone against it in the past or examples from case law. The principle of expediency often means that an unauthorised development, whether intentional or accidental, may not be enforced against at all if it complies with national and local policy. However, if an unauthorised development would not be granted planning permission, then it is expedient to take enforcement action.

It is general practice for an LPA to invite the relevant type of application so that an unauthorised development can gain formal planning permission. Such an approach demonstrates reasonableness on the part of the LPA and is generally considered good practice. Where there is very little chance of receiving planning permission, the LPA should relay this information to the landowner and/or occupant and advise them as to what works they should carry out next to avoid enforcement action. Steps may include rectifying the breach of planning control or turning the development (or use) into an acceptable form of development.

Not only can the receipt of retrospective planning permission provide the landowner with peace of mind that they have a lawful development, but it can allow the LPA to apply planning conditions to the grant of permission, giving the authority additional control over what would have been an unrestricted, but acceptable, unauthorised development. In instances where retrospective planning permission is not forthcoming the LPA must then decide whether it is expedient to take enforcement action. This situation may arise after a prolonged period of investigation. Where no enforcement action is taken, this can create the public perception that an individual has 'got away with it'. Normally, however, the LPA will have considered all of the relevant facts. As already stated, this arm of the planning system is not predicated on punishing those who have fallen foul of it.

Planning conditions cannot be attached to enforcement notices. If a development is potentially acceptable, but only with conditional control, the LPA may choose to over-enforce. This avenue involves issuing an enforcement notice with requirements; for example, the cessation of an unauthorised change of use of a building or land and will often lead to a Planning Inspector granting planning permission for the development on the basis that the steps for complying with the Notice are excessive. The benefit of this however is that it can lead to a permission with conditional control, ultimately achieving an acceptable form of development, if the conditions are complied with. With respect to enforcement notice appeals, the LPA can also suggest conditions to the relevant appeal body (for example PINS in England or the PAC in Northern Ireland), which has the power to attach conditions where it is minded to grant planning permission (see Chapter Eleven). An important consideration is control over the longer term. In the instance of an unauthorised change of use, for example, the new use may become acceptable if hours of operation can be controlled, even if the development is currently not operating outside the prescribed time.

Beyond the primary planning legislation, other legislation is also used for the purposes of enforcement. This means that the relevant legislation may not relate directly to the concept of development. Sometimes other council departments, or even the police, can be involved in an enforcement case, as a range of complicated issues can come into play. The role of planning enforcement officers may thus be varied in practice and include dealing with graffiti under anti-social behaviour legislation, unauthorised works under listed building legislation or Leylandii under high hedges legislation, to name some of the most common. Enforcement officers have also started to utilise other powers available to them, for example through the legislation on proceeds of crime. Where successful, such actions can be a deterrent to others making financial gain from unauthorised development. Moreover, taking action demonstrates that the law is being upheld.

Box 10.1: Enforcement action in practice

Despite having three planning applications to convert a property into flats turned down, a developer decided to rent out four flats while he again sought planning permission. The LPA issued a planning enforcement notice demanding that the unauthorised use of the property be stopped. Failure to comply with the enforcement notice led to a claim by the Council under the relevant Proceeds of Crime Act. The company was ordered to pay more than £175,000 as a result. The Deputy Leader of Lambeth Council commented: 'Our planning system is there for a reason – to ensure any development is in the best interests of Lambeth – and anybody caught flouting the rules will be prosecuted.' (Lambeth Council, 2014)

What is a breach of planning control?

The legal definition of development governs whether a breach of planning control has occurred. Before deciding whether enforcement action is expedient, the first thing an LPA enforcement officer must establish when investigating a case is whether a breach has actually occurred.

A breach of planning control is defined as:

- the carrying out of development without the required planning permission; or
- failing to comply with any condition or limitation, subject to which planning permission has been granted.

Matters become more complicated when deciding whether or not a change is material, and this can depend on the context of a particular development, rather than simply a list of criteria. It is a matter of judgement. A central difficulty in planning enforcement is often making that judgement. Faced with the same 'facts', another officer in another area might reach a different opinion. Moreover, if the matter reaches appeal there is a chance that a planning inspector (England and Wales), reporter (Scotland) or commissioner (Northern Ireland) may also take a different view. In carrying out enforcement activities, specialist officers must use their knowledge not only of case law, legislation and established principles but of local policy and relevant appeal decisions to help them form a judgement in respect of each case, and then decide what action, if any, to take. Since the scope of planning enforcement often extends beyond a narrow concern with development that requires consent, knowledge of whether a breach of other legislation has occurred is also required by LPA enforcement officers.

Legislation

Enforcement legislation is mainly contained within the primary planning acts of each national jurisdiction, namely, the Town and Country Planning Act 1990 in England and Wales, Part V of the Planning Act (Northern Ireland) 2011 and Parts V and VI of the Town and Country Planning (Scotland) Act 1997, with each Act having a section dedicated to the area of planning enforcement.

Slight variation in enforcement controls may be discerned between the four administrations. In Northern Ireland and Scotland, for example, a system of fixed penalty notices exists for breaches of planning control. In Wales, Enforcement Warning Notices were introduced through the Planning (Wales) Act 2015. Certain basic principles and practices of planning enforcement are nonetheless fairly consistent.

Time-limits

Statutory time-limits exist for taking enforcement action, providing some reassurance to the landowner that after a certain period has passed no enforcement action will be taken against their unauthorised development. Two time-limits exist in England, Wales and Scotland for the taking of enforcement action:

1. a four-year rule on enforcement action against operational development and change of use of a building to a single dwelling-house
2. a ten-year time-limit, which applies to all other breaches of planning control (for example, changes of use or breaches of conditions).

The four-year residential rule refers only to single dwelling-houses. Hence, the ten-year time-limit applies to the creation of two or more dwelling-houses.

Taking action within the time-limit is essential. For example, if enforcement action is taken against a single dwelling-house within the time-period, the LPA can take further enforcement action up to four years later. Thus, if the LPA needs to withdraw the original notice, for example due to an error, it effectively gets a 'second bite' to pursue the case within a further four-year time frame (DCLG, 2014). In Northern Ireland the time limits changed in December 2011: enforcement action must be taken within five years for all breaches of planning control. Further enforcement action can be taken up to five years after the original action in respect of the breach. The removal of time-limits was considered in the review of the enforcement system in Wales (Welsh Government, 2013) but not implemented through the Planning (Wales) Act 2015.

Concealment

Box 10.2: Deliberate concealment?

Fidler v Secretary of State for Communities and Local Government (2010) EWHC 143;

Fidler v Secretary of State for Communities and Local Government (2011) EWCA Civ 1159.

Mr Fidler attempted to gain immunity from enforcement action for a house built in the Green Belt in Surrey without planning permission. He constructed the house behind hay-bales and lived in it, with his family, for four years, after which time he removed the hay-bales. Reigate and Banstead Borough Council served an enforcement notice requiring the removal of the house.

The Courts determined that Mr Fidler had deliberately sought to deceive the LPA and could not therefore rely on the statutory time-limit. The hay-bales were considered an integral part of the building operations and it was stated that the enforcement notice should be upheld because it was issued within four years of their removal.

Welwyn Hatfield Borough Council v Secretary of State for Communities and Local Government and Beesley (2011) URSC 15.

Mr Beesley obtained planning permission for a hay-barn, but instead used it as a dwelling-house. The LPA served an enforcement notice. Mr Beesley argued that the LPA could not do this, as the four-year time-limit for enforcement action had elapsed. Originally the High Court found in his favour, but its decision was overturned by the Supreme Court. The Supreme Court's decision was on the basis that no change of use had occurred as Mr Beesley had never used the building as intended, and one should not be allowed to profit from one's own wrong-doing.

Despite the principles established in the cases presented in Box 10.1, the Localism Act 2011 introduced Enforcement Orders to the Town and Country Planning Act 1990 in England. Section 171B allows the LPA to apply to the Magistrates' Court for an order, where it has sufficient evidence to show that a breach of planning control has occurred. The Court must be satisfied that the development was deliberately concealed and, if it issues the order, the LPA can take enforcement action against the development within that year, whether or not the statutory time-limits have expired. This provision has not been commenced in Wales, as it was considered that the principle of concealment had been adequately established in law to enable such development to be addressed. This position does not prevent the Welsh Government from implementing this part of the 1990 Act in the future, if it so wishes.

Planning Contravention Notice

Planning Contravention Notices (PCN) are a means for the LPA to obtain information to substantiate a breach of planning control. PCNs are a useful tool because the evidence obtained through the completion of a PCN often assists the LPA in deciding whether or not to take enforcement action.

A PCN can be served on the owner and/or occupier of land where a suspected breach has occurred, or on any person using the land or carrying out operations on it. The legislation prescribes what information must be included in a PCN and the parameters of what information the LPA can seek to obtain. The PCN can require the person on whom it is served to give information as to any operations being undertaken on the land, any use of the land and any other activities being carried out on the land and relating to the conditions or limitations subject to which any planning permission has been granted.

A PCN can also require the person, as far as they are able, to:

- state whether the land is being used for any purpose specified in the notice, or if any operations or activities specified in the notice are being or have been carried out on the land;
- state when any use, operations or activities began;
- give the name and address of any person known to use or to have used the land for any purpose, or to be carrying out or to have carried out any operations or activities on the land;
- give any information they hold as to any planning permission for any use or operations, or any reason for planning permission not being required for any use or operations;
- state the nature of their interest in the land, and the name and address of any other person known to have an interest in the land.

Although the issue of a PCN is not considered enforcement action, it is an offence not to respond to the notice within 21 days. It is also an offence to provide false or misleading information. Unless the LPA has any evidence to the contrary, it must assume that the PCN has been answered honestly. It is thus of particular importance that the LPA ask the relevant questions in the PCN. There is nothing in legislation to prevent it serving further PCNs if it wishes to obtain more information.

Stop notices and temporary stop notices

The four administrations have powers to issue stop notices and temporary stop notices. A stop notice can be served only where it is expedient that the relevant activity should cease before the expiry of the compliance period specified in the enforcement notice. This information must be annexed to the stop notice. Stop notices are used for the most urgent or serious cases, such as where issues of public safety are involved.

Once the enforcement notice takes effect, a stop notice cannot be served. Nor can a stop notice be served to prohibit the use of any building as a dwelling-house, or in relation to any activity that has been carried out for more than four years (except for any activity consisting of, or incidental to, building, mining, engineering or other operations, or the deposit of refuse or waste materials). In Northern Ireland, stop notices cannot be used to prohibit a person using a building, caravan or other structure as their main residence. Stop notices can be served on any person who appears to have an interest in the land or who is engaged in any activity prohibited by the notice.

Stop notices cannot come into force earlier than three days after being issued, unless there are special reasons for doing so. In Northern Ireland, stop notices come into effect on the date they are served and special reasons must be given for a later date. Stop notices cease to have effect when the activities prohibited by it cease; if the associated enforcement notice is withdrawn; if the period of compliance with the enforcement notice expires; or if the stop notice is withdrawn. It is an offence to contravene a stop notice and a fine of up to £20,000 can be imposed by the Courts, or up to £100,000 in Northern Ireland.

Compensation can be payable in respect of stop notices, but the grounds set out in the respective legislation are limited. The circumstances relate to errors made by the LPA, resulting in a notice being quashed, or varied to the extent that the breach alleged is no longer included in the accompanying enforcement notice, or if the LPA withdraws the notice on the grounds that planning permission is later granted for the matter to which the notice related.

The Planning and Compulsory Purchase Act 2004 inserted sections 171E to H in relation to temporary stop notices into the Town and Country Planning Act 1990. Temporary stop notices have been used in England since 2005; the legislation was not commenced in Wales until June 2015. In England approximately 250 to 300 temporary stop notices are issued each year (Welsh Government, 2013). A benefit of temporary notices over stop notices is that they come into force immediately in all instances and do not have to be served with an enforcement notice. Temporary notices last for a period of 28 days, giving LPAs the power to take immediate action where they consider it expedient in respect of an unauthorised activity, or part of an unauthorised activity. Importantly, the legislation specifies that the LPA must serve a temporary stop notice where it considers it expedient to do so. A second temporary stop notice can be served when further enforcement action has been taken.

The same restrictions to serving stop notices apply to temporary stop notices. England revoked the 2005 regulations in 2013, which prevented the service of temporary stop notice on caravans being used as a person's main residence. The justification for doing so was based on the fact the human rights issues must be considered in each individual case (DCLG, 2013). This consideration included the rights of those affected by the continued unauthorised use, as well as the rights of those upon whom the notice would be served. Weighing up these considerations is intended to govern the LPA's decision whether or not to serve a temporary stop notice in respect of residential caravans.

In implementing the temporary stop notice legislation, the Welsh Government has not put any restriction on their service on caravans used as a person's main residence. In Scotland the Town and Country Planning (Temporary Stop Notice) (Scotland) Regulations 2009 may not prohibit the stationing of a caravan on land, provided that:

• the caravan is stationed on land immediately prior to the service of the temporary stop notice; and
• the caravan is, at the time, occupied by a person as her/his main residence.

However, temporary stop notices can be used to prevent more caravans being moved onto a site.

As with stop notices, it is an offence to contravene a temporary stop notice and a fine of up to £20,000 is payable, or £100,000 in Northern Ireland. Because temporary stop notices do not rely on the service of an enforcement notice the grounds under which compensation is payable are more restricted. These do not relate to the outcome of an appeal associated with an enforcement notice for a related breach of planning control; only where planning permission is granted for the activity or where the local authority withdraws the notice.

Enforcement notices

Enforcement notices are the primary means by which LPAs seek to resolve unauthorised and expedient breaches of planning control. There is very little difference in the legislation between the four administrations. When considering issuing an enforcement notice, the LPA needs to have: investigated the matter, established that there is a breach and decided that planning permission will not be granted, and will have given the landowner and any occupier opportunity to resolve the situation either informally or through a retrospective planning application, which would allow sufficient control. When investigating an alleged or apparent breach of planning control, a crucial first step is for the LPA to attempt to contact the owner or occupier of the site in question. Section 330 of the Town and Country Planning Act 1990 provides LPAs with the power to require information as to interests in land. Where possible, early engagement is vital to establish (a) whether there is a breach of planning control and the degree of harm that may be resulting; and (b) whether those responsible for any breach are receptive to taking action to remedy the breach.

Under the legislation, the LPA may issue an enforcement notice where it appears to it that there has been a breach of planning control and it is expedient to issue the notice, having regard to the provisions of the development plan and any other material considerations. A copy of the notice must be served on the owner and occupier of the land to which it relates, and on any other person having an interest that is materially affected by the notice in the land. The notice comes into effect not before 28 days after the date on which it is served.

The legislation is prescriptive as to what an enforcement notice should contain. LPAs therefore need to ensure that they draft an enforcement notice correctly, in order to reduce the possibility of the enforcement notice being either quashed or varied on appeal. The notice must state the matters that appear to the LPA to constitute the breach of planning control and the relevant paragraph of the Act under which, in its opinion, the breach falls. A notice will not comply with these requirements if it does not enable the person upon whom it is served to know what those matters are. In other words, the enforcement notice must be clear about what the breach is.

The notice must also specify the steps that need to be taken, or the activities that should cease, in order, wholly or partly to:

- remedy the breach by making it comply with the terms of any planning permission that has been granted in respect of the land, by discontinuing any use of land or by restoring the land to its condition before the breach took place; or
- remedy any injury to amenity that has been caused by the breach.

An enforcement notice can require, for example:

- the alteration of any building or works;
- the carrying out of any building or other operations;
- any activity on the land not to be carried out, except to the extent specified in the notice;
- the contour of a deposit or refuse or waste materials on land to be modified by altering the gradient or gradients of its sides; or
- the construction of a replacement building that is as similar as possible to the demolished building, where the notice relates to a breach consisting of the demolition of a building.

The enforcement notice should also specify the date upon which the requirement(s) is/are to come into effect and the period for compliance. Different periods for compliance can be specified for different steps in the notice.

Once the notice has been complied with, LPAs can, in effect, grant planning permission for the remaining development. The legislation specifies that this is the case where a notice could have required any buildings or works to be removed or any activity to cease but does not do so, and the requirements of the notice have been met. It may be an LPA's intention to do this, and this is known as 'under enforcement'. Care needs to be taken, however, when drafting a notice and its requirements to ensure that unintentional under enforcement is not permitted in this way. Similarly, where a notice requires the construction of a replacement building, and all the requirements of the notice have been complied with, planning permission shall be treated as have being granted.

After issuing an enforcement notice the LPA is able to withdraw it, relax or waive any requirement in it or extend the period for compliance. This arrangement creates a degree of flexibility, in effect giving an LPA discretion to consider the notice complied with when steps may have been taken to resolve the breach of planning control to an acceptable level, although not to the extent originally specified.

Where an enforcement notice is not complied with, LPAs can enter the land to fulfil the requirements of the notice and seek to recover the cost from the landowner.

Breach of condition notice

For England and Wales S.187A of the Town and Country Planning Act 1990 relates to the specific enforcement of conditions relating to a planning permission. The respective section of the Planning Act (Northern Ireland) 2011 is S. 152, and for the Town and Country Planning (Scotland) Act 1997 it is S. 145. Although it is an offence not to comply with a breach of condition notice (BCN), there are some important differences from enforcement notices.

Firstly, BCNs must specify the condition(s) not complied with in the notice. Although a BCN comes into force immediately upon being served, the LPA must allow a minimum period of 28 days for compliance. The notice can specify the steps necessary for compliance. Secondly, there is no right of appeal against a BCN. However, the recipient would have had an opportunity to appeal the condition when planning permission was granted, or is able to seek to vary or to remove the condition through a separate planning application, and can appeal refusal of such an application.

Although BCNs can specify steps for compliance with a condition they cannot seek the submission of information for consideration by the LPA, even if the submission of details may have formed part of the original condition. Instead, the correct procedure for a BCN is to specify what the LPA considers acceptable. For example, if a condition attached to a grant of planning permission for a housing estate required the submission of a landscaping scheme, and for that scheme to be implemented as approved, the LPA must provide a scheme for the developer to implement if one has not already been agreed.

The LPA can choose to serve an enforcement notice in respect of a breach of condition. However, this would allow the recipient of the notice an avenue for appeal, and if the appeal were to be successful the condition could be varied or removed by the appeal body (for example, PINS in England).

Listed building enforcement notices

As discussed in Chapter Nine, it is an offence to execute or to cause to be executed any works for the demolition of a listed building, or for its alteration or extension in any manner that would affect its character as a building of special architectural or historic interest, unless the works are authorised. It is also an offence not to comply with a listed building enforcement notice.

Where unauthorised works have been carried out to a listed building the LPA may serve a listed building enforcement notice if it is considered expedient to do so. Powers variously exist under the following sections: S. 38 Planning (Listed Building and Conservation Areas) Act 1990; S. 35 Planning (Listed Building and Conservation Areas) (Scotland) Act 1997; S. 157 Planning (Northern Ireland) Act 2011. However, works that require an LBC do not always require planning permission and so it is not always necessary to serve an enforcement notice if those works did not also constitute development and need planning permission.

The listed building enforcement notice should specify the breach and set out the required steps to restore the listed building to its former condition or to alleviate the effect(s) of the unauthorised works or to bring the building into a state to comply with the terms of an LBC. Who the notice can be served upon, the timings and the ability of the LPA to amend or withdraw the listed building enforcement notice are consistent with enforcement notices.

When drafting a listed building enforcement notice the LPA enforcement officer will often seek assistance from a listed building or conservation expert (typically an internal member of council staff). This expert is more likely to have the necessary knowledge of what particular features originally looked like or comprised of, or at least to have an informed idea of the typical design elements a specific feature, such as a window or fireplace should have. This knowledge is critical where features may have been removed. In some cases official list descriptions of buildings may not be sufficiently detailed or inadequate evidence may be available for an enforcement officer to draft specific-enough requirements for rectifying a listed building offence. In practice, then, while a listed building enforcement notice can specify that a building is returned to its previous condition, in reality such work may be difficult to achieve without photographs, plans or an accurate description.

Injunctions

The LPA can apply to the Courts for an injunction, or interdict as referred to under S. 146 of the Town and Country Planning (Scotland) Act 1997, for any actual or apprehended breach of planning control if it thinks it is expedient to restrain the breach in this way. Injunctions can also be sought in relation to listed buildings. To contravene an injunction made by the Courts is very serious and a person can be committed to prison or held in contempt of Court. Therefore, injunctions are normally applied for only as a last resort or where other enforcement options would be ineffective (DCLG, 2015b), and so they are not commonly used.

Appeals

Appeals are discussed further in the following chapter and are discussed here only in the context of enforcement matters.

There are several grounds of appeal against enforcement notices, and different appeal procedures in relation to the routes the LPA might take. For example, there are appeals not only against enforcement notices, but against listed building enforcement notices and notices served under S. 215 of the Town and Country Planning Act 1990 in respect of unsightly land, for example. In England the majority of appeals are determined by PINS, but appeals in respect of unsightly land are determined in a Magistrates' Court.

Briefly, the grounds of appeal in respect of an enforcement notice are similar across the four administrations, namely:

1. in respect of any breach of planning control that may be constituted by the matters stated in the notice, planning permission ought to be granted or, as the case may be, the condition or limitation concerned ought to be discharged;
2. those matters have not occurred;
3. those matters (if they occurred) do not constitute a breach of planning control;
4. at the date when the notice was issued no enforcement action could be taken in respect of any breach of planning control that may be constituted by those matters;
5. copies of the enforcement notice were not served as required;
6. the steps required by the notice to be taken, or the activities required by the notice to cease, exceed what is necessary to remedy any breach of planning control that may be constituted by those matters or, as the case may be, to remedy any injury to amenity that has been caused by any such breach; or
7. any period specified in the notice falls short of what should reasonably be allowed.

An appeal body can correct or vary an enforcement notice, providing it does not cause injustice to the appellant or LPA; or it can quash the notice completely and grant planning permission for the development that is subject to the notice.

Other powers

Unsightly land

In England, Wales and Scotland, LPAs have powers to serve notices, commonly known as unsightly land notices, to require proper maintenance of land where they consider that the condition of a building or land is having an adverse effect on the area. The notice can require steps to be taken to remedy the condition of the land. It is an offence not to comply with such a notice. In England and Wales appeals against these notices are made to the Magistrates' Court; in Scotland, they are made to the Secretary of State. The Planning Bill (Wales) 2014 set out measures to transfer responsibility for appeals to the Secretary of State.

Advertisement control

Each administration has its own set of regulations to control the display of advertisements (see Chapter Nine). Each of the primary planning acts provides powers for LPAs to require the removal of any advertisement displayed in contravention of its regulations and to require the discontinuance of land for the use of display of advertisements. It is an offence to display an advertisement in contravention of the regulations.

Advertisement control provides us with a good example of how challenging enforcement can be in practice; a regulatory construct is often necessarily quite rigid and difficult to translate into the dynamic reality of the real world. As an example, an advert on a vehicle normally used as a vehicle is excluded from control, but when is a vehicle actually being used as a vehicle? This can be difficult to prove sometimes, and can lead to interesting situations such as presented in Photograph 10.1.

Photo 10.1: Enforcement challenges

Fixed penalty notices

Fixed penalty notices are part of the Scottish enforcement toolkit. They are also included within the Northern Irish primary legislation, through the Planning (Amount of Fixed Penalty) Regulations (Northern Ireland) 2015. Fixed penalty notices can be issued where a person is in breach of an enforcement notice or a BCN. They offer a person the opportunity to avoid liability in respect of non-compliance by paying a fine or fixed penalty. A second fixed penalty notice cannot be served, but one can be served for each step that is not complied with in an enforcement notice (Scottish Government, 2009). Once the penalty has been paid, the LPA cannot pursue any further action, with the exception of direct action, in respect of that breach. Stated another way, a decision has to be made whether the fixed penalty is commensurate with the scale of the breach. The maximum fixed penalty for a breach of an enforcement notice is £2,000, and £300 for a BCN in Scotland and Northern Ireland.

Enforcement warning notices (Wales)

The Planning (Wales) Act 2015 includes new provisions to allow LPAs to serve enforcement warning notices where they think that an unauthorised development is likely to be granted planning permission with conditional control. If a development is not likely to gain planning permission the LPA cannot serve one of these notices. The premise is that enforcement warning notices will encourage landowners to regulate unauthorised development, rather than the LPA having to over enforce by serving an enforcement notice. The notices will provide a date by which a planning application should be submitted, and failure to do so will result in the service of an enforcement notice. Enforcement warning notices will count as taking enforcement action. Serving such a notice will give the LPA a further four years within which to take enforcement action, similar to the service of an enforcement notice.

Chapter summary

The enforcement system in the four UK administrations is broadly similar, although some procedural differences and fines vary. However, a consistent principle is that the enforcement system is designed to be effective and fair. Enforcement is recognised to be complex, with case law and practice evolving. Here we have sought to simplify the key legislation to help you understand the nature of the UK's enforcement system.

In the enforcement of planning control there is often a party who feels that the outcome achieved is not the most satisfactory one. Enforcement investigations can be lengthy and the process of notice, appeal and prosecution can often mean that an unauthorised development is present for a number of years before a case is resolved. Bodies such as the National Association of Planning Enforcement

(NAPE) within the RTPI are actively promoting best practice among enforcement professionals and this, coupled with existing and forthcoming legislation, should help to make the future enforcement system in the UK more effective and efficient.

Despite this, how each local authority approaches planning enforcement may vary, with some being more proactive than others, and this can often be a result of resources and experience. Local authorities are under pressure to cut budgets and justify their services, and reduced resources may have led some planning departments to rationalise and cut staff numbers. The impact on specialist enforcement professionals is yet to be seen, but research (Sheppard et al, 2014) suggests that it is important that specialist skills are retained to some degree to ensure continued improvement of the service.

Recommended reading

Harris, N.R. (2013) 'Surveillance, social control and planning: citizen engagement in the detection and investigation of breaches of planning control', *Town Planning Review*, vol 84, no 2, pp 171–96.

McKay, S. and Murray, M. (2014) 'In pursuit of regulatory compliance: a study of planning enforcement structures in Northern Ireland', *Town Planning Review*, vol 85, no 3, pp 387–410.

McKay, S., Murray, M. and Macintyre, S. (2015) 'Pitfalls in protection: how theory can enrich our understanding of regulatory compliance problems in planning practice', *International Planning Studies*, vol 20, no 3, pp 270–91.

Sheppard, A., Britnell, S. and Cooke, J. (2014) *Planning enforcement England: At the crossroads*, Bristol: University of the West of England.

Enforcement is, perhaps, the most technical area of planning with respect to the legal issues involved. To read further detail on this, you should consult a law book such as:

Duxbury, R. (2012) *Telling & Duxbury's planning law and procedure*, 15th edn, Oxford: Oxford University Press, chapter 12.

McMaster, R. and Smith, G. (2013) *Scottish planning law*, London: Bloomsbury Publishing, chapter 9.

Moore, V. and Purdue, M. (2014) *A practical approach to planning law*, 13th edn, Oxford: Oxford University Press, chapter 20.

ELEVEN

Planning appeals, Judicial Review and the Ombudsman

Chapter contents

- Planning appeals
- Judicial Review
- The Ombudsman
- Chapter summary

Introduction

Thus far we have presented a very positive account of the benefits offered by the planning system. However, there are, occasions where individuals, developers or local communities may be disappointed or frustrated by a decision outcome or the imposition of a planning condition. Perhaps the system for issuing a decision has been slower than the time frame specified in the planning legislation. What remedy exists, if any? Or it may be the case (though very infrequently) that the formal administrative processes for taking a planning decision have not been followed correctly or appropriately. What can be done? Or, perhaps you have a complaint about the way your engagement with the planning process has been handled. Are there any means for redress? This chapter considers the different ways in which the actions and decisions of those operating the planning system can be reviewed. The processes of review, challenge and improvement under the different arrangements operating in the four administrations of the UK vary. However, the basic principles are very similar. In this chapter we highlight some important differences.

Firstly, we consider the different appeals systems. A scalar set of arrangements exists for examining and reviewing decisions, based on the principle with which we have now become familiar: that of proportionality. Some applications are relatively minor, while others may involve major infrastructure. Some decisions may be fairly clear cut, while others may be highly contentious, with considerable third-party interest. Different appeal formats apply. However, whatever type of appeal route is taken, the fundamental point is that an appeal revisits the legal and factual basis of a decision. Stated simply, appeals enable another decision maker to exercise their judgement in relation to a particular case.

Secondly, we discuss Judicial Review (JR), whereby the process of decision-making is reviewed, rather than the conclusion reached. The remit of JR turns on the legality of the decision-making process, and so it differs from the appeal route, which is concerned with the decision itself. Moreover, JR is open to any individual or party who has been actively involved in the specific decision-making process, including a third party such as a neighbour, a community group or a charity, such as the RSPB. JR concerns 'due process' and the JR mechanism exists for any aspect of public law activity, including challenging issues in relation to the allocation of school places or welfare rights. Finally, we consider the complaints procedure and the role of the Local Government Ombudsman in seeking to put things right.

Planning appeals

The right to challenge a decision is essential to the effective and equitable working of the planning system. Philosophically, the nationalisation of development rights – which enabled the state to intervene in the public interest and on the grounds of social justice – represents a significant compromise of the rights of private individuals. Given this exercise of state power over the individual, it is important that an opportunity for challenge or redress should exist to ensure oversight and fairness in the system. In the majority of cases an appeal is made by the applicant (developer) in relation to a refusal, conditions imposed on a permission or consent or non-determination of an application – that is, where a decision has not been made within the specified statutory time-period. Over the years, the remit of planning appeals has extended beyond permissions in relation to development, to include appeals relating to various forms of consent (for example, listed buildings, minerals and hazardous substances); enforcement notices; and the requirement for an environmental statement to accompany an application. Grounds for appeal are set out in related country-specific guidance notes.

Unlike in the Republic of Ireland there are no third-party rights of appeal in the UK, so this route is only available to the applicant and not someone who has objected to a grant of permission. The absence of an equal right to appeal in the planning system is seen by some as very unfair (see recommended reading below). Those not in favour of extending appeal rights to third parties raise issues, such as adding delays to the system and increasing uncertainty for investors, developers and communities (Beveridge et al, 2016). There does not currently appear to be an appetite to introduce this right.

Below we consider the different bodies involved in the four administrations, differentiating between national and local appeal procedures. We then outline the broad processes involved and set out the types of appeal route available.

National-level appeal bodies

Although the legislation in relation to the conduct of planning appeals has changed and been amended over the years, and despite there being some differences between arrangements in England, Wales, Scotland and Northern Ireland, the basic right of appeal has remained the same. The main difference in relation to the UK's four administrations is who 'hears' the appeal against the initial decision. Interestingly, these same bodies play an important role in reviewing draft development plans (see Chapter Four). The existence of different levels or scales of planning authority effectively separates different powers, allows for impartiality to be exercised and provides for what we might term peer reviewing of the actions of (lower) authorities. Although reference is made to the right of appeal being at ministerial level (for example, to the Secretary of State) in practice the majority of appeal decisions are delegated by central government to a dedicated appeals body. The important point remains, however, that planning decisions are reconsidered by an entity separate from the original decision maker.

In England and Wales appeals are decided by a planning inspector working for PINS, an executive agency that is sponsored by DCLG and the Welsh Government. In Scotland, reporters from the Scottish Government Directorate of Planning and Environmental Appeals (DPEA) decide appeals. In practice, appeals are rarely 'recalled' to be dealt with at ministerial level. Use may also be made of other 'appointed persons'. In Northern Ireland the situation is different. Here, planning appeals are made to the PAC, with appeals being decided by commissioners. Uniquely, the PAC is not part of or linked to any governmental department, but is an independent body receiving its administrative and financial support from the Northern Ireland Courts and Tribunal Services. The PAC deals primarily with land-use planning and related matters (PAC, 2016). Its functions extend to appeal decisions arising from local councils and the decisions or proposals of Northern Ireland Assembly departments. Despite these organisational differences, the essential processes and principles for pursuing appeals are broadly similar.

Local-level appeal route (Scotland)

An interesting variation exists in Scotland in relation to who deals with planning appeals with respect to delegated decisions. In order to improve the timeliness, efficiency and transparency of appeals, the Planning etc. (Scotland) Act 2006 introduced certain changes to the planning system, including removing an applicant's right of appeal to a separate authority in relation to a local development dealt with under a scheme of delegation (see Chapter Six). Instead the applicant has a right to a local review by the planning authority itself of the delegated decision or the failure to determine the application within the statutory period.

The Town and Country Planning (Schemes of Delegation and Local Review Procedure) (Scotland) Regulations 2013 – stipulate that the review must be undertaken by a committee – a Local Review Body (LRB) comprising of at least three elected members identified from a bigger pool and who were not involved in the determination of the application (thereby constituting a separate authority). LRB meetings must be held in public and the appellant has no right to be heard.

Different operations are in place across Scotland. For example, the LRB of the Loch Lomond and National Park Authority (as the local planning authority) comprises up to five members. The quorum of the LRB for the National Park is three members, where one such member must be either the Chair or the Deputy Chair. In contrast, Dundee City Council's (2009) LRB comprises three elected members, with a further six identified who may act as substitutes when required. Where an applicant wishes to appeal (seek a review) they need to give written notice, a so-called 'notice of review', to the local authority. Forms are available from the Scottish Government or relevant local authority and specific time-limits apply, depending on the nature of each case. The LRB can agree to accept written or oral evidence.

A more detailed discussion and critique of LRBs is highlighted in the 'Recommended reading', but it is useful to note that while this approach is considered to have increased local accountability, there are concerns about the Scotland-wide consistency of the LRBs and an identified need to enforce elected member training (Beveridge et al, 2016). A similar 'local member review body' system was not taken forward in England in 2008 (McMaster et al, 2013). Where an applicant seeks a local review because the planning authority official had not decided the planning application within two months, and the LRB then fails to make a decision within a further three months, the case can be appealed to Scottish Ministers. Having looked briefly at this local variance, we now focus on the broad system of appeals at the national level.

Remit of appeals

Planning appeals allow for a planning decision to be challenged on its merits. The applicant may also appeal where a decision has not been made within the statutory time-period. The right to appeal is limited to the original applicant or their legally recognised appointee (which may be a planning consultant or a legal representative). In determining appeals the relevant appeals body can, against a refusal of planning permission, or in relation to conditions on an approval or to an enforcement notice, take the following actions:

- allow the appeal
- dismiss the appeal
- reverse the decision
- vary any part of the decision.

It is generally the case that the appeal is examined as if the application is being considered 'in the first instance'. This qualification is important because it means that the appeal process does not constitute a review of the decision; rather, it involves a separate and independently taken decision. This principle is important because it gives the planning system integrity by allowing for a second, impartial decision, and one taken apart from the original planning authority.

The existence of different types of appeal reflects one of the underlying principles that you will have noted running throughout this book, that of proportionality. It would be inappropriate for a single model of appeal to be utilised in all scenarios, since a one-size-fit-all approach would be either inadequate or excessive, depending upon the nature of the decision concerned.

As well as different forms of appeal, the terminology varies slightly across the UK. For our purposes, we focus on presenting the broad process, which is essentially very similar across the four administrations. The appeal processes are scaled, reflecting the hierarchy of development. Three procedures exist: written, informal and formal (Table 11.1).

Table 11.1: Reviews and appeals

UK	Local	Written	Informal	Formal
Scotland	Local Review Body	Written submission	Hearing	Inquiry
England		Written representation (including fast-track version)	Hearing	Inquiry
Wales		Written representation	Hearing	Inquiry
Northern Ireland		Written appeal	Informal appeal	Hearing

General process

The appeal system follows a defined structure and time frame. Underlying the process is an effort to provide for the effective exchange of information and robust decision-making. Word counts and time-scales for the submission and exchange of information vary between the different appeal types but must be rigorously followed. The use of online facilities is encouraged. Figure 11.1 provides a general flow-chart, although bear in mind that the terminology varies. In the following sub-sections we address some key points of the appeal process.

Time-limits and submissions

An applicant wishing to appeal must generally do so within six months of the decision to refuse planning permission (but note that there are reduced time-periods for appealing an enforcement notice or advertisement consent, for example). To apply for an appeal (and subject to the differences discussed in relation to LRBs), the applicant must obtain and complete the relevant form, namely, from PINS (for England and Wales), the PAC (for Northern Ireland) or the DPEA (for Scotland).

Figure 11.1: A generalised flow chart of the appeal process

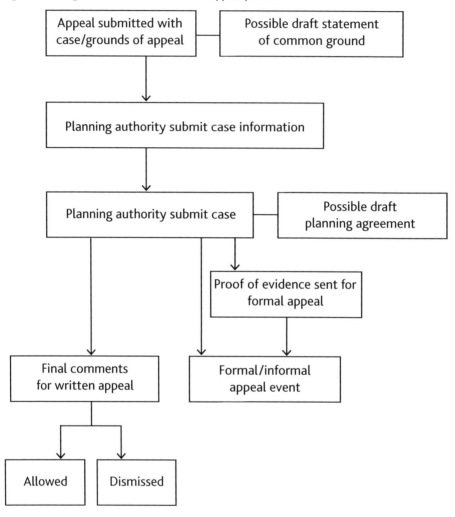

The submission of an appeal application is accompanied by the following documents:

- the application made to the planning authority on which the appeal is based;
- all plans, drawings and documents in connection with the appeal;
- all correspondence relating to the case from the planning authority;
- any notices or certificates provided to the authority (for example, certificate of ownership);

- any other plans, drawings or documents that were not sent to the planning authority;
- the notice of the decision or determination (if any); and
- if the application concerns reserved matters, the application and documentation in relation to the outline planning permission.

Appeal types

Written methods

The written appeal is the most commonly used procedure. This format is used for all appeal scenarios where the matters for consideration are modest and attracted limited controversy. At its most basic level, a written appeal involves an exchange of documentation. The local authority and applicant both submit their case to the respective decision-making body (PINS, the PAC or DPEA).

Each party submits a statement of case, which contains the full argument of that party. Although a site visit will be made by the relevant individual (an inspector, reporter or commissioner), there is no face-to-face discussion in the written process. This approach is designed for the less problematic cases and the underlying intention is that the appeal should not be unnecessarily lengthy or costly to all involved. Indeed, in England and Wales, the written model has been taken further for minor matters. Householder applications (and shop-front and advertisement appeals) in England are now subject to a 'fast-track' variant of the written appeals process. The same basic steps are involved, but with a compressed time-scale and fewer information requirements. This logic again follows the proportionality principle, with the process attempting to reflect the procedure that is necessary to allow for a decision to be made.

Informal methods

This route is suitable for appeals where there is a need for face-to-face discussion, given the issues associated with the scheme. Again, the development is unlikely to be large in scale or to raise complex legal or technical issues. There will be little or no third-party interest and no need for cross-examination. An informal 'event' will be held, essentially involving a round-table meeting chaired by an inspector (a reporter in Scotland). In Northern Ireland a PAC commissioner will lead the informal hearing of the case. This procedure is intended to offer the opportunity for a constructive conversation and a robust consideration of the issues. As with the written process, a full statement of case must be provided.

The fact that the proceedings are discussion based is intended to avoid making the event overly adversarial and to minimise conflict. Even though the appeal is less formal, the person leading the discussion must act (and be seen to act) fairly, ensuring that all the relevant information is taken into account. Where necessary, a site visit may be appropriate and the protocols for how the visit is carried out must be followed.

Formal methods

Formal appeals are best suited to complex development proposals where there may be third-party representation or where there is a need to cross-examine witnesses as part of the 'inquiry' (hearing in Northern Ireland). Already you can see that the tone and style of this procedure are different from the preceding ones.

Formal appeals have a prescribed 'starting date', after which there is an exchange of statements of case. The statement of case contains the full details of the appeal that each party (that is, the appellant or planning authority) intends to use as their evidence. The purpose of the exchange of these documents a few weeks before the appeal hearing is so that issues are shared between the principal actors concerned and no time is lost at the event itself in dealing with background matters or matters that are not central to the appeal.

In very simple terms, the formal event involves the planning authority speaking first, followed by the appellant. Generally, legal teams of barristers and solicitors are used. Finally, it is the turn of any other persons permitted to speak, such as expert witnesses in relation to environmental or wildlife matters, landscape or transport issues or, for example, acoustics. During the inquiry (or hearing in the case of Northern Ireland) each party to the appeal may call upon persons, including private planning consultants, to give evidence and to be cross-examined by the legal representation. Again, a site visit generally forms part of this process.

Major infrastructure projects

Appeals in relation to major infrastructure projects, such as new airport terminals, nuclear power stations, or large offshore wind farms, require the formal public inquiry procedure. In practice, such appeals tend to extend over several days, in contrast to the 'simpler' appeal format, which may be counted in hours. Formal inquiries (hearings in the case of Northern Ireland) may therefore be extremely expensive, both financially and in terms of the time involved. Quite often aside from the main purpose of the inquiry, there can be other matters associated with the case, such as multiple planning applications, environmental aspects, scheduled monument orders or transport works. A question then arises as to who bears the costs involved.

Award of costs

Parties in planning appeals normally meet their own expenses and appeal costs. However, an 'award of costs' in informal and formal appeals is quite common, although this has only recently come into force in Northern Ireland (2015). This is not to say that an award of costs follows the decision; it is possible for the appellant to be successful at appeal (in that a refusal is overturned, or a condition removed) but to have costs awarded against them.

The basis of an award of costs is to ensure appropriate behaviour during the appeals process, rather than to act as any sort of reward or compensation. All parties are expected to behave reasonably to support an efficient and timely planning appeals process. For example, appropriate behaviour involves providing all the required evidence in line with the timetable. Where a party has behaved unreasonably, incurring another party unnecessary or wasted expenditure, the latter may be entitled to an award of costs.

Two types of costs award are available, and may result in the payment of either partial or whole costs, namely:

- *Procedural costs* – that is, relating to the appeal process, where costs are based upon whether a party followed the procedures correctly and their behaviour was reasonable;
- *Substantive costs* – that is, relating to the planning merits of the appeal and whether or not the decision made could be considered reasonable.

Applications for costs should be made at the inquiry, with the amount to be awarded then agreed. If no agreement is possible the parties can have the amount determined through the Courts.

Box 11.1: 'Untitled 1986': the case of the Headington shark

A celebrated planning case in the 1980s involved the installation of a fibre-glass shark in the roof-space of a terraced property. The shark's tail protruded above the roofline. The sculpture was designed to commemorate the falling of the atomic bomb on Nagasaki. It was considered as unauthorised development by the LPA; enforcement action followed and the owner of the house was subsequently refused retrospective planning permission by Oxford City Council. Undeterred, the property-owner then appealed to the (then) Secretary of State for the Environment.

In relation to the said development ('the shark') the inspector commented as follows:

> It is not in dispute that this is a large and prominent feature. That was the intention, but the intention of the appellant and the artist is not an issue as far as planning permission is concerned. The case should be decided on its planning merits, not by resorting to 'utilitarianism', in the sense of the greatest good to the greatest number. And it is necessary to consider the relationship between the shark and its setting ... In this case it is not in dispute that the shark is not in harmony with its surroundings, but then it is not intended to be in harmony with them. The basic facts are there for almost all to see. Into this archetypal urban setting crashes (almost literally) the shark. The contrast is deliberate ... and, in this sense, the work is quite specific to its setting.

As a 'work of art' the sculpture ('Untitled 1986') would be 'read' quite differently in, say, an art gallery or on another site. An incongruous object can become accepted as a landmark after a time, becoming well known, even well loved in the process. Something of this sort seems to have happened, for many people, to the so-called 'Oxford shark'. The Council is understandably concerned about precedent here. The first concern is simple: proliferation with sharks (and Heaven knows what else) crashing through roofs all over the City. This fear is exaggerated. In the five years since the shark was erected, no other examples have occurred. Only very recently has there been a proposal for twin baby sharks in the Iffley Road. But any system of control must make some small place for the dynamic, the unexpected, the downright quirky. I therefore recommend that the Headington shark be allowed to remain. (Jenkins, undated)

Photo 11.1: Unauthorised development? The so-called Headington shark

Source: Deborah Peel

Judicial Review

JR is a relatively complex process. In contrast to the administrative systems of planning with which we have primarily been concerned, JR is a particular type of Court action. The procedure is available in all spheres of public life to enable individuals or groups to challenge the decision(s), or action(s) of a body performing a public function. For our purposes, this might mean an LPA or government department, such as the DfI, for example.

Commentators have pointed to an increased use of JR. In part, the prevalence of JR stems from 'greater preparedness on the part of developers to mount legal challenges' (Orbinson et al, 2009, p 21). This point was also made by Field (2005, p 67), who noted that JR has become:

> a vehicle to vent frustrations and disappointments with the planning system as well as an instrument to protect commercial interests … [and] a central part of third party opposition strategy.

These insights suggest two important distinctions. First, JR may be used as a legitimate form of redress – this being its original institutional intention. A petitioner may thus challenge a public body on the basis of illegality, procedural impropriety or irrationality.

Second, JR may be used by third-party interests as a de facto right of appeal. In the UK, when a planning application is granted permission, the only way for a third party to challenge the decision is by JR in the Courts (Barclay, 2002). In practice, however, scope to mount a JR is a very confined option, limited in both procedural and practical ways. Anyone mounting a JR must be able to demonstrate sufficient interest in the case and must initiate proceedings within three months of a planning decision. Consequently, there are time, financial and capacity costs associated with engaging in JR action. The environmental campaign group Friends of the Earth (2006, p 32) has cautioned:

> Judicial Review can only be used where there is no right of appeal or all other appeal opportunities have been exhausted. It is not equivalent to or a substitute for a third party right of appeal. Instead, Judicial Review is applicable in only a very few cases and is not open to anyone who simply is not satisfied with a decision […] The process is a very lengthy and potentially very costly one. […] The length and expense of this process underlines the need for initial legal advice to assess the strength of the case and the potential costs involved in seeking the review.

Grounds for Judicial Review

The grounds for bringing a JR against a public body fall under four broad headings. The public body must have:

1. acted illegally;
2. acted in a procedurally unfair manner;
3. acted irrationally; or
4. acted contrary to an individual's legitimate expectation as protected by law. (PILS, 2012, p 7)

The focus of JR, then, is whether or not that body observed all relevant legal rules, standards and requirements; and whether it acted within the limits of its powers (that is, was not ultra vires). While planning appeals allow for the merits of a planning decision (or the lack of a decision, in non-determination cases) to be challenged, the JR procedure serves a different purpose. Specifically, JR is used to determine the legality of a decision and whether it is lawful and 'reasonable'. In consideration of what is reasonable behaviour, reference may be made to English case law and, specifically, *Associated Provincial Picture Houses Ltd v Wednesbury Corporation [1948]1KB 223*. This was not a planning matter. The case concerned the limitations on the showing of films in a cinema. The Court considered the concept of reasonableness. It was noted that an unreasonable decision can be considered to mean: 'so unreasonable that no reasonable authority could ever have come to it'.

A final point, by way of introduction, is important: JR is a remedy of 'last resort', which means that there must be no other way to resolve the issue. It follows that efforts are made to provide other alternatives for redress and to avoid this route where possible.

Who can take a Judicial Review?

Notwithstanding the slight differences across the four administrations, there are similarities in who can pursue a JR. Whether or not a group, individual or body can take action turns on the notions of capacity and standing. Larkin and Scoffield (2007, p 93) note that 'capacity' focuses on the legal entitlement of the applicant to litigate generally. In relation to 'standing', this concept is normally based on an assessment of the relationship between the individual or group and the subject matter of the particular application. Individuals must have 'sufficient interest in the matter to which the application relates' (Northern Ireland's RCJ Order 53 Rule 3 (5)). For example, applicants for planning permission may be considered to have sufficient interest in the outcome of that decision.

Nevertheless, limitations apply. In *Re D's Application [2003] NI 295 CA* – the Lord Chief Justice stated that 'standing' is a relative concept, to be deployed according to the potency of the public interest content of the case. Importantly, the test of standing is a flexible one. As Orbinson and colleagues clarify (2009, pp 10–11), an important aim is to weed out 'a crank, mere busybody(s) or mischief maker(s)', as they have no standing to seek JR.

In practice, the concept of standing has proved to be quite extensive. For example, standing exists on human rights grounds, where the individual must be a 'victim' of the disputed decision. Local authorities that can show that a planning decision in another council area may impact upon their own district will have standing. Participants in planning inquiries may have standing to challenge the decision. Neighbours affected by a planning decision have been recognised to have standing, as well as the 'environmentally concerned' individual. Affected developers can have standing if they can establish that there is a real possibility that the grant of planning permission would affect the likelihood of their own development proving successful. Those with a financial or commercial interest may have standing. Groups of interested persons, such as Greenpeace, Friends of the Earth, the RSPB, international professional bodies such as the RTPI, or locally -based environmental pressure groups such as the Royal Society of Ulster Architects may also have standing.

The Judicial Review process

In order to initiate JR in England and Wales and Northern Ireland, there is a two-stage procedure. An application for JR must be initiated within three months of the date when the disputed decision was made. The first stage is the application for leave to apply for JR. The second stage involves applying to the Court for the substantive hearing, through an originating motion. In England and Wales this step is known as the permission stage of the application (Larkin and Scoffield, 2007).

In Northern Ireland, JR is governed under the Judicature (Northern Ireland) Act 1978 (S. 18–S. 25) and Order 53 of the Rules of the Court of the Judicature (RCJ) (Northern Ireland) 1980. Guidance is laid out in the *Judicial Review Practice Note 1/2008*. The Northern Irish model corresponds to the procedure used in England and Wales under Part 54 of the Civil Procedures Rules of 1998, which has seen some minor amendments in terminology.

In Scotland, the Courts Reform (Scotland) Act 2014 introduced some amendments within the Scottish system of JR. The intention is to reduce the number of JR hearings by introducing a preliminary stage at which permission to proceed to JR is granted or refused. A judge will consider if there is interest in the matter, and if there is a chance of success.

Application for leave

The purpose of 'leave' is to find a means of filtering out applications without merit and to free up Court time to deal with cases for which leave has been granted. In this first stage of the process the JR application is brought before the High Court in England and Wales and Northern Ireland, and the Court of Session in Scotland. Recent reforms in Scotland have introduced an equivalent to this leave stage and time-limit.

The Court then makes a determination as to whether the application should proceed to the substantive hearing. Orbinson et al (2009, p 7) explain that the test for granting leave is:

> whether the applicant has an arguable case on each of the grounds on which the applicant seeks to challenge the impugned decision.

There can be occasions where the respondent may be able to persuade the Court that leave should not be granted, by providing reasons such as the applicant has insufficient interest in the subject matter of the challenge, the application has been made too late, the applicant has been guilty of material non-disclosure or the applicant has access to an alternative remedy. This latter point about having an alternative remedy is important, as JR is viewed as an option of last resort.

After the grant of leave

Once leave is granted, the process moves to the next stage, with an 'originating motion' being issued and served on the respondents (on all persons directly affected). A 'notice of motion' follows this, setting out the grounds upon which leave has been granted and the relevant information (for example, affidavits, exhibits and so on) associated with the matter.

The respondent's affidavit(s) must then be drafted in response, setting out the evidence (but not the arguments). An affidavit is a written sworn statement of fact, voluntarily made under oath, and administered by a person authorised to do so by law.

It is up to the Court to refuse or grant permission for third-party interventions, by written and/or oral submissions.

Format of hearings

There is no fixed requirement for an oral hearing in all cases, and it may be that written submissions will suffice if there is no dispute as to the primary facts (Anthony, 2014, p 243). Nevertheless, it should be remembered that the right to a hearing is regarded as a fundamental precept of both common law and the European Convention on Human Rights.

The applicant's counsel opens the case and makes their submissions as to why the application should be allowed, providing affidavit evidence and dealing with points of law or authorities (Larkin and Scoffield, 2007, p 182). The respondent's counsel will then make their submissions, similarly outlining their case, dealing with points of law and explaining why the application should be dismissed.

The applicant can respond, but can deal only with matters raised by the respondent in their submission. It is not permissible to introduce new arguments or materials. Larkin and Scoffield (2007) note that it is generally not the case that oral evidence is relied upon at the hearing; rather, the evidence contained in the affidavits is used. On occasion, parties can call witnesses for cross-examination, such as where affidavits are unsatisfactory and so cannot be accepted with any confidence without cross-examination. In this context, Orbinson and colleagues (2009, p 101) noted that the English Courts have held that it is:

> undesirable that inspectors, given their quasi-judicial office, should be cross-examined and have only allowed it when there was unsatisfactory evidence leading to an inference of improper behaviour by an inspector.

The judge may give a decision at the end of the hearing, although it is more common in JR for a written judgment to be given at a later date (Larkin and Scoffield, 2007). The judge will generally indicate what relief is to be provided at the same time as the judgment. Occasionally, a separate hearing for remedies can be set up, although this is quite rare and usually occurs where there is controversy or debate between the parties as to what relief is appropriate.

Upon receiving the High Court judgment, respondents may wish to pursue the matter further. Leave may then be sought to appeal to the Courts of Appeal, to the House of Lords and, ultimately, to the European Courts (Orbinson et al, 2009). While this is currently the position, the implications of the result of the UK's EU referendum are unclear. We note that the UK's relations with the EU will be affected only once Article 50 is triggered to initiate the so-called 'Brexit'. Interestingly, for some, the UK's subjection to a foreign Court was intrinsically problematic (Ekins, 2016). For others, the EU was an important source of environmental protection. Nonetheless, as the Law Society (2016) observed in terms of people's legal rights, leaving the EU does not remove the UK's membership from either the European Convention of Human Rights, or from the jurisdiction of the European Court of Human Rights.

Remedies

Five remedies are available under JR. Remedies are entirely discretionary and not available as of right. Morcover, remedies do not enable the High Court to substitute its decision for that of the original decision maker (Anthony, 2014, p 267). In exercising their discretion, factors that may be taken into account include: the impact on third parties, the impact on good administration, the consideration of the public interest in having the decision in question made lawfully, the sufficiency of interest, the availability of other remedies and, inter alia, whether granting the relief sought would secure a practical benefit (Orbinson et al, 2009, p 106).

Section 18(1) of the Judicature Act 1978 and RCJ Order 53 set out the following forms of relief: an order of mandamus; an order of certiorari; an order of prohibition; a declaration; or an injunction. The first three of these remedies are known as the 'prerogative' orders and were formerly known as writs, issued by the Crown (Anthony, 2014). The latter two forms of relief have their origins in equity and are traditionally more flexible, being unconstrained by strict rules of precedent.

An order of mandamus is a coercive order requiring a public authority to perform a public (statutory) duty (Larkin and Scoffield, 2007). Such an order would be sought where the applicant wants to force the respondent to do something that it is under a public obligation to do. Here, the applicant should have called upon the respondent to perform the relevant duty. Anthony (2014) notes that failure to comply with an order of mandamus may be considered contempt of Court, punishable by means of a fine. An example of this remedy in practice is provided by Orbinson and colleagues (2009), where an order of mandamus could be used to compel the government department responsible for planning to determine a long-standing planning application, even though the applicant had not appealed to the PAC on grounds of non-determination within the statutory period.

Larkin and Scoffield (2007) provide an explanation of the remedy of certiorari, otherwise known in the English Courts as 'a quashing order' for unlawful decisions. In cases where a decision, order or policy is being challenged, the applicant will want the decision to be set aside or invalidated. As such, certiorari is the most commonly requested remedy in JR. The Court may quash a decision in whole or in part. The effect of certiorari is to render the decision or other measure in respect of which it is made as having been without any legal effect, enabling the decision to be taken again – but this time legally (Anthony, 2014).

An order of prohibition restrains a public authority from doing something unlawful, going beyond its jurisdiction or acting unlawfully (that is, going beyond its powers) (Larkin and Scoffield, 2007). An English example, *Allen v City of London Corporation [1981] JPL 685*, concerns where the Court declined to issue an order of prohibition restraining the planning authority from reaching a decision on a planning application before the conclusion of a local plan inquiry (Orbinson et al, 2009). Prohibition can be used to prevent the respondent from making the same decision in the future. Failure to observe an order of prohibition can lead to contempt of Court (Anthony, 2014).

A declaration confirms the legal state of play between parties (Orbinson et al, 2009), involving a judicial statement on the legal position. How such declarations are used in practice varies. Where the conduct of a public body, such as the PAC, is challenged, the Court may choose to declare the conduct unlawful, rather than issuing a formal order of prohibition forbidding the body from acting in that way. Orbinson and colleagues (2009) go on to state that that body will accept the declaration and mend its ways without being formally compelled to do so.

Finally, injunctions are one of the most useful and flexible aspects of JR. Larkin and Scoffield (2007) note that injunctions can, like a mandamus order, require the respondent to do something or to refrain from doing something. However, injunctions tend to be sought as a form of interim relief, rather than a final order. The use of injunctions is consequently quite rare. Where used, a final injunction is issued only when the grounds for review have been demonstrated and where the Court considers that this form of remedy should be granted.

Box 11.2: Dylan Thomas's views from writing-shed at risk

A JR was granted after plans were agreed for a wind turbine across the estuary from Dylan Thomas's writing-shed. Planning permission for a 45-metre single wind turbine in Llansteffan was granted by Carmarthenshire Council Planning Committee in May 2014, despite council planning officers recommending its refusal. It was argued that the turbine would be visible across the estuary from the famous poet's boat-house and writing-shed in Laugharne.

There were close to 500 objections from the public in relation to the proposed development. Objectors said that the turbine would blight the view that has attracted international tourists and Dylan Thomas fans for decades. The officer's planning report had highlighted that tourism is an important economic driver for Wales and that the negative impact on tourism would be significant, since the proposed development would adversely affect visual amenity and visitors' perceptions of the attraction. The residents of Laugharne were granted a JR to challenge the Council's decision to grant permission on a number of grounds, including that the planning committee acted irrationally in departing from the officer's advice on landscape and cultural harm. The campaigners won their legal challenge in January 2015. The Council was required to pay £21, 275 in costs. (*Davies v Carmarthenshire CC [2015] EWHC 230 (Admin)*)

The Ombudsman

Where a government body is considered not to have acted properly or fairly, or to have given a poor service and not to have put things right, there are two levels available for making a complaint. The Parliamentary Ombudsman exists in relation to central government departments. The Local Government Ombudsman provides an impartial service, investigating complaints on behalf of people who believe they have been treated unfairly as a result of 'maladministration' by a local authority.

Although there is no strict definition of 'maladministration', the concept covers issues such as bias, neglect, delay, incompetence and inaptitude. For example, an LPA may take an excessive length of time to deal with a matter without good reason, or not follow its own rules and guidelines, or act corruptly or fraudulently, or provide incorrect information. Maladministration also includes knowingly giving advice that is misleading or inadequate, offering no redress or disproportionate redress, or refusing to answer reasonable questions. Such behaviour is simply not acceptable, or professional, planning practice.

In the case of a local planning matter, for example, the Local Government Ombudsman investigates the circumstances surrounding how the LPA conducted itself. Importantly, the role of the Ombudsman is not to arbitrate on a decision of the council, nor to overturn a decision because someone may disagree with it. The remit of the Local Government Ombudsman is to investigate complaints by members of the public who believe they have suffered injustice due to maladministration. The issue here is not the decision (an appeal), nor the process (JR), but the (poor) exercise of 'administrative functions'. Moreover, one does not have to be the applicant or appellant to pursue a complaint through the Ombudsman.

The role of the Ombudsman has been considered by the Law Commission (2005), which stated that the Ombudsman provides a cost-free and more informal method of dealing with grievances against the state (than the Courts). Indeed, it has been said that the Ombudsman may, in some ways, be a better long-term complaints-resolution mechanism where public bodies are concerned, on the grounds that the service is more able to deal with the systematic nature of some public law disputes. Moreover, in contrast to Court proceedings, the Ombudsman offers an informal alternative. The approach taken is inquisitorial rather than adversarial, and the objective is to focus on the facts of the case, rather than the complaint as presented, or who presents the most persuasive legal argument.

Complaints are generally channelled through the local authority chief executive. If the council's response is unsatisfactory, or if there is no response, then the Ombudsman will launch an investigation. An investigator is appointed to determine if there is a case to answer and advise on proceedings. A formal report is then prepared by the Ombudsman as to whether there has been maladministration and the extent to which the complainant suffered as a result. The Ombudsman may recommend a course of action to the council in order to rectify the matter, such as paying compensation or carrying out remedial actions, although s/he cannot force the council to take the recommended action. Where appropriate, this procedure can go some way to addressing third-party concerns.

Box 11.3: Poor service? Failing to act properly

An LPA gave planning permission for a two-storey side and single-storey rear extension. The complainant had written to the council, objecting to the proposed development, since it would: (i) be out of keeping with the street-scene; (ii) encroach on his boundary; and (iii) impact on the light to his kitchen. Despite carrying out a site visit prior to making the recommendation, the planning officer failed to take account of the relationship between the neighbouring properties, particularly with respect to the likely effects of the proposed extension on the light to the complainant's kitchen window. An Ombudsman case ensued.

The Local Government Ombudsman found fault in the way the council had considered the impact of the proposed extensions on the complainant's house. Specifically, the Ombudsman identified significant adverse impact in relation to the reduction in light to the kitchen. In addition, the Ombudsman observed that the council had failed to take into account its own relevant development plan policies in reaching its decision. The cost to the council of remedying the injustice and paying for the kitchen to be reconfigured was £7,000. ('Tariq's story' – Local Government Ombudsman, 2014)

Chapter summary

In this chapter we have explored the different means of redress and challenge that exist in relation to the planning system. First we looked at the ways in which a state decision can be re-examined by means of an appeal. We highlighted similarities across the four administrations, noting that the type of appeal is intended to be proportionate to the nature of the case. As further enhancements are sought to improve the efficiency, transparency and accountability of the appeals system, we noted that changes are being introduced. Notably, in Scotland, the use of LRBs was highlighted as a way to strengthen local accountability by enabling locally elected members to review delegated decisions. Three points here are important: separation of decision-making entities is retained; local autonomy is strengthened; and resources can be targeted at major or more contentious appeals. In England, fast-tracked appeals have been introduced as a way to provide timely decisions. There are no third-party rights of appeal in the UK: the appeals process focuses on individual decisions from the perspective of first party interests only.

While appeals concern the merits of the decision, JR turns on the legitimacy of the way in which the decision was made, or the use of statutory powers by a public body. We noted that JR is a mechanism of last resort. Given the number of stages involved, and the nature of this process, JR tends to be very costly and, as such, lies beyond the reach of private individuals or charities. However, both the planning appeals system and the broader route of JR, are very important philosophically to the operation of the planning system, since they are designed to ensure the legitimacy and accountability of state controls over the private interest. State powers must be used appropriately.

Finally, we looked at the complaints procedures that exist through the Ombudsman, highlighting that this process is open to third parties. Interestingly, when the function of Local Government Ombudsman was established in 1974, there were more complaints about planning in that first year than in any other area. It remains one of the areas most complained about today (Local Government Ombudsman, 2014), demonstrating that considerable care must be taken when following planning rules and procedures. In contrast to the appeals system, both JR and the Ombudsman may be understood as concerned with the proper functioning of state processes and, as such, they address public-interest concerns.

Recommended reading

For more information on Appeals and Local Review Bodies see:

Ferguson, A.C. and Watchman, J. (2015) *Local planning reviews in Scotland*, Edinburgh: Avizandum Publishing Ltd.

Green Balance, Leigh Day & Co Solicitors, Popham, J. and Purdue, M. (2002) *Third party rights of appeal in planning*, Available at: http://www. civicvoice.org.uk/uploads/files/Third_party_rights_of_appeal_Orgs.pdf [Accessed: 28 July 2016]

Moore, V. and Purdue, M. (2014) *A practical approach to planning law*, 13th edn, Oxford: Oxford University Press, chapter 18.

For an overview of the Judicial Review process, see:

Anthony, G. (2014) *Judicial Review in Northern Ireland*, 2nd edn, Oxford: Hart Publishing.

Duxbury, R. (2012) *Telling & Duxbury's planning law and procedure*, 15th edn, Oxford: Oxford University Press, chapter 19.

Law Commission (2015) *Remedies against public services, a scoping report*, available at http://www.lawcom.gov.uk/wp-content/uploads/2015/04/ Remedies_Public_Bodies_Scoping.pdf [Accessed: 28 July 2016]

Orbinson, W., McGhee, G. and Warke, J. (2009) *Planning and judicial review*, Belfast: SLS Legal Publications (NI).

To learn more about the role of the Local Government Ombudsman see:

Local Government Ombudsman (2014) *Not in my backyard: Local people and the planning process. Focus report: learning lessons from complaints*, Coventry: LGO. Available at: https://www.lichfielddc.gov.uk/Council/Planning/ Planning-guidance/Downloads/Local-people-and-the-planning-process-Local-Government-Ombudsman-report.pdf [Accessed 28 July 2016].

You should also consult with the information that is available for you online given the dynamic nature of planning to ensure you have the most current information:

England: Planning Portal (remembering to identify 'England' as your location): http://www.planningportal.gov.uk
Northern Ireland: Planning Portal: https://www.planningni.gov.uk/
Scotland: ePlanning Scotland: https://eplanning.scotland.gov.uk/WAM/
Wales: Town Planning Portal (remembering to identify 'Wales' as your location): http://www.planningportal.gov.uk

TWELVE

Reflections on planning law

Chapter contents

- Sustainable development
- Well-being
- Local democracy
- Community planning
- Public participation
- New styles of joint working
- Permitted development
- Conditions
- Marine planning
- Transboundary working and combined consents
- Final word

Introduction

This book has sought to stimulate your interest in planning law by setting out why and how it works in practice. The Town and Country Planning Act 1947, a major milestone in the development of a dedicated town planning regime, was a core element of the post-war state apparatus and the welfare state. Seventy years on, and against a backdrop of neoliberal ideology, the 1947 legislation remains a cornerstone of British planning. The anniversary year of 2017 provides a timely occasion for reflection. Moreover, as Sir Desmond Heap, a leading authority on planning law, noted in 1978, "Town Planning law never stops!" (Heap, 1978, p 24). So, whither planning law?

We have seen in the preceding chapters that planning law provides the legal framework and operational context for how the state, market and civil society interrelate. Importantly, the various rules of planning set out who must do what, and with what authority, and who can do what. Planning law provides the rules of the game. A range of public servants and political (elected) actors then implement the planning system on a range of national, regional, local and neighbourhood scales. Judicial actors play a central role in interpreting planning law through the Courts. Here, the common law system and precedence are of paramount importance to the functioning of the UK's discretionary planning tradition.

Planning is a normative activity. We began by reflecting on the fact that land is a precious resource, and that we all hold a stake in thinking about and debating the best use of land. However, social constructions of what is best vary. The Foresight Land Use Futures Project (2010), for example, pointed to the multifunctionality of land (while acknowledging the potential conflicts over its use and development) both in the short term and over the longer term. The Foresight report identified a number of systemic issues in relation to land management, including the disconnect between institutional arrangements and private ownership, where there is a need to strike a balance between protecting the interests of landowners, local priorities and the wider public interest. Land-use planning, as part of a wider land governance framework, involves decisions taken at different spatial scales. These scales do not always best reflect the level at which impacts are felt, nor correspond to how natural systems operate, as with water resource management (Foresight Land Use Futures Project, 2010). This book has sought to show how, over time, planning law has evolved and expanded to reflect changing appreciations of what society wants from the land resource and to minimise the adverse effects of negative impacts.

Decisions about the nature and scope of planning law are clearly influenced by the wider context and prevailing political ideology. Notably, the UK's constitutional context continues to be questioned. The Scottish Independence referendum in 2014, for example, is illustrative of particular spatial dynamics. Further changes to the UK constitutional settlement are to be expected as a continuing commitment to devolve powers from Westminster is translated into local actions on the ground. This political context is important, as planning is a devolved power. Since the millennium, planning law across the devolved UK has been re-shaped in relation to other areas of state activity, such as community planning in Scotland, community relations in Northern Ireland and health and well-being in Wales. Further constitutional change can be expected as a consequence of the result from the UK's 2016 EU referendum.

This final chapter comments on certain key aspects and speculates on some potential future directions. Two fundamental questions are: What should planning law seek to do? Do the legal provisions work in practice? A number of key concepts and issues are likely to influence planning law in the coming years. Some of these are familiar, others less so. The following are our top 10.

Sustainable development

Since the 1980s, principles of sustainability have become relatively more established. Land has also become more sought after as a commodity, with significant financial implications that are not evenly distributed. Concerns over climate change and an ever-increasing global and urbanised population have raised public awareness of the vulnerability and ultimate scarcity of the land resource. We are beginning to see more deliberate attempts, through planning law, to put a stronger emphasis on the economic, social and environmental dimensions of sustainable development. While there continue to be arguments over what an appropriate balance of sustainable development might look like in practice, sustainability has become an accepted and overarching principle informing state thinking and requiring proactive intervention. The Planning Act (Northern Ireland) 2011 S. 5-(1), for example, states:

> Any person who exercises any function under this Part must exercise that function with the objective of furthering sustainable development.

What 'furthering sustainable development' means in each case, however, will be contested. Interpretation through case law will no doubt offer meaning, but decision makers will need to take this objective into account when determining planning applications.

Well-being

Linked to sustainable development is the more recent concern with well-being. In some ways this reflects planning law's original concerns with public health, but the concept of well-being extends beyond narrow issues of sickness, to incorporate cultural and intellectual values. The policy context emphasises prevention and is proactive in nature, rather than reactive. As we confront an aging population, actively promoting well-being is in the public interest. But what does this mean for planning?

Chapter 25 of the Planning Act (Northern Ireland) 2011 specifically highlights that the Act makes provision for matters relating to planning and 'connected purposes' and the remit of the new planning legislation specifically includes 'promoting or improving well-being'. Similarly, the Scottish Government's overarching purpose emphasises flourishing, with all government activities, including planning, required to work towards sustainable economic growth and reducing inequalities. In Wales, planning must now take account of the Well-being of Future Generations (Wales) Act 2015. This requirement includes paying attention to seven well-being goals, alongside the sustainable development principle. Such ambitions may be considered progressive objectives, and also suggest concerted efforts to reconnect with and to better articulate ideas around the public interest. Critically, a focus on outcomes (rather than process) is a core aspect of this agenda with a clear emphasis on different public sector providers aligning their activities for better effect.

Local democracy

An important principle of planning is that decisions should be taken at the local level. The development of neighbourhood planning in England is one area where planning powers are being decentralised. The May 2016 Queen's Speech, which included a new Neighbourhood Planning and Infrastructure Bill, identified the need to address aspects of resourcing neighbourhood planning to further empower local people. This is a powerful statement of the commitment to strengthening local powers.

A related matter turns on the use of delegated powers. The use of delegated schemes in relation to development management helps to focus political time and effort on significant rather than minor planning matters. The further delegation of powers to enable elected members in Scotland to review locally determined delegated decisions through LRBs is an example of an attempt to establish a proportionate appeals system, while enhancing local accountability. This may be another area for experimentation in planning law as a way to expand local autonomy.

Community planning

Organisational arrangements with respect to planning essentially mean that different legal duties and responsibilities fall to different departments and agencies. In part, these arrangements help to hold decision makers to account and provide a context for strategic and locally sensitive decision-taking. Coordinating these governmental activities across different layers (multi-level governance) clearly requires a systematic approach and awareness of how different components conform to the different tiers and responsibilities. Critically, there is a need to coordinate plans that will have shared outcomes.

The statutory linkage between land-use planning and community planning in Northern Ireland can be regarded as a step-change in linking community visions with the management and development of the local land resource. In Northern Ireland the community plan will become the overarching plan for a partnership of actors from across the public, voluntary and private sectors. Local government will have an important facilitative role in preparing and implementing this vision, but other service providers, such as the police, fire-safety and health, for example, will also be taking forward their statutory obligations. In this context, the land-use development plan will be subservient to a wider and holistic agenda of community planning. Within this changing context, a well-functioning planning system will foreground the land resource. Ideally, planning law will accommodate and mediate between the fullest range of different actors and actively seek to engage as many people as possible. The planning system will recognise that degrees of power and influence are distributed differently; and will provide opportunities for different parties to participate in decisions that affect them, taking account of future generations. As the new local government boundaries and planning system in Northern Ireland bed in, we will be better able to see how this active linkage between community planning and land-use planning works in practice.

Emerging thinking in Scotland, arising from the review of the Scottish planning system (Beveridge et al, 2016) also emphasises the need for improvements. Key aspects identified include: greater synthesis between development and infrastructure planning; a more collaborative mind-set; and for planning to be positioned at the heart of local authorities' corporate agendas. This line of argument points to the need for the coordination of different statutory requirements at the community level.

Public participation

Public participation has been a tenet of the planning system since the Skeffington Report on People and Planning in 1969. Interestingly, while the right to participate in planning decision-making is fully accepted – and indeed has been reinforced by the 1998 Aarhus Convention in relation to environmental justice – concerns regarding the timing and amount of public engagement continue to be raised in relation to the efficient operation of the planning system.

For example, the Planning Act (Northern Ireland) 2011 stipulates the preparation and publication of a statement of community involvement at both central and local government levels. Explanations for disinterest or non-engagement by the public vary, but the important point here is that the existence of a statutory provision to prepare and publish a statement of community involvement does not of itself result in individuals and communities participating in planning. There is a qualitative judgement to be made about how well a given LPA has involved the public, and many a research project or council strategy has sought to improve public engagement.

Compliance with the law by producing a statement of involvement and timetable does not necessarily produce the desired outcomes in terms of a community-informed plan. The level of participation will depend in part upon the quality of the processes put in place: how convenient, timely, easy, accessible, inclusive and so on these arrangements are. The Independent Review of the Scottish Planning System (Beveridge et al, 2016) highlighted the potential of using social media and 3D visualisation in improving approaches to engagement. Particular emphasis was placed on young people, with a recommendation that consideration should be given to introducing a new statutory right for young people to be consulted on the development plan. Such a right would realise the terms of Article 12 of the UN Convention on the Rights of the Child. More generally, however, Beveridge and colleagues (2016) noted that views were mixed in terms of whether early and equitable community engagement could be enhanced through improved practice alone or necessitated legislative change.

New styles of joint working

Throughout this book, we have outlined the ways in which state–market relations have evolved. Our intention has been to illustrate that planning law has sought to clarify and strengthen responsibilities for joint working – both in terms of actively engaging civil society in new ways, such as neighbourhood planning, and through new relations with the market, such as public-private partnerships. There is clear evidence of shifting responsibilities to enhance working arrangements in terms of the planning process. For example, in relation to monitoring the implementation of planning permissions, the Planning etc. (Scotland) Act 2006 initiated provisions with respect to developers' responsibilities for notification about both the initiation and completion of development. The statutory provisions also make the commencement of development without prior notification of the local authority an offence.

Similarly, the Town and Country Planning (Hierarchy of Developments) (Scotland) Regulations 2009 introduced Planning Processing Agreements as a project management tool in development management. Such agreements exist between developers, the LPA and relevant stakeholders and are intended to set out the key stages involved in determining a planning application. They cover what information is required and from whom, and the time-scales involved. A commitment to joint working underpins this idea, but it is also an effort to improve the transparency, responsibility and predictability of action of the different sectors involved. Changes to planning law may be seen as having introduced a subtle shift from the planner as regulator to planner as facilitator and enabler.

Permitted development

Core to planning is the concept of development. A particular area of reform relates to permitted development rights. Changes introduced in England in 2015 were designed to support growth in the economy and make development in a range of areas easier for businesses and house-holders, including: use of premises, housing, domestic extensions, retail premises and use of solar-panels on commercial buildings. Related to this are certain changes to procedural aspects, including deemed discharge of planning conditions in cases where the LPA does not respond within a given time-period. Such modifications to planning law are intended to speed up decision-making. They involve a reduction in state controls and limit third party input. For example, extension of permitted development rights on the one hand increases what individual landowners and developers can do; but on the other hand such changes effectively constrain the rights of others to comment on or challenge development schemes or the use of the land resource. Have we got the balance right?

Conditions

Change is constant, and the planning system continues to evolve. For example, in England the Neighbourhood Planning and Infrastructure Bill 2016 identified a reduction in the use of pre-commencement planning conditions. This agenda is indicative of the on-going commitment to streamlining the system. A commitment to continuous improvement and performance monitoring means that no area of planning law can escape scrutiny. Roles and responsibilities will change as a result.

Marine planning

Another area to watch with respect to planning law is the whole area of marine planning. There is a potential risk that marine planning legislation will develop separately from terrestrial planning. We have sought to show that a sound appreciation of the land–sea interface is required for both systems to work as part of a bigger whole or 'system of systems'. This connection is critical if we wish to ensure the resilience of our coastal infrastructure, manage our energy needs and maintain a productive and healthy relationship with the marine environment.

Transboundary working and combined consents

The twin ideas of reform and modernisation of the planning system have sought to legislate for change since the 1980s. Part of this agenda necessitates changing the legal framework, but it also requires a culture change. For example, given the sustained emphasis on promoting economic growth and supporting the delivery of housing and infrastructure, it is only to be expected that further changes will be introduced that are presented as improving the workings of the planning and related systems, such as the combining of consents, including for roads and drainage. New areas of development, such as aquaculture, also tend to require multiple consents.

Efforts to ensure a more integrated approach to environmental protection mean that it is important that those professionals whose duty it is to implement and enforce planning law need to work effectively as part of an integrated environmental approach. Such joint working is already necessary with respect to Environmental Impact Assessment, Strategic Environmental Assessment, Habitats Regulations Assessment and Flood Risk Assessment. As we noted earlier, the result of the 2016 EU referendum, and consequential renegotiation of the UK's relationship with the EU will very likely change the authority and remit of a common European environmental protection regime. It remains to be seen how the different parts of the UK proceed in terms of both their land and marine planning legal frameworks and how they go about finding an appropriate balance between environmental, economic and social priorities. An important issue to watch will be how the different legal frameworks mesh together and manage transboundary and – particularly in the case of Northern Ireland – cross-border planning issues. While putting a legal 'duty to cooperate' in place may well be seen as a good starting point, how we work together in the future to plan and manage development in the public interest may prove more challenging in practice.

Final word

Our intention in this book was to stimulate wider interest in the legal frameworks underpinning planning practice, to explain how and why planning decisions are made, and specifically to improve understanding of development management. As the nature, scope, impacts and effects of 'development' change in light of societal demands and technological innovation, planning law will likely continue to adapt as further controls are considered necessary. Public interest in air quality, coastal erosion, employment opportunities or fuel security is illustrative of just some of the related pressures claiming political attention. As the rules of the game change and state–market–civil relations are inevitably re-adjusted, rights and responsibilities with respect to the environment and future generations will also evolve. We may see a further shift from state legal powers and controls to a planning regime involving enhanced developer responsibility towards the environment and local communities. In tandem, there may be an extension of community rights in managing development in individual localities. The precise role of the planning professional will also change. We hope that this book enables you actively to participate in these discussions.

References

Aldridge, H. (1915) *The case for town planning*, London: The National Housing and Town Planning Council.

Anthony, G. (2014) *Judicial Review in Northern Ireland*, 2nd edn, Oxford: Hart Publishing.

Barclay, C. (2002) 'Third party rights of appeal in planning', Research Paper 02/38, 22 May, London: House of Commons.

Bell, S., McGillivray, D. and Pederson, O.W. (2013) *Environmental law*, 8th edn, Oxford: Oxford University Press.

Beveridge, C., Biberbach, P. and Hamilton, J. (2016) *Empowering great places: An independent review of the Scottish planning system*, Edinburgh: Scottish Government.

BGS (British Geological Society) (2016) 'Why do we need minerals?' NERC. Available at: http://www.bgs.ac.uk/mineralsuk/mineralsyou/whydo.html [Accessed 11 November 2016].

Booth, P. (2003) *Planning by consent: The origins and nature of British development control*, Abingdon-on-Thames: Routledge.

British Geological Survey (2016) 'Minerals UK, Centre for Sustainable Mineral Development'. Available at: http://www.bgs.ac.uk/mineralsUK/ [Accessed 11 November 2016].

Britnell, S., Cooke, J. and Sheppard, A. (2014) *Planning enforcement: At the crossroads*. Available at: http://eprints.uwe.ac.uk/24531/ [Accessed 11 November 2016].

Cabinet Office (2006) *The UK Government's approach to public sector reform, the Prime Minister's Strategy Unit*, London: Public Service Reform team.

Cardiff Capital Region (2015) *Powering the Welsh local economy*, Cardiff: Welsh Government.

Cave, S. (2016) 'A new mandate, a new environment', Blog, 3 May. Available at: http://www.assemblyresearchmatters.org/2016/05/03/a-new-mandate-a-new-environment/#more-71 [Accessed 11 November 2016].

Cave, S., Rehfisch, A., Smith, L. and Winter, G. (2013) *Comparison of the planning systems of the four UK countries*, Research paper 13/39, Inter-Parliamentary Research and Information Network, Stormont: Northern Ireland Assembly.

CBI (Confederation of British Industry) (2011) 'Distributing minerals to future markets'. Available at http://www.ukmineralsforum.org.uk/downloads/CBI%20UKMF_Distributing%20minerals%20to%20future%20markets.pdf [Accessed 11 November 2016].

Claydon, J. (2006) 'Marine spatial planning: A new opportunity for planners', *The Town Planning Review*, vol 77, no 2, pp 1–6.

Clifford, B.P. and Tewdwr-Jones, M. (1998) *The collaborating planner: Planning in the neoliberal age*, Bristol: Policy Press.

Climate-KIC (2016) 'PLACE'IN: Planning Circular Economy for Industrial areas', project website. Available at: http://www.climate-kic.org/projects/placein/# [Accessed 11 November 2016].

Cullingworth, B., Nadin, V., Hart, T., Davoudi, S., Pendlebury, J., Vigar, G., Webb, D. and Townshed, T. (2015) *Town and country planning in the UK*, 15th edn, Abingdon-on-Thames: Routledge.

Day, J. (2008) 'The need and practice of monitoring, evaluating, and adapting marine planning and management'. *Lessons from the Great Barrier Reef*, no 32, pp 823–31.

DCLG (Department for Communities and Local Government) (2012) *National Planning Policy Framework*, London: The Stationery Office.

DCLG (2013) 'Explanatory Memorandum to the Town and Country Planning (Temporary Stop Notice) (England) (Revocation) Regulations', London: DCLG.

DCLG (2014) 'Ensuring effective enforcement', Planning Practice Guidance, paragraph: 004 Reference ID: 17b-004-20140306. Available at: http://planningguidance.communities.gov.uk/blog/guidance/ensuring-effective-enforcement/ [Accessed 11 November 2016].

DCLG (2015a) *Plain English guide to the planning system*, London: The Stationery Office.

DCLG (2015b) 'Ensuring effective enforcement', Planning Practice Guidance, 17b (01/09/2015). Available at: http://planningguidance.communities.gov.uk/blog/guidance/ensuring-effective-enforcement/ [Accessed 11 November 2016].

DEFRA (Department of Environment, Food and Rural Affairs) (2002) *Safeguarding our seas: A strategy for the conservation and sustainable development of our marine environment*, London: The Stationery Office.

DEFRA (2006) *A Marine Bill: A consultation document*, London: The Stationery Office.

DEFRA (2007) *A sea change. A Marine Bill White Paper*, London: The Stationery Office.

DEFRA (2009) *Our seas – a shared resource, high level marine objectives*. Available at: http://www.gov.scot/resource/doc/1057/0080305.pdf [Accessed 11 November 2016].

DEFRA (2011) *Marine policy statement*. Available at: https://www.gov.uk/government/publications/uk-marine-policy-statement [Accessed 11 November 2016].

DEFRA (2012) *UK statistics on waste*. Available at https://www.gov.uk/government/uploads/system/uploads/attachment_data/file/487916/UK_Statistics_on_Waste_statistical_notice_15_12_2015_update_f2.pdf [Accessed 11 November 2016].

DOE (Department of the Environment) (2011) *Tree preservation order: A guide to protecting trees*, Advice Leaflet 4. Available at: http://www.planningni.gov.uk/index/advice/advice_leaflets/8pp_tree_preservation_order_lores.pdf [Accessed 11 November 2016].

DOE (Department of the Environment (2014) *Living Places: An Urban Stewardship and Design Guide for Northern Ireland*, Belfast: DOE. Available at: http://www.planningni.gov.uk/index/policy/supplementary_guidance/guides/livingplaces_-_web.pdf [Accessed 30 November 2016].

DOE (Department of the Environment) (2015) *Strategic Planning Policy Statement*, Belfast: DOE. Available at: http://www.planningni.gov.uk/index/policy/spps_28_september_2015-3.pdf [Accessed 3 November 2016].

DRD (Department of Regional Development) (2001) *Shaping our future: Regional development strategy for Northern Ireland 2025*, Belfast: DRD.

DRD (2012) *Building a better future: Regional development strategy 2035*, Belfast: DRD.

Duck, R. (2011) *This shrinking land: Climate change and Britain's coasts*, Dundee: Dundee University Press Ltd.

Dundee City Council (2009) *Local reviews and Dundee City Council's local review body. A users guide*. Available at: http://www.dundeecity.gov.uk/dundeecity/uploaded_publications/publication_1374.pdf [Accessed 11 November 2016].

Duxbury, R. (2012) *Telling & Duxbury's planning law and procedure*, 15th edn, Oxford: Oxford University Press.

Ekins, R. (2016) 'Brexit and judicial power', Policy Exchange. Available at: https://policyexchange.org.uk/publication/brexit-and-judicial-power/ [Accessed 11 November 2016].

Exeter St James Forum (2013) *Exeter St James neighbourhood plan*, Exeter: Exeter St James Community Trust Limited. Available at: http://exeterstjamesforum.org/st-james%20plan [Accessed 11 November 2016].

Feeny, D., Hanna, S. and McEvoy, A.F. (1996) 'Questioning the assumptions of the "tragedy of the commons" model of fisheries', *Land Economics*, vol 72, no 2, pp 187–205.

Ferguson, A.C. and Watchman, J. (2015) *Local planning reviews in Scotland*, Edinburgh: Avizandum Publishing Ltd.

Field, D. (2005) 'Planning in court – the rules and the role of judicial review in planning, *Journal of Planning Law*, December, pp 49–76.

Foresight Land Use Futures Project (2010) *Final project report*, London: The Government Office for Science. Available at: http://www.foresight.gov.uk/OurWork/ActiveProjects/LandUse/lufoutputs.asp [Accessed 11 November 2016].

Friends of the Earth (2006) *Planning for the environment in Northern Ireland*, Belfast: FOE.

GAUFRE (2006) *A flood of space: Towards a spatial structure plan for sustainable management of the North Sea*, Brussels: University of Ghent, Maritime Institute for Belgian Science Policy.

Giddens, A. (1998) *The third way: The renewal of social democracy*, Cambridge: Polity Press.

Gilg, A. (2005) *Planning in Britain: Understanding and evaluating the post-war system*, London: Sage.

Gloucestershire County Council (2006) *Waste minimisation in development (incorporating reduction, re-use and recycling requirements): Supplementary planning document.* Available at: http://www.gloucestershire.gov.uk/CHttpHandler. ashx?id=12849&p=0 [Accessed 11 November 2016].

Greed, C. and Johnson, D. (2014) *Planning in the UK: An introduction,* Basingstoke: Palgrave Macmillan.

Hall, P. (1997) *Cities of tomorrow: An intellectual history of urban planning and design in the twentieth century,* Oxford: Blackwell.

Hardin, G. (1968) 'The tragedy of the commons', *Science,* vol 162, no 3859, pp 1243–8.

Hardy, D. and Ward, C. (1984) *Arcadia for all: The legacy of a makeshift landscape,* London: Mansell.

Harris, N.R. (2013) 'Surveillance, social control and planning: citizen engagement in the detection and investigation of breaches of planning control', *Town Planning Review,* vol 84, no 2, pp 171–96.

Heads of Planning Scotland (2014) *Planning Performance Framework,* Version 3. Edinburgh. Available at: http://www.gov.scot/Resource/0044/00448461.pdf [Accessed 11 November].

Heap, D. (1978) *An outline of planning law,* 7th edn, London: Sweet & Maxwell.

HES (Historic Environment Scotland) (2016) *Scottish Historic Environment Policy,* Edinburgh: Historic Environment Scotland: https://www.historicenvironment. scot/archives-and-research/publications/publication/?publicationId=f41371 1b-bb7b-4a8d-a3e8-a619008ca8b5 [Accessed 12 November 2016]

Jenkins, S. (undated) 'The Headington Shark'. Available at: http://headington. org.uk/shark/ [Accessed 11 November 2016].

Jones, L.A. (2009) speaking on BBC Radio 4, *Wildlife and the Marine Bill,* 9 March.

Jones, P. and Evans, J. (2013) *Urban regeneration in the UK: Boom, bust and recovery,* 2nd edn, London: Sage.

Judicial Review Office (2013) 'Judicial review practice note', 1/2008. Available at: http://www.Courtsni.gov.uk/enGB/Judicial%20Decisions/Practice%20 Directions/Documents/PN%201–2008/j_j_PN%201–2008%20–%20 revised%2010%20October%202013.htm [Accessed 11 November 2016].

Kidd, S. (2013) 'Rising to the integration ambitions of marine spatial planning: reflections from the Irish Sea', *Marine Policy,* no 39, pp 273–82.

Kidd, S. and Shaw, D. (2014) 'The social and political implications of marine spatial planning: some land-based reflections', *ICES Journal of Marine Science,* vol 71, no 7, pp 1535–41.

Lambeth Council (2014) 'Lambeth uses Proceeds of Crime Act powers to go after planning cheats'. Available at: https://lambethnews.wordpress. com/2014/09/15/lambeth-uses-proceeds-of-crime-act-powers-to-go-after-planning-cheats/ [Accessed 11 November 2016].

Larkin, J.F. and Scoffield, D.A. (2007) *Judicial review in Northern Ireland. A practitioner's guide,* Belfast: SLS Legal Publications (NI).

Law Society (2016) 'Legal sector does not need further instability in the wake of Brexit'. Available at: http://www.lawsociety.org.uk/news/press-releases/legal-sector-does-not-need-further-instability-in-the-wake-of-brexit/, 28 June [Accessed 11 November 2016].

Lloyd, M.G., Peel, D. and Duck, R.W. (2013) 'Towards a social-ecological resilience framework for coastal planning', *Land Use Policy*, vol 30, no 1, pp 925–33.

Local Government Ombudsman (2014) *Not in my backyard: Local people and the planning process. Focus report: learning lessons from complaints*, Coventry: LGO. Available at: http://www.lgo.org.uk/assets/attach/2301/FR%20-%20Not%20in%20my%20back%20yard%20planning%20Dec%202014.pdf [Accessed 30 November 2016].

Maes, L. (2009) speaking on BBC Radio 4, *Wildlife and the Marine Bill*, 9 March.

McAuslan, P. (1980) *The ideologies of planning law*, Oxford: Pergamon.

McCarthy, J.P. (2008) 'Is all tourism beneficial? The impacts of port-city regeneration initiatives'. Paper presented at the conference 'On the waterfront: Culture, heritage and regeneration in port cities', Liverpool, 19–21 November. Available at: https://content.historicengland.org.uk/images-books/publications/on-the-waterfront/waterfront-part8.pdf/ [Accessed 11 November 2016].

McHarg, A. (2013) *Access to judicial review in Scotland*, UK Constitutional Law Association. Available at: http://ukconstitutionallaw.org/2013/07/30/aileen-mcharg-access-to-judicial-review-in-scotland/ [Accessed 11 November 2016].

McKay, S. and Murray, M. (2014) 'In pursuit of regulatory compliance: a study of planning enforcement structures in Northern Ireland', *Town Planning Review*, vol 85, no 3, pp 387–410.

McKay, S., Murray, M. and Macintyre, S. (2015) 'Pitfalls in protection: how theory can enrich our understanding of regulatory compliance problems in planning practice', *International Planning Studies*, vol 20, no 3, pp 270–91.

McMaster, R. and Smith, G. (2013) *Scottish planning law*, London: Bloomsbury Publishing.

MMO (Marine Management Organisation) (2014a) 'Inshore and East Offshore Marine Plan'. Available at: https://www.gov.uk/guidance/east-inshore-and-east-offshore-marine-plan-areas [Accessed 11 November 2016].

MMO (2014b) 'South Inshore and South Offshore Marine Plan'. Available at: https://www.gov.uk/guidance/south-inshore-and-south-offshore-marine-plan-areas [Accessed 11 November 2016].

Moore, V. and Purdue, M. (2014) *A practical approach to planning law*, 13th edn, Oxford: Oxford University Press.

Newman, P. and Thornley, A. (1996) *Urban planning in Europe: International competition, national systems and planning projects*, Abingdon-on-Thames: Routledge.

Northern Ireland Assembly (2010) *Sustainable Development Strategy for the Northern Ireland Assembly Commission*, April, Belfast: Northern Ireland Assembly. Available at: http://www.niassembly.gov.uk/globalassets/documents/corporate/sustainable-development/sustainable_development_strategy_april2010.pdf [Accessed 30 November 2016].

Orbinson, W., McGhee, G. and Warke, J. (2009) *Planning and judicial review*, Belfast: SLS Legal Publications (NI).

Oxford Economics (2015) *The economic impact of the UK's maritime services sector*, London: Oxford Economics. Available at: http://maritimelondon.com/wp-content/uploads/2014/10/The-economic-impact-of-the-UK-maritime-services-sector_Combined_Final.pdf [Accessed 11 November 2016].

PAC (Planning Appeals Commission) (2016) 'Planning Appeals Commission Functions (as at 15th March 2016)'. Available at: https://www.pacni.gov.uk/sites/pacni/files/media-files/Functions%20-%20March%202016.pdf [Accessed 11 November 2016].

Peel, D. and Lloyd, M.G. (2004) 'The social re-construction of the marine environment: towards marine spatial planning', *Town Planning Review*, vol 75, no 3, pp 359–78.

Peel, D. and Lloyd, M.G. (2010) 'Strategic regeneration: an integrated planning approach to managing a coastal resort in South Wales', *Environmental Hazards*, vol 9, no 3, pp 310–18.

Peel, D., Lloyd, M.G. and Ritchie, H. (2010) 'An introduction to land use planning and business in Northern Ireland', in H. Browne (ed) *Aspects of law relating to business*, Harlow: Pearson Education Limited, pp 55–78.

PILS (Public Interest Litigation Support) (2012) *Judicial review in Northern Ireland: A guide for non governmental organisations*, Belfast: PILS.

Planning Portal (2016) 'Lawful development certificates', V1. Available at: https://ecab.planningportal.co.uk/uploads/1app/guidance/guidance_note-lawful_development_certificates.pdf [Accessed 11 November 2016].

Plant, G. (2003) 'Offshore wind energy development: the challenges for english law', *Journal of Planning Law*, August 945, pp 939–64.

Poustie, M. (2014) *Scottish planning law and procedure*, 2nd edn, Edinburgh: W. Green.

Ritchie, H. and Ellis, G. (2009) *Across the waters. Implementation of the UK Marine and Coastal Access Act and devolved marine legislation, cross-border case studies: The North Channel*, Belfast: Queen's University Belfast for WWF, pp 1–14.

Rowan-Robinson J., Lloyd M.G. and Elliot, R.G. (1987) 'National Planning Guidelines and strategic planning: matching context and method?' *Town Planning Review*, vol 58, no 4, pp 369–81.

RTPI in Scotland (Royal Town Planning Institute in Scotland) (2012) Response to the Better Regulation Bill in Scotland. Available at: http://www.rtpi.org.uk/media/12501/better_regulation_bill_-_covering_letter_-_26_october_2012.pdf [Accessed 11 November 2016].

Russ, G.R. and Zeller, D.C. (2003) 'From Mare Liberum to Mare Reservarum', *Marine Policy*, no 27, pp 75–8.

Rydens (2015) *Planning for Infrastructure final report*, Livingston: Scottish Government Local Government and Communities Directorate.

Scottish Government (2009) *Planning circular 10/2009, planning enforcement*, Edinburgh: The Scottish Government.

Scottish Government (2010) *Designing streets: A policy statement for Scotland*, Edinburgh: The Scottish Government.

Scottish Government (2011) *Scotland's cities: Delivering for Scotland*, Edinburgh: The Scottish Government.

Scottish Government (2013) *Creating places: A policy statement on architecture and place for Scotland*, Edinburgh: The Scottish Government.

Scottish Government (2014a) *National Planning Framework 3*, Edinburgh: Scotland. Available at: http://www.gov.scot/Resource/0045/00453683.pdf [Accessed 3 November 2016].

Scottish Government (2014b) *Scottish Planning Policy*, Edinburgh: Scotland. Available at: http://www.gov.scot/Resource/0045/00453827.pdf [Accessed 3 November 2016].

Scottish Government (2015) *Scotland's National Marine Plan: A single framework for managing our seas*, Edinburgh: Marine Scotland. Available at: http://www.gov.scot/Topics/marine/seamanagement/national [Accessed 11 November 2016].

Scottish Government (2016) 'Marine planning partnerships'. Available at: http://www.gov.scot/Topics/marine/seamanagement/regional/partnerships [Accessed 11 November 2016].

Shetland Islands Council (2015) *Supplementary guidance: Shetland Islands' Marine Spatial Plan*. Available at: http://www.shetland.gov.uk/planning/documents/SIMSP_2015.pdf [Accessed 11 November 2016].

Singh, U. (2008) *A history of ancient and early medieval India: From the Stone Age to the 12th century*, New York: Pearson Education

Tallon, A. (2013) *Urban regeneration in the UK*, 2nd edn, London: Routledge.

Taylor, N. (1998) *Urban planning theory since 1945*, London: Sage.

Thomas, K. (1997) *Development control: Principles and practice*, London: UCL Press.

Thornley, A. (1993) *Urban planning under Thatcherism: The challenge of the market*, 2nd edn, Abingdon-on-Thames: Routledge.

Unwin, R. (1994) *Town planning in practice: An introduction to the art of designing cities and suburbs*, New York: Princeton Architectural Press.

Welsh Government (2004) *Wales spatial plan - people, places, futures*, Cardiff: Welsh Government.

Welsh Government (2012a) *Towards a Welsh Planning Act: Ensuring the planning system delivers, report to the Welsh Government by the Independent Review Body*, Cardiff: Welsh Government.

Welsh Government (2012b) *City regions – final report*, Cardiff: Welsh Government.

Welsh Government (2013) *Research into the review of the planning enforcement system in Wales*, Cardiff: Welsh Government.

Welsh Government (2016) *Planning policy Wales*, Cardiff: Welsh Government.

Winter, A. (2012) 'Axed tree costs man record £125,000', *Daily Echo*, 23 November. Available at: http://www.bournemouthecho.co.uk/news/10068984. Axed_tree_costs_man_record___125_000/ [Accessed 11 November 2016].

Wood, D., Chynoweth, P., Adshead, J. and Mason, J. (2011) *Law and the built environment*, Chichester: Wiley-Blackwell.

Yale University (2008) *The Code of Hammurabi*, The Avalon Project. Available at: http://avalon.law.yale.edu/ancient/hamframe.asp [Accessed 11 November 2016].

Index

References to figures, tables and boxes are shown in *italics*

Case law index